Oliver Wendell Holmes Jr. and Legal Logic

Oliver Wendell Holmes Jr. and Legal Logic

FREDERIC R. KELLOGG

THE UNIVERSITY OF CHICAGO PRESS CHICAGO AND LONDON

The University of Chicago Press, Chicago 60637
The University of Chicago Press, Ltd., London

Published 2018
Printed in the United States of America

27 26 25 24 23 22 21 20 19 18   1 2 3 4 5

ISBN-13: 978-0-226-52390-3 (cloth)
ISBN-13: 978-0-226-52406-1 (e-book)
DOI: 10.7208/chicago/9780226524061.001.0001

Library of Congress Cataloging-in-Publication Data

Names: Kellogg, Frederic Rogers, author.
Title: Oliver Wendell Holmes Jr. and legal logic / Frederic R. Kellogg.
Description: Chicago ; London : The University of Chicago Press, 2018. |
Includes bibliographical references and index.
Identifiers: LCCN 2017026676 | ISBN 9780226523903 (cloth : alk. paper) |
ISBN 9780226524061 (e-book)
Subjects: LCSH: Holmes, Oliver Wendell, Jr., 1841–1935. | Law—Philosophy. |
Law—Methodology.
Classification: LCC KF8745.H6 K449 2018 | DDC 347.73/2634—dc23
LC record available at https://lccn.loc.gov/2017026676

♾ This paper meets the requirements of ANSI/NISO Z39.48–1992 (Permanence of Paper).

FOR MOLLY

Contents

INTRODUCTION

The Law Lectures

The Storrs Lectures at Yale Law School are an annual occasion for the reflections of preeminent judges or legal scholars, as were the Oliver Wendell Holmes Lectures, supported by Holmes's devise to Harvard Law School. Endowed lectureships at American law schools have, on rare occasions, become great lectures, remembered in posterity for their enduring influence on legal thought.

So it was that Columbia law professor Philip Bobbitt, author in 1982 of *Constitutional Fate*,[1] spoke in his 2014 Storrs Lecture of an enduring Storrs Lecture forty years earlier by his professor at Yale, Grant Gilmore, later published as *The Ages of American Law*. Gilmore had decried our "age of anxiety," caused by "the conundrum into which Holmes and the legal realists had led American law."[2]

What conundrum? The twentieth-century legal realists, influenced by Holmes, who died in 1935, challenged the view that judicial decisions are mechanical deductions from existing rules or principles, and argued instead that there are always *opposing* rules and principles; so judges had to decide first and baldly rationalize their decisions. Law was simply (as Holmes had apparently said) judicial behavior. "If law was simply what the judges did," asked Bobbitt, "then how could they ever—from a legal point of view—be wrong? But judges often contradicted and reversed each other and themselves—so how could they ever be right?"

1. Bobbitt, *Constitutional Fate: Theory of the Constitution*. Bobbitt also authored *Constitutional Interpretation*, *The Shield of Achilles: War, Peace and the Course of History*, and *Terror and Consent: The Wars for the Twenty-First Century*.

2. Philip Bobbitt, "The Age of Consent," *Yale Law Journal* 123 (May 2014): 2334, 2336.

But Holmes had not said that. What he actually said, and thought, is subtle, original, and widely, if not uniformly, misread by legal scholars. It concerns the logical method of law. Rather than judicial behavior, Holmes viewed legal adjudication as part of the struggle among active and often opposing forces: a struggle not just between rules, or even ideas, but patterns of belief and conduct. Legal knowledge must be grounded, then, in the ultimate resolution of broad conflicts. If so, how are such resolutions achieved?

Reassessing Holmes's legal logic requires a new understanding of the role of judges in controversial cases. The conundrum of legal realism is still a problem, but I want to absolve Holmes of responsibility for it, and introduce another, much more indispensable, Oliver Wendell Holmes Jr. Demonstration will take the reader back to Holmes's post–Civil War diaries, through his early reading in philosophy and science, his discussions with peers, especially Chauncey Wright and William James, his response to lectures on logic and scientific induction by Charles Peirce in 1866, and his own early essays probing and responding to John Stuart Mill's *A System of Logic*. It will then advance critically through the recent history of American jurisprudence.

The conundrum problem is rooted in logic. Holmes and his friends, in the period before and during meetings of their famous Metaphysical Club of Cambridge in the 1870s, were caught up with examination of traditional or "classical" logic, with their own reassessments of epistemology (or how humans know), the legacy of early modern philosophy, great figures like René Descartes, David Hume, Immanuel Kant, and G. W. F. Hegel. Holmes and his friends were also heavily influenced by the recent and dramatic progress of scientific discovery.

Classical logic since Aristotle has been framed by two procedures, deduction and induction, governing the relation between (as Holmes would have put it) "generals and particulars."[3]

What, in a difficult legal case, is the logical problem? In an easy case, it is whether I brought my car to a complete stop at a stop sign; there is a clear rule and a clear act, a plain particular covered by a general, decided by deduction. Difficulty increases with the complexity of unanticipated acts that have combined to cause a claim of loss or harm. Where deduction from existing rules is inconclusive, the question approaches becoming an inductive one. Properly understood, induction seeks to find, from experi-

3. On the philosophy of logic in New England before and during Holmes's legal research, see generally Flower and Murphey, *History of Philosophy in America*, 2:365–87.

ence, the general rule that will resolve not just the case, but the problem. The problem may be a new one, not yet covered by settled authority. Is medically assisted death suicide or murder? The relevant "particulars," then, are not just the particular facts of this new case, but the judgments, or *findings*, in a *succession* of cases, very like a succession of experiments in chemistry or physics.

Students in high school physics pour liquid mercury into a clean test tube, and turn it upside down. A space unexpectedly appears between the tube's rounded bottom and the heavy liquid through which no air could have passed. Is this an *empty* space, or is there some substance in that visible area? How, thought Thomas Hobbes in the seventeenth century, could such a space paradoxically be "filled with *nothing*"? It took a *succession* of experiments to find an answer.[4]

This example will elucidate where Holmes was (and is) misunderstood, and why he is innocent of blame for the conundrum. Surely, when deduction works, law is what the judges say it is. But where a new matter falls cleanly *outside* or *between* settled general rules and propositions, induction from experience is required to revise, or renew, prevalent belief and conduct. Sufficient experience may take time to gather and evaluate. *That* is when judges may understandably, and quite legitimately, appear to contradict and reverse themselves and each other, as also have scientists, at least since the eighteenth century, working with successions of experiments to see whether, say, the empty space in the test tube is something we can now (often inexactly) call a "vacuum."

Like scientists, judges don't and shouldn't "choose first and rationalize"; rather, like juries, they must surely choose, but not *prematurely* rationalize, as did Hobbes in opposing (and actually denouncing) Robert Boyle's famous air-pump experiments.[5] What scientists have used is an inductive process, which Holmes and his friends knew to be regrounded

4. This is an oversimplification of a famous demonstration originally made by Evangelista Torricelli in 1644 (where the test tube would have been set within a dish of mercury), and refers to the question raised as to the nature of the "Torricellian space," and whether or not a true vacuum could exist in nature. The question also arose as to the cause of the suspension of the mercury above the dish. Hobbes was a "plenist," a view opposed to "vacuism," and opposed Robert Boyle's air-pump experiments to explore the complex controversy on several grounds, including Hobbes's favoring a "demonstrative" (and largely deductive) method of inquiry. Steven Shapin and Simon Shaffer, *Leviathan and the Air-Pump: Hobbes, Boyle, and the Experimental Life*, 21, 41–49.

5. Ibid.

in Francis Bacon's seventeenth-century empiricism, and which they also knew had recently been reexamined by Mill and William Whewell in the 1840s. It was examined and refined again by Holmes, in the years following the American Civil War.

Law lectures have played a prominent role, not always positive, in understanding Holmes and American law, and they will hopefully elucidate this book and keep it readable. Especially so is Holmes's own notorious lecture to Boston University law students in 1897, which accounts for his blame for the conundrum. In "The Path of the Law," he defined law as "prediction" of what judges decide, which was unfortunately interpreted as meaning *whatever any* judges decide. By "prediction" he really meant the outcome of his reconceived inductive process, but he was taken to mean the entire set of judicial acts, including all the conflicting opinions of Bobbitt's conundrum. That he actually meant the outcome of the extended inductive process should have been evident from his other writings, in particular another lecture just two years later.

In 1899, before the New York State Bar Association, Holmes sketched, in broad strokes and colloquial language, his inductive theory, worked out twenty-five to thirty years earlier, observing in essence that law has been an inquiry, over time, into the general problem of legal liability, or blame. It operates in a succession of particular *problems*. Broad practices, reinforced by general beliefs, dominate the path of law, from local rules on up to the nature of legal liability. Patterns of conduct and belief, often conflicting, are the grounding source of legal meaning, and they may be just flexible enough to permit consensual resolutions.[6]

This practice-based notion of meaning introduces an element missing in classical logic, which assumes fixed similarities of objects under inquiry. The continuing function of law is the consensual finding of similarities. Stopping or not stopping at stop signs are plainly similar acts, but not so *novel* cases where, for example, a gravely ill patient has been taken off life support, or has been provided with a button to release a deadly substance into his or her body. New questions must be addressed: what is a voluntary act, what condition is sufficiently debilitating, can these issues be addressed in a "living will" or some other statement of intent not to be kept alive? Is there a governing basic right, to *life*, or to personal *autonomy*? Is assisted death suicide, or is it homicide?

6. Holmes's 1899 address is discussed in greater detail in chaps. 4 and 5, and his 1897 address in chap. 8.

I use this controversial example to focus attention; I should add that there are innumerable less controversial examples of disputed similarity in everyday legal matters, involving the rights of neighboring landowners, contracting parties on the internet, even fender benders on the roads and intersections. Examples are found throughout Holmes's writings and judicial opinions. Disputes over similarity affect even fundamental constitutional questions.[7]

After Holmes's death, great lectures took over his legacy, deeply affecting his reputation. In 1940 and 1942, Harvard law professor Lon Fuller, his severest critic, misread what Holmes had said in 1897, leading to his guilt for the conundrum. Fuller further (in 1940) reprimanded the late Holmes, who had warned the law students against misinterpreting legal language with moral overtones, taking him to mean *removing morals from law*.[8]

Properly understood, the warning was against premature rationalization. Yet, in the 1950s, Fuller's charge merged into a larger debate over the fundamental relation of law and morals. This was raised to a philosophical level when H. L. A. Hart of Oxford University, visiting Harvard Law School, delivered in 1957 what is surely the greatest Holmes Lecture of all time, "Positivism and the Separation of Law and Morals." In defending the separation, Hart took Holmes to be on his own side, as a "legal positivist."

In conceiving law as a multilevel system of rules, Hart sought to remove the conundrum of legal realism (which he later called a "nightmare") by granting that judges must occasionally "legislate," but only modestly, in a small but empty "penumbra" around inherently vague words. But a decade later, Ronald Dworkin countered powerfully that, when the rules offer no clear deductive solution, judges must turn to "moral principles." This turned the conundrum of American law into an ideological trap, where judges must either legislate, or find a moral principle to decide the controversial case.[9] By accepting deductive recourse to moral principles instead

7. This will be discussed in greater detail in chaps. 6, 7, and 10.

8. This will be discussed in greater detail in chaps. 7 and 8. Fuller's 1940 "The Law in Quest of Itself" was delivered as three lectures provided by the Julius Rosenthal Foundation for General Law, delivered at the Law School of Northwestern University at Chicago in April 1940. His "Reason and Fiat in Case Law" was the second annual Benjamin N. Cardozo Lecture before the Association of the Bar of the City of New York on October 27, 1942.

9. The Holmes Lectures at Harvard had also in the 1950s turned to the nature and use by judges of "principles." Judge Learned Hand would take a skeptical position regarding judicial recourse to constitutional principles in his 1958 Holmes Lecture, which Professor Herbert Wechsler would oppose in 1959, defending judicial use of "neutral principles." Alexander

of inductive inquiry, the predominant theory of law has now come to reinforce the political polarization that now infests American judicial politics, casting doubt on the legitimacy of the judicial process.[10]

The controversy over Holmes and the conundrum comes from a deeply perceived inconsistency; there is no clear consensus on his underlying theory of law and judging. This is due to a failure to connect his early research, and its sources, with his later writing and decisions. His post–Civil War diaries reveal readings in philosophy and science that (through conversations with his friends) led to an original logical method. It grew from law, but had general logical application. It was applied consistently throughout his judicial career. It is the missing piece of a long-standing Holmes puzzle, and I hope to show that, even in the context of contemporary theory, his is still an original contribution to the philosophy of logic.

The order of presentation is in ten chapters. In chapter 1, setting the scene, I examine Holmes's reading and meetings in Cambridge during the period in which his interest was focused on science and philosophy. In the second, I trace how his reading of Mill's *A System of Logic*, noting a passage dealing with the syllogism, was influenced by questions raised by Charles Peirce in lectures on logic and induction in late 1866. In chapter 3, I examine the influence on Holmes of writings on science by Mill, Whewell, and John Herschel, and the debate between Mill and Whewell over the role of ideas in induction. In chapter 4, I address past criticisms based on an erroneous view of Holmes's thought, and explain the application of his commitment to induction, extending even to the appellate stage of litigation. In chapter 5, I explain how Holmes is wrongly associated with legal realist concerns over "indeterminacy" in the difficult case.

In chapter 6, I discuss how social conflict affects the process of comparison of experience, through which general propositions are consensually developed and shared, comparing it with Mill's account in his *Logic*. In chapter 7, I apply the lessons of Holmes's inductivism to the operation and understanding of legal principles. In chapter 8, I address the association of Holmes with the "positivist" separation of law and morals, and compare

Bickel of Yale Law School would attempt to unravel the difficulty, unwittingly coming close to Holmes's actual position. This is discussed in greater detail in chap. 7.

10. A polarization between realism and formalism has underlain debates over American law, given another expression by H. L. A. Hart in 1973, calling it a standoff between the "nightmare" of realism undermining the "noble dream" of formalism. American efforts in legal thought simply oscillate between them. This is discussed in chap. 9.

his perspective with that of H. L. A. Hart, Ronald Dworkin, and Lon L. Fuller. In chapter 9, I trace the development of Holmes's inductivism to elucidate what Hart saw as an "oscillation" between the "nightmare" of legal realism versus the "noble dream" of deductive formalism in American jurisprudence, and clarify its import for logical theory. In chapter 10, I address Holmes's implicit approach to validation, in the context of free expression in time of war.

In his introduction to a collection of essays on Holmes in 1992, Robert Gordon wrote:

> Holmes . . . has served for several generations as a representative man, an iconic figure. His influence, magnified into legend by the attention he has received, has helped to constitute the identity of the legal profession, the conception of the judicial function, and the role of the public intellectual, in modern American culture. Perhaps that helps explain why a Victorian legal theorist and judge who happened to be carried by longevity into the New Deal era should have inspired, and should continue to inspire, both lawyers and intellectuals to passionate attempts to come to terms with that legend—to appropriate it to their own purposes, to denounce and resist it, or simply to take it apart to see what it is made of.[11]

This book is not concerned with appropriating Holmes to "anterior purposes," but is the third effort on my part to "take apart" Holmes's thought and legacy and "see what it is made of."

In *The Formative Essays of Justice Holmes: The Making of an American Legal Philosophy* (1984), I sought to focus more scholarly attention upon his early research, to inform and understand his later writings. I reprinted the key early essays, which are now available in Sheldon M. Novick's *The Collected Works of Justice Holmes*. In *Oliver Wendell Holmes Jr., Legal Theory, and Judicial Restraint* (2007) I emphasized the element of judicial self-restraint implicit in Holmes's resistance to general propositions.

I had not looked, until more recently, carefully enough at the influence on Holmes of nineteenth-century English science, despite clear evidence of the importance of science in the development of Holmes's thought.[12] The chronological edition of the previously unpublished papers of Peirce, still

11. Robert W. Gordon, introduction to Gordon, ed., *The Legacy of Oliver Wendell Holmes Jr.*, 5.

12. See Howe, *The Shaping Years*, and discussion in chap. 3 below.

being gathered and published at the Indiana University Press, has made accessible the development of Peirce's own thought and interests during the 1860s, in particular the content of lectures that were attended by Holmes in 1866, leading (as noted in Holmes's diaries) to his careful reading of Mill's *A System of Logic*. Lately, Laura J. Snyder's detailed examination of Mill's debate with Whewell, and the common influence on both men of Francis Bacon, brings greater clarity to Holmes's shared interests with his confessed mentor Chauncey Wright. I rely further on the comprehensive analyses of early American philosophy by Bruce Kuklick, Elizabeth Flower, and Murray G. Murphey.

My treatment of other writers concerning Holmes's legacy, and their alternative viewpoints, has been selective and limited to the goal of elucidating the theme of induction. Holmes's resistance to general propositions has stood as the characteristic theme of his career for me since I encountered it in law school fifty years ago. Having found convincing reasons to associate it with Chauncey Wright's Baconian empiricism, it now appears clear, given his attendance at Peirce's lectures on induction and the timing of Holmes's reading of Mill's *System of Logic*, that it led to a significant contribution by Holmes to the logic of induction, the empiricism of conflict, the social dimension of deriving meaning and reference for disputed terms, and naturalizing the way in which the dialectic among concepts is understood. It outlines the logical framework of a sociology of legal knowledge.[13]

Holmes strongly implied in the 1899 New York lecture that not only law, but science and other forms of knowledge, commonly develop through an analogous inductive process.[14] One obvious question would be how it might apply to ethics. While this bears closer examination than space here permits, the insight his thought can provide to ethical theory is the importance of practice in the continuum, over time, of inductive inquiry. A major issue in ethics is the relation of particular reasons to general propositions.[15]

13. This phrase is now common in studies of natural science but is largely missing in studies of law. See Barry Barnes, David Bloor, and John Hanson, *Scientific Knowledge: A Sociological Analysis*. Julius Stone in 1966 anticipated a sociology of legal knowledge in *Social Dimensions of Law and Justice*.

14. O. W. Holmes Jr., "Law in Science and Science in Law," *Harvard Law Review* 11 (1899): 443; *The Collected Works of Justice Holmes*, ed. Sheldon Novick, 3:406 (hereafter *CW*). See chap. 6 below.

15. Jonathan Dancy, *Moral Reasons*. The issue of ethical generalism and particularism as putatively rival accounts of moral knowledge and motivation, rather than (as implied by Holmes) stages of social inquiry, is examined in chap. 9.

Holmes's continuum of legal inquiry, influenced by Mill's empiricism, addresses that relation, and provides a means of understanding how the general, or abstract and conceptual, element is socially derived through experience and adjustment of (often conflicting) practice. By analogy from law, ethical particularism and generalism would not be rival accounts of moral knowledge and understanding, but rather stages of inquiry into *actual* urgent moral problems, not *hypothetical* moral dilemmas.[16]

An examination of Holmes's sources, his early meetings and readings, particularly Mill's *A System of Logic* and nineteenth-century English debates over the logic of science, helps to clarify Holmes's ideas and to sharpen his relevance to contemporary controversies about law. It also renews a comparison of legal and scientific knowledge, that influenced his early research and his Millian "inductive turn." His philosophy should be viewed as a post–Civil War response to Mill's thought and its context—Mill's debates with Richard Whately, William Hamilton, and William Whewell—rather than only to the legal-ideological issues of his time.[17]

How judges decide the difficult or "hard" case[18] is the focus of much controversy, in theory, and also in public conversation—for example, regarding abortion, assisted death, affirmative action, same-gender marriage, or freedom of expression as it relates to other public purposes. Addressing the nature of the difficult case, Holmes emphasized an aspect of uncertainty distinct from the problem one often envisions challenging the deciding judge: semantic unclarity or contradiction within the settled law, or vagueness in the meaning or application of the terms of an applicable rule or standard.[19]

While cognizant of these factors,[20] Holmes focused on the relation of novel or unanticipated fact to an underlying and emergent social problem.

16. See my "The Snake and the Roundabout: Ethical Particularism and the Patterns of Normative Induction."

17. See, e.g., Morton Horwitz, *The Transformation of American Law, 1870–1960: The Crisis of Legal Orthodoxy*; David Rosenberg, *The Hidden Holmes: His Theory of Torts in History*; David M. Rabban, *Law's History: American Legal Thought and the Transatlantic Turn to History*.

18. Richard Posner notes that the meaning of "hard" is now "difficult," but previously (in Holmes's time) meant emotionally compelling, or "tugging at the heartstrings" as in the lawful eviction of an elderly widow. Richard Posner, *The Problems of Jurisprudence*, 161n.

19. Brian Bix, *Law, Language, and Legal Determinacy*, and "Vagueness and Political Choice in Law," in Geert Keil and Ralf Poscher, eds., *Vagueness and the Law: Philosophical and Legal Perspectives*.

20. Holmes wrote the opinion in *McBoyle v. United States*, 283 U.S. 25 (1931), holding

For him the appearance of legal uncertainty, where opinions and authorities are sharply divided in a controversial case, signaled a stage of a broader societal continuum of inquiry. It would not then be strictly a *legal* uncertainty, and it is a category mistake to expect that judges alone can effectively decide the broader question. Their role is recast by Holmes, whose thought recognizes the importance of input from outside the law—the importance, as I hope to demonstrate, of the *social dimension* of logical induction.

The common interpretation of the term "legal logic" is mainly a deductive form of legal reasoning, a meaning familiar to the law student. The body of settled law is massive and must regularly be applied to the analysis of complex fact situations. The typical law examination presents complex situations that the student must analyze, drawing on the body of existing law. Like many actual cases where deduction may indeed lead to resolution, it tests both the knowledge of authoritative law and the ability to identify and evaluate its application to all aspects of a hypothetical problematic situation.

Holmes's model accepts, but goes beyond, this model. It concerns, in particular, what in 1873 he called the *growth* of the law, through the negotiation of disputed meanings and the eventual entrenchment of similarities and differences. General positions that appear at first blush to be "incommensurable" may eventually, through a piecemeal process of contextual convergence, be reconciled through public adaptation and judicial specification. Where this *convergence* of opposing positions is successful, it is a stabilizing force; where it is not possible, as in the disputes over treating humans as private property that preceded the American Civil War, any resolution must be reached through other forms of struggle for dominion.

I will explore Holmes's application of these insights to his decisions as a judge, and illustrate their relation to the path of legal theory since his death: legal realism, legal positivism, conceptual and principled jurisprudence, the legal process school, and critical legal studies. This is done with a broad brush, as I cannot hope to address comprehensively the massive literature on these movements (although I will address salient work in footnotes). I can best try to emphasize a few key themes, having in mind

---

that the National Motor Vehicle Theft Act, U.S. Title 18, § 408, which punishes "whoever transports, or causes to be transported, in interstate or foreign commerce a motor vehicle knowing it to have been stolen," and which defines "motor vehicle" as including "an automobile, automobile truck, automobile wagon, motor cycle, or any other self-propelled vehicle not designed for running on rails," does not apply to aircraft.

the relevance and importance of opening up for consideration Holmes's original view of legal uncertainty. The conventional view, which focuses on language, is roughly characterized by the comment "Nothing internal to language compels a particular result." Simplified, Holmes's response is: If a key term is subject to a process of contested application through litigation, it may in time acquire a practical specification; although, where there is a recalcitrant underlying problem, it will not be resolved without practical *adjustment*, of the future conduct of contesting interest groups.

This suggests that a focus on language alone limits and obscures attention to the process of conceptual change; and much contemporary theory is heavily committed to linguistic analysis. One issue that deserves continued emphasis is that the process of resolving uncertainty can be protracted, affecting the *appearance* of uncertainty. It is useful then to consider the implications of *stages* of inquiry. At the initial stage, a comparison of factual situations with existing doctrine may appear at its most uncertain, indeed closest to a description as "indeterminate." At a later stage, relevant factors will have been identified and addressed both within and outside the law, as, for example, private and public policy in disputes over medically assisted death. It is then that uncertainty and its resolution may yield to description by "general principle," but again, within *and outside* the legal arena.

A final comment is due, on the underlying epistemology, or conceptual grounding, of Holmes's inductivism. A question implied is: What would be Holmes's account of validation, or the justification of legal knowledge? Is his viewpoint a form of banal conventionalism, equating legal truth with social "convention," as when Holmes appears to defer to input into the continuum of inquiry from contemporary opinion? What exactly are the "nonlegal resources" referred to above, and why does he defer? Is there any recognition or pursuit of "real" or "right" answers to legal questions, or merely of answers designed to accommodate opposing parties and keep order? What standard of objectivity is attainable by a social induction? What, if any, account is there of a relation of legal answers to ethics and morals?

I will argue that Holmes's perspective does address these matters, but it is easy to misread his overall views from comments like "I do not know what is true. I do not know the meaning of the universe," "man's destiny is to fight," "my Can't Helps," and defining truth "as the majority vote of that nation that can lick all the others."[21] I claim in the final chapter that his

21. Holmes to Learned Hand, June 24, 1918, Papers of Learned Hand. This remark, and its application to social inductivism, is examined in chap. 10.

theory of validation lies less in the metaphor of war than in "naturalizing" the *dialectic* among opposing concepts, dialectic being a phenomenon that philosophy has explicitly recognized since Zeno, Plato, and Aristotle.[22]

Among the innumerable debts accumulated while working on this book, I should thank, for their comments and support, Paul Churchill and the philosophy faculty at George Washington University; Professor George Browne and the graduate students and law faculty at Universidade Federal de Pernambuco in Recife, Brazil, where I have been a visiting professor since my Fulbright Fellowship in 2008; and students and faculty at the School of Law of the University of Edinburgh, Scotland, where I was a MacCormick Fellow in 2009. I also thank the Department of Philosophy at the University of Warsaw, Poland, where I did early research on legal logic as a Senior Fulbright Fellow in 1996.

A formative stage of this project came from my interaction with David Bloor and the Science Studies Unit of the Department of Sociology at the University of Edinburgh. While the sociology of scientific knowledge is a vital topic of interest and inquiry, the same cannot yet be said of law. This book is a hopeful step in the confirmation of the sociology of legal knowledge as a coherent research project.

In working out the early development of Holmes's philosophy I should also recognize the influence of Beth Singer, Susan Haack, Peter M. Hare, Joseph Margolis, and Ralph Sleeper, all of whom I met through the Society for the Advancement of American Philosophy. For their comments and encouragement on various working portions of this text I also thank Brian Butler, Alexander Lian, Paul Churchill, Mark Medish, Judge Pauline Newman, Roberto Frega, Charles Karelis, referees and reviewers at the University of Chicago Press, as well as reviewers and commenters at the American Philosophical Association, and the Charles S. Peirce International Centennial Congress in 2014.

Finally, I should recognize the importance of the views of other scholars on Holmes and jurisprudence, without whose work mine would be impossible. This includes several whom I subject to criticism, such as Grant Gilmore in chapter 4 and Lon Fuller and Mark Howe in chapter 8. Their work in particular has inspired my own, and Gilmore's encouragement in

22. "It was partly because Aristotle had to work out for himself the theory and methodology of dialectic that he made himself into the first logician philosopher." Gilbert Ryle, "Dialectic in the Academy," in G. E. L. Owen, ed., *Aristotle on Dialectic, The Topics: Proceedings of the Third Symposium Aristotelicum*, 73. This is addressed in greater detail in chap. 10 below.

1980 for my exploration of Holmes's interaction with the early pragmatists was essential to the direction of my research. I am greatly indebted also to Philip Bobbitt for his comments and encouragement.

* * *

NOTE ON INDUCTION. This book is intended mainly for lawyers and general readers interested in law and Holmes, not as a technical account for specialists. However, in just a few paragraphs, I should briefly summarize Holmes's view within the broader context of the philosophy of logical induction.[23] (This will be further addressed in chapter 6.)

David Hume opened the modern understanding of logical induction by arguing that there was no necessary connection between a present fact and that which is inferred from it. No one has succeeded in rejecting this thesis, and contemporary scholars have come to agree that inductive inferences lack the perceived necessity of deduction; hence the response has been to see skepticism as intrinsic to all inductive inquiry.

Skepticism defines an attitude, and its application can readily become a conversation stopper, an end of inquiry. The question of inductive and logical necessity may be further investigated, as it has in the study of scientific research, asking how deductive necessity itself is defined and achieved. Bertrand Russell made the following observation in 1914, regarding the relation of induction and deduction:

23. Principles sources are Peter Manicas, *Logic as Philosophy*; Susan Haack, *Philosophy of Logics*; Hilary Putnam, *Philosophy of Logic*; W. V. Quine *Philosophy of Logic*; and Bertrand Russell, *Problems of Philosophy*.

Holmes's approach is an extension of (rather than a deviation from) classical logic. Its salient point lies in an original approach to the principle of "bivalence," that of "p or not-p": a proposition must be either true or false. This is also known as the "excluded middle" (hence *bi*valence) because there are only *two* logical options. There are three formal analytical approaches to bivalence, that is, attempts by logicians to account for the excluded middle: they are "modal," "many-valued," and "fuzzy" logics. Haack, *Philosophy of Logics*. Holmes deviates from all three of these, in a manner that is not accounted for in classical or formal philosophies of logic, which seek to formalize uncertainty. Modal logic derives from Aristotle's insight that propositions about the future cannot be analyzed as bivalent. Many-valued logics are designed to specify the third value, e.g., by denoting it as indeterminate or uncertain. Fuzzy logic has attempted to assess the middle as a matter of degree. Holmes's idea of logical uncertainty rests on the notion of degrees, but not of semantic degrees, and rather degrees of completeness in the process of finding similarity in the succession of experience or experiments. Bivalence is a quality of the successful completion of inquiry resulting in settled propositions

> But induction, important as it is when regarded as a method of investigation, does not seem to remain when its work is done: in the final form of a perfected science, it would seem that everything ought to be deductive. If induction remains at all, which is a difficult question, it will remain merely as one of the principles according to which deductions are effected.[24]

Russell observes here that induction may actually precede and lead to deduction. How? In the following pages, the answer will be sought through exploration of the notion of similarity itself.

In conventional explanations of the inductive process, similarity among objects of inquiry is commonly presumed. The similarity among red balls repeatedly drawn from a bag, leading to an inference that the remaining objects in the bag are red balls, discounts individual differences, presuming them minute or otherwise irrelevant to the inquiry.[25] That is because the question at hand doesn't concern the qualities of redness or ballness, but rather the numerical contents of the bag. The possibility that the color of each ball may have slight differences, or that the shapes of the balls are not precisely identical, is not at issue.

An important question for this book will be: What indeed *is* similarity in logic and induction; is it a natural or conventional quality, and how is it perceived and/or derived?[26] The importance of similarity in induction was

24. Bertrand Russell, "Logic as the Essence of Philosophy," 33.

25. I use the example of red balls drawn from a bag because it appears in the 1866 lectures by Peirce attended by Holmes, as will be explored in chap. 2 on the origins of Holmes's early inductive turn.

26. As the philosopher Hilary Putnam observes, "In fact, *everything is similar to everything else in infinitely many respects*. For example, my sensation of a typewriter at this instant and the quarter in my pocket are both similar in the respect that some of their properties (the sensation's occurring right now and the quarter's being in my pocket) are *effects of my past actions*" (*Reason Truth and History*, 64–65; Putnam's italics). Peirce raised questions regarding how similarity and uniformity are perceived in induction, in an 1866 lecture attended by Holmes. *Writings of Charles S. Peirce: A Chronological Edition*, 1:415–20. See also Nelson Goodman, "Seven Strictures on Similarity," in *Problems and Prospects*, 437: "Similarity, ever ready to solve philosophical problems, is a pretender, an imposter, a quack. It has, indeed, its places and uses, but more often is found where it does not belong, professing powers it does not possess." W. V. Quine and J. S. Ullian, *The Web of Belief*, 87: "What counts as similarity? Everything is similar to everything in some respect." For a recent approach to "naturalizing" similarity in induction, see Hilary Kornblith, *Inductive Inference and Its Natural Ground: An Essay in Naturalistic Epistemology*.

clearly noted by Hume. No matter how many repetitions of uncontroversially similar events, runs his skeptical claim, we can still have no warrant regarding the occurrence of the next one: that the next object removed from the bag (even after an infinite number of red balls) will also be a red ball, even that the sun will again rise over Boston tomorrow morning. This is because it is the inductive process itself that is called upon to validate any particular induction regarding the bag or the sun.[27]

This uncertainty affects general ideas: Hume wrote, crediting Berkeley, "[A]ll general ideas are nothing but particular ones, annexed to a certain term, which gives them a more extensive significance, and makes them recall upon occasion other individuals, which are similar to them."[28] "Similarity," then, is for Hume a critical constitutive element in logic: "When we have found a resemblance among several objects, we apply the same name to all of them, whatever differences we may observe in the degrees of their quantity and quality, and whatever other differences may appear among them."[29] The term "we," with which Hume here refers to the perceiver of a similarity, has by implication already found the resemblance and discriminated away the differences.

But this approach to similarity implies completion of an unexamined process, as Charles Peirce noted in lectures given in late 1866, attended by Holmes. The above passage (from Hume's *Treatise on Human Nature*) hides two critical questions: who indeed is the "we" to whom he refers, and how was the resemblance "found"?

Hume's expository use of "we" is a commonly accepted discursive practice. But its use can leave out the possibility of disagreement over the purpose and consequences of a *disputed* resemblance. The expository "we" deploys an ideal observer of a paradigmatic situation; it obscures whether, in actual life, the general statement of resemblance applies to all possible communities of speakers. It obscures the social dimension of *establishing* similarity. The issue of similarity doesn't arise unless there is a practical uncertainty regarding the resemblance in question. Such practical uncertainty arises constantly in the operation of legal adjudication. It may also be found in science and other branches of human inquiry.

27. David Hume, "Skeptical Doubts concerning the Operations of the Understanding," in *An Inquiry concerning Human Understanding*, 1748, secs. 4 and 5.

28. David Hume, *A Treatise on Human Understanding*, bk. 1, pt. 1, sec. 7, para. 1.

29. Ibid.

Naming is another crucial constitutive element in logical theory.[30] What if the reach of application by a particular "name" is disputed by opposing interests within the same linguistic community? Parties to legal disputes may seek to gain coverage of a legal term ("liberty," "equality," even "murder") for their own interests, and to exclude other interests. This can be seen in minor disputes, or in major ones like the extension of the constitutional right of free expression to political campaign donations (hence the extension of "liberty"), of murder or homicide to doctor-assisted suicide, or of marriage to same-gender partners (implicating the extension of "equality"). With his famous aphorism "general propositions do not decide concrete cases," Holmes (drawing on influences that will be examined below) resisted responding to such disputes axiomatically, through premature deduction from a general statement or statements about law or rights, rather than inductive exploration, a process informed by experiential feedback into the legal process from society at large. Precisely what induction means in this context is the principal subject of this book.

For one thing, it implies social resolution of borderline cases. The ancient "Sorites paradox" questions at what point the addition (or subtraction) of an individual grain of sand governs defining a collection of grains as a "heap." "Heap" has thus been accounted an *inherently vague* term, as are many other terms when removed from context. Philosophers of law and language commonly treat semantic vagueness as a natural, in the sense of intrinsic, quality of discourse.[31] This ignores that the *legal* extension of "heap," or any other practically disputed term, can in the process of litigation take on a specific extension: it will be subject to increasingly precise determination through abstraction from particular decisions exploring the context of an emergent or ongoing actual dispute.

Thus, induction is not immediate; it is often connected with social conflict, with real-world instantiations of dialectical opposition. Its resolution is, moreover, experimental, and engages human creativity in the introduction of ideas or hypotheses; and the enterprise of extending human knowledge is intimately linked to the contentious nature of human conduct. Moreover, the process of legal inquiry is inadequately understood only as an examina-

30. See John Stuart Mill, *A System of Logic Ratiocinative and Inductive*, 1:23–82; Quine, *Elements of Logic*, 120–21.

31. See, passim, Timothy A. O. Endicott, *Vagueness in Law*; Timothy Williamson, *Vagueness*; see also Quine, *Word and Object*, 125–28. The issues of vagueness and the borderline case are examined in following chapters, especially chap. 9.

tion of authoritative texts, or of only *judicial* activity and the operation of *legal* institutions alone.

Critical to the resolution of conflicting positions is the influence of opposing social standards and the patterns of conduct supporting them. It is not possible for detached individuals, no matter how great their expertise, to resolve a deeply rooted dispute at a single moment, or even a succession of such experts to do so over time, without input from and adjustments within society at large. Knowledge, conduct, language, and conflict are all actively interrelated. Inductive inquiry and inference takes place (using terms later favored by John Dewey) in a "continuum" over time. It is, moreover, socially "transformative," and its success in practical terms (which I will define as the "convergence" of opposing positions) is never assured.[32]

Prompted by the early readings in his diary and his post–Civil War discussions, especially with William James, Charles Peirce, and Chauncey Wright, Holmes came to focus on the method of inductive generalization by judges in the common law tradition: how the elusive property of similarity, which is at the essence of logic in law (and logical induction in general), is found among novel and complex circumstances, and projected into future cases where opposing authorities conflict. In so doing he reconceived logical induction as a social process, a form of inference that engages adaptive action and implies social transformation. Rather than Hume's famous problem (the impossibility of attributing validation to inductive inference from uncontroversially similar events), I focus instead on the logically prior question of *finding* similarity—of how, in legal or everyday inquiry, the objects of induction come to be recognized as similar, such that inductive inference itself (Hume's doubt notwithstanding) becomes even conceivable.

Exploring this aspect of Holmes's thought engages his early philosophical and scientific interests, which are revealed in his early diary and readings. I will explore the mechanism of his legal induction, which relies on consensus regarding similarities and differences that the law seeks among various classes of human activity. His approach, focusing on the social process through which legal similarity is found amidst often bitter controversy and eventually entrenched, has been almost entirely missing in

32. It is upon the convergence of opposing positions that expository use of "we," implying an objective observer, is cognizable. Wilfrid Sellars has spoken for many contemporary pragmatists in saying, "Awareness—all of it—is a linguistic affair." Cheryl Misak, *The American Pragmatists*, 222. In Holmes's depiction of law, the linguistic expression of awareness follows the role of reconciled practice.

accounts by other writers.[33] It implies an original insight, of social inductivism as a general philosophical perspective. It is drawn from John Stuart Mill's psychologistic approach to logical theory, which predated the flourishing of formal logic, wherein the issue of similarity is largely removed from consideration.[34] Holmes's contribution to logic consists, in essence, of what might be called a "social-psychologistic" derivation from Mill, a line of logical theory that has yet to be fully recognized and carried forward.

Holmes's social induction, which bears a genetic but not identical relation to the philosophy now known as pragmatism, informs many claims and opinions that he advanced in his long career. Avoiding (until the final chapter) the presumptions and complexities of the label "pragmatism" (some of which are clearly antithetical to Holmes's position), I will mainly refer to his program as social inductivism. In engaging law this way, Holmes provides ground for recognizing the essentially unfinished nature of law and restraining ideology in the legal process. Logic is conceived as proceeding through stages of inquiry, accounting for the social dimension of the acquisition of conceptuality.

33. "Entrenchment" in this usage includes general belief and action. This is stronger than linguistic assertion and cognitive acceptance, as in Frederick Schauer's definition in *Playing by the Rules: A Philosophical Examination of Rule-Based Decision-Making in Law and Life*, 38–39: "Instead of being continuously malleable in the service of changing circumstances, generalizations become entrenched, and the entrenchment of past generalizations impedes the possibility of an infinitely sensitive and adaptable language" (42).

34. See chap. 9, n. 34, and accompanying text.

CHAPTER ONE

Prologue

In January of 1860, a U.S. senator from Mississippi, Jefferson Davis, proposed that southern states should secede from the United States of America, and a committee of the Harvard Board of Overseers reported unfavorably on instruction in "intellectual and moral philosophy." An attack by Confederate troops on Fort Sumter would take place in the spring of 1861. Twenty-year-old abolitionist Harvard senior Oliver Wendell Holmes Jr. would enlist immediately in the Fourth Massachusetts Battalion of Infantry (he would soon receive a commission as lieutenant in the Twentieth Massachusetts Volunteer Regiment of Infantry). The cause of poor instruction in philosophy was attributed to overwork of a professor who had been teaching Holmes and other Harvard students: the influential but now almost forgotten Francis Bowen.[1]

The returning thrice-wounded soldier, turned legal scholar and then judge, was elevated from the Massachusetts Supreme Judicial Court to the U.S. Supreme Court in 1902, lived just short of ninety-four years, and died between the two world conflicts in 1935. This book will explore his thought, with an emphasis on its genesis in the years after returning from the Civil War. Although immersed in its worst violence, he showed little posttraumatic stress in plunging into law and philosophy, living with his parents in Boston, visiting the woman whom he would marry at age thirty, regularly commuting to Cambridge, surrounded by and engaged with intellectually motivated friends.[2]

1. See Bruce Kuklick, *The Rise of American Philosophy*, 28–45.

2. See G. Edward White, *Justice Oliver Wendell Holmes: Law and the Inner Self*; Sheldon M. Novick, *Honorable Justice: The Life of Oliver Wendell Holmes*; Liva Baker, *The Justice from Beacon Hill: The Life and Times of Oliver Wendell Holmes*.

Philosophy was not a rigorous academic discipline at Harvard as it is today, despite the best efforts of the overworked Bowen. Yet it was taken up with genuine commitment and surprising rigor by recent graduates, Holmes, William James, Charles S. Peirce, and others, in particular the solitary but welcoming bachelor Chauncey Wright. As did they, Holmes broke new ground in his chosen field, ground that has been obscured by subsequent commentary and criticism.

Almost from the moment of his death, another life for Holmes began. An often-disputed Holmes has been brought into contemporary debates over the nature and theory of law, even if later dismissed for misunderstood views. This is yet another extended conversation about the deceased, but with a closer look and a wider audience in mind, as it explores aspects of his thinking that have not been adequately recognized.[3]

The reason for this has been failure to follow his early train of thought, and the context of concerns among his teacher Bowen, mentors, and friends, leading to misinterpretation of later writings and addresses. This has obscured the fact that his perspective stems from a surprising source, the reformism and logic that drove John Stuart Mill's empiricism, the view that human progress was contingent upon education and study of facts, and of logical induction from them to a correct understanding. Mill's hopeful meliorism would collide in Holmes with the experience of violent ideological conflict, leading to a profound appreciation for the precariousness of human hopes and accomplishments. Holmes would apply this attitude to the work of the courts. Yet his underlying insights grew from philosophical inquiry, and as such they carry wider implications.

How humans think, communicate ideas, form beliefs, and act upon them—these are critical questions. Answers have been posed, to be reconsidered in the face of new difficulties. They are never entirely settled, as the patterns of human thought and action are not rigid, but change with new problems, new habits and beliefs, and new generations. While my topic

3. The legal historian Robert Gordon writes that legal history can have the effect of "softening existing structures by becoming aware of conflicts and ambiguities," and "recovering suppressed alternatives less to establish them as a new orthodoxy than to suggest the perpetual malleability of structures and the possible experimental directions for their revision." Robert Gordon, "The Past as Authority and as Social Critic," 356. Gordon has questioned the persistent faith in the "progressive paradigm of progress." Returning cycles of conflict, in the last century as well as this, have undermined the faith, and may permit a new look at Holmes not just for his skeptical view of that faith but also for his original conception of the role of conflict in human knowledge.

has a legal and historical reference, it concerns questions about logic and its relation to the formation of knowledge. Holmes contributed to a new perspective on these matters in the late nineteenth century. The influences on him ranged from Professor Bowen's Scottish realist empiricism and familiarity with British and German philosophy, to the community of recent Harvard graduates that populated Cambridge in the postwar years, informing his early theoretical essays on law and his eventual treatise, *The Common Law*, published in 1881.[4] And, of course, the Civil War itself.

A famous Holmes refrain (especially in dissenting opinions) was "general propositions do not decide concrete cases."[5] An aversion to deductive reasoning, and perhaps to ideology, is implied. Holmes would later resist a tendency among some members of the Massachusetts and U.S. Supreme Courts to ground decisions on sweeping constitutional propositions, potentially obscuring subjective bias. But where does the refrain, and his resistance, come from? When we see that it derives from a line of thought traceable in his reading back to the English scientific debates earlier in the nineteenth century, the line can be extended further back to the early seventeenth-century English lawyer-scientist and philosopher Francis Bacon (1561–1626), whose perspective on scientific discovery—and knowledge in general—illuminated for Holmes the growth of normative knowledge in the common law.

Bacon's own reformist empiricism guided English scientific progress in the period before the American Civil War, and Holmes and several Cambridge friends followed a renewed debate in England over the ground of knowledge and discovery, contextualized by what is now called "early modern philosophy" (seventeenth- to early nineteenth-century writers from Descartes and Hume to Kant and Hegel), debate engaged in by the scientists William Whewell, John Herschel, and Charles Darwin, encompassing a vigorous disagreement over scientific method between Whewell and John Stuart Mill.[6]

The issues were related to Aristotle's distinction between deduction and induction.[7] The former is characterized by the syllogism, the various forms in which conclusions may be drawn from general premises. Content

4. O. W. Holmes Jr., *The Common Law*; *CW*, 3:109.

5. E.g., *Lochner v. New York*, 198 U.S. 45, 76 (1905).

6. See generally Laura J. Snyder, *Reforming Philosophy: A Victorian Debate on Science and Society*.

7. Snyder examines the manner in which the legacy of Aristotle was revived and debated in nineteenth-century England. Ibid., 36, 38–39.

is less important than form. For induction, content is the focus, how particular experience may be transformed into the general statements from which deductions may usefully be made.

Deduction:

All men are mortal

Socrates is a man

Socrates is mortal

Induction:

The ball drawn from this bag is red

This ball also drawn is also red; as is this ball, this ball, etc.

All balls in the bag are red

Law, of course, engages both. Deduction from existing rules is essential to the application of law, while induction from novel facts aids in establishing new or revised rules and principles.[8] Meanwhile, law influences human action, and provides a forum for resolving conflict. Deduction and induction offer different approaches to conflict. The former privileges logical form, the latter emphasizes specific circumstances.

How best, then, to resolve complex and controversial cases? Addressing the relation of the two methods came fortuitously, from British philosophy and science, tinctured with German idealism, into the life of the young Holmes after his return from the Union Army. It was fortuitous because of the inquiring spirit of his time, his intense early engagement with philosophical peers, and his ambition to understand and excel; and likely also, his experience as a soldier, bringing intimacy with conflict to bear on the nature and growth of normative knowledge.

In the wake of Bacon and the British empiricists, and particularly influenced by Mill's criticism of the syllogism in his 1843 *System of Logic*, Holmes's preference for induction is suggested by his remark (at the beginning of *The Common Law*), "The life of the law has not been logic: it has

8. Edward H. Levi, *An Introduction to Legal Reasoning*, 27: "It is customary to think of case-law reasoning as inductive and the application of statutes as deductive," citing C. K. Allen, *Law in the Making*, 249.

been experience. The felt necessities of the time, the prevalent moral and political theories, intuitions of public policy, avowed or unconscious, even the prejudices which judges share with their fellow-men, have had a good deal more to do than the syllogism in determining the rules by which men should be governed."[9] What is the background to this remark, and what did he mean by "experience"? And how might this connect with broader currents of thought?

Another Holmes phrase was "Great cases, like hard cases, make bad law."[10] Today's Supreme Court has occasionally been (as have previous courts) accused of ignoring or discarding settled lines of precedent to decide controversial matters like presidential elections and campaign financing. This comment comes from a further extension of the same thinking, its conception of the process of inquiry as it draws on prior experience.

Still another locution of his was the necessity of judicial "line drawing," as in, "[A]ll legal lines are more or less arbitrary as to the precise place of their incidence, although the distinctions of which they are the inevitable outcome are plain and undeniable."[11] When this comment is placed in the context of Holmes's overall thought, it expresses a theory of social (and consensual) resolution of uncertainty, maintaining behavioral as well as cognitive order by managing the extension of statutes, precedents, and constitutional rights as they oppose one another in litigation. Line drawing was his logical mechanism, and I examine in detail how he got there.

Holmes's contribution to legal logic is manifest but not explicit in his writings, which lack the transparency of contemporary academic practice. Remarkably little mention of his early reading and research is found in his voluminous later correspondence. It is necessary to seek out the origins of his thought and connect his judicial writing with the early research. His achievement is worth recovering, as it connects the disparate fields of law and natural science. The track of his thought, evident in the early essays from 1870 to 1880, reveals a pronounced inductive turn guiding his analysis of legal doctrine. It is focused on the method of induction as retrospective translation of clusters of judgments into precedent and legal doctrine. In accounting for this process, Holmes adds a uniquely social element to contemporary understanding of the logic of induction.

9. Holmes, *Common Law*, 1; *CW*, 3:115.

10. *Northern Securities Co. v. United States*, 193 U.S. 197, 400 (1904). Regarding the meaning of "hard cases," see introduction, n. 18.

11. *Lincoln v. Dore*, 176 Mass. 210, 213, 57 N.E. 336, 338 (1900).

The tension between deduction and induction is present in natural science, if under different conditions than law—and, indeed, recent scholarship has increasingly explored the social dimension of scientific inquiry.[12] Do separate domains of knowledge have methods in common? This has been at least an open question, and stimulated Francis Bacon in the seventeenth century, David Hume (and others) in the eighteenth, Mill, Whewell, and their colleagues in the early nineteenth, and the young members of the Cambridge, Massachusetts, "Metaphysical Club" in the later nineteenth century.

It is the social component that connects Holmes's view of logic with legal and social order. I will claim that Holmes came to interpret the Aristotelean logical forms with a recognition that the social context surrounding both the "particular" and the "general" can be in flux in controversial matters. Belief in certain legal "generals" may be emergent or flexible. Judicial response to a changing situation implicates the maintenance of social cohesion. Holmes addressed how the particular relates to the general in an unsettled, dynamic context, and how abstraction amidst conflict works to generate belief and inform conduct. As will be seen, it offers a theory of the stabilization and entrenchment of ideas.

Entrenchment, a term of increasing currency in philosophy since Nelson Goodman's "new riddle of induction,"[13] concerns the phenomenon of a conception gaining not just tentative belief but broad, undisputed, even intuitive, acceptance. The term implies both an end state and a spectrum. To become "entrenched" is to reach a final condition, implying that conceptions may be only partially so. Use of the term implicates a move away from fixed and necessary conceptual categories. It opens up questions missing from the analysis of fixed concepts: how they acquire firmness and stability, and how they might be susceptible to modification or change.[14]

While Holmes did not use the term, I will suggest that his model of legal knowledge reflects an overriding concern with this phenomenon. Much of

12. Barry Barnes, David Bloor, and John Henry, *Scientific Knowledge: A Sociological Analysis*.

13. Nelson Goodman, *Fact, Fiction, and Forecast*, 59–83.

14. Holmes's notion of entrenchment, described in 1899 as the "ideals of society have been strong enough to reach that final form of expression, or what have been the changes in dominant ideals from century to century," is a subject addressed in the following chapters; as noted above, it is distinct from Frederick Schauer's "entrenchment of generalizations," in *Playing by the Rules: A Philosophical Examination of Rule-Based Decision-Making in Law and Life*, 38–50.

the obscurity surrounding his thought derives from a failure to recognize his transformative conception of legal inquiry, even while the culture surrounding legal language, to which he was naturally committed as a lawyer and judge, demands that its concepts not appear to be in transition. Law is more readily analyzed, from law school on, as a fixed system. I will sharply distinguish Holmes's position from an influential conceptual view of law, and of legal logic, associated with now-dominant analytical and conceptual philosophies of law.

Holmes took few pains to formalize his philosophical perspective, which has left others to select among his writings and speeches for its essence. Many have focused on a provocative 1897 address to Boston University law students, "The Path of the Law." The next chapter focuses instead on much earlier texts of 1870 and 1873, in which is found a distinctive move, radical for both legal and logical theory, that I refer to as a socially informed "inductive turn." The inductive turn was tentative at first, but would be elaborated in the context of his theory of legal history set forth in *The Common Law*. The turn brought him to address the social dimension of logical induction, connecting conflict with the finding of legal similarity and the entrenchment of legal concepts.

Evidence of his concern with entrenchment can be found in his 1899 address to the New York State Bar Association, by then Chief Justice Holmes of the Massachusetts Supreme Judicial Court. The title of this talk, notably, was "Law in Science and Science in Law."

> It is perfectly proper to regard and study the law as a great anthropological document. It is proper to resort to it to discover what ideals of society have been strong enough to reach that final form of expression, or what have been the changes in dominant ideals from century to century. It is proper to study it as an exercise in the morphology and transformation of human ideas. The study pursued for such ends becomes science in the strictest sense.[15]

Here Holmes suggests a broad view of entrenchment, applicable to both ideas and "ideals." Holmes's inductive turn, in looking at the "morphology and transformation of ideas," was unlike every canonical exposition of later legal realism. The legal realists of the twentieth century, energized by Holmes, also favored empirical and inductive methods, but their choices of what to adopt as the empirical base of law were different. The

15. "Law in Science and Science in Law," *Harvard Law Review* 11 (1899): 443; *CW*, 3:407.

legal realists focused on the particular judicial decision, and the influences immediately surrounding it. Holmes focused on the relation of court decisions to the problems underlying them, and thence to the process by which, in addressing those problems, general legal knowledge grows and becomes stable through a process that will be called convergence.

His approach may be compared to Mill's reformism, as it is generically related to the latter's zealous opposition to thinking from general axioms. Holmes accepted Mill's idea that concepts are grounded in particular experience, and amended it with an admonition drawn from dispute, conflict, and warfare. Louis Menand has written that Holmes "had gone off to fight because of his moral beliefs, which he held with singular fervor. The war did more than make him lose those beliefs. It made him lose his belief in beliefs. It impressed on his mind, in the most graphic and indelible way, a certain idea about the limits of ideas." This is true, as far as it goes; but Holmes went further than mere skepticism, grounded in "limits." The war motivated him to reconsider authoritative texts on logic, and to reexamine the *operation* of ideas. Menand has this to say about the Civil War:

> [T]he outcome of the Civil War was a validation, as Lincoln had hoped it would be, of the American experiment. Except for one thing, which is that people who live in a democracy are not supposed to settle their disagreements by killing one another. For the generation that lived through it, the Civil War was a terrible and traumatic experience. It tore a hole through their lives. To some of them, the war seemed not just a failure of democracy, but a failure of culture, a failure of ideas.[16]

This is also accurate, and it applies, as Menand writes, also to Wright, Peirce, James, and Dewey. They sought a reconstruction of human thought in the wake of a terrific conflict, but Holmes was the one who took the fact of *perennial* conflict seriously, and brought it into a theory of knowledge. He looked at legal (and by inference also human) development with an eye for the mechanism of success and failure: the process, which I will analyze in detail, of conflict and "convergence," the nature of resolution by practical adaptation as well as cognitive resolution. His view of law was not of an autonomous force, but as a field of inquiry. Into it came critical nonlegal input, through the network of social practices.

16. Louis Menand, *The Metaphysical Club*, x–xi.

Ironically, Holmes's severest academic critic, Harvard law professor Lon L. Fuller, unknowingly shared his view of the role of the network of informal customs and practices in defining law and obligating citizens, but mistook his position mainly from remarks made in 1897 in "The Path of the Law." Largely through this misreading, Holmes was roundly criticized, first by Fuller in 1940, and lately in a 1999 monograph by Professor Albert W. Alschuler of the University of Chicago Law School. Fuller's criticism in 1940 set a negative tone that has never been entirely redressed. The error lay in mistaking a caution against confusing moral terms as an ontological rather than a methodological claim.

As a visiting professor at Harvard Law School, Oxford University professor H. L. A. Hart gave the 1957 Oliver Wendell Holmes Lecture, "Positivism and the Separation of Law and Morals." Later, in his influential *The Concept of Law* (1961), Hart refocused jurisprudence toward a rigorous analytical positivism. Hart's strict separation of law and morals reignited interest in moral principles and natural law, stimulating Hart's debates with Lon Fuller and later Ronald Dworkin. Meanwhile, Holmes's warnings against judicial moralizing continued to lead many scholars (including Hart) to place him on Hart's side of the separation debate.

Recovery of Holmes's initial position and its origins opens insight into issues of interest to historians of legal thought. It is also relevant to the continuing path and relevance of philosophical pragmatism.[17] I will define his views within the developing perspective of legal philosophy, and of pragmatism as an increasingly influential movement worldwide. With this in mind, my first task is to recover his earliest concerns. I begin with the intellectual milieu into which he entered on returning from the Civil War in 1864.

Philosophy in Nineteenth-Century Cambridge

In April 1876 Holmes wrote to Ralph Waldo Emerson (whom he had known from youth) enclosing a just-published article[18] on law with the comment,

17. This will include examination of Holmes's social inductivism regarding the sources of knowledge in general, coming from early modern philosophy. As noted in chap. 10, contemporary pragmatism has been transformed by linguistic analytical philosophy. See Cheryl Misak, *The American Pragmatists*.

18. Mark De Wolfe Howe, *Justice Oliver Wendell Holmes: The Shaping Years, 1841–1870*. The article was "Primitive Notions in Modern Law No. I," *American Law Review* 10 (April 1876): 422; Kellogg, *Formative Essays*, 129; *CW* 3:4.

"law provides a way to philosophy . . . and I hope to prove it before I die." What exactly did he mean, and intend, by this? It has not given rise to a consensus among Holmes's biographers and other commentators. Holmes was not given to idle remarks during this period of his life, especially to Emerson. What evidence do we have of Holmes's philosophizing, and its sources, prior to this letter?[19]

The word "pragmatism" was not used by any of the Cambridge intellectuals until much later.[20] The term has gained scope as it has come to encompass a distinct vision of American thought since the nineteenth century, sometimes including Holmes. We should keep in mind, as Bruce Kuklick and others have written, that immediate concerns took precedence—the context of religious thought in New England, foundational issues raised by European philosophy, and Darwin's work on evolution, influences that are well known. Less so are nineteenth-century reflections on the early modern philosophers, especially Berkeley, Hume, Hegel, and Kant, and less well-known writers like Thomas Reid, William Hamilton, Herbert Spencer, and William Whewell. Darwin's theory of evolution was shaking claims of certainty, and led the Cambridge intellectuals to question philosophical premises for the source and nature of concepts, like abstract space, which had played a role in Immanuel Kant's eighteenth-century response to British empiricism.[21]

Pragmatism has been closely connected with the group called the Metaphysical Club, of which Charles Peirce records the founding in 1871. The suggestion of such a group came from James in a letter from Europe to Holmes in 1868. Looking back in 1906, Peirce included himself, Holmes, William James, Chauncey Wright, John Fiske, and N. St. John Green, but in two other accounts he omits Holmes. Much has been written about the

19. He added, "Accept this little piece as written in that faith and as a slight mark of the gratitude and respect I feel for you who more than anyone else first started the philosophical ferment in my mind." Holmes to Emerson, April 16, 1876, Harvard University Archives, quoted in Howe, *The Shaping Years*, 203; White, *Justice Oliver Wendell Holmes*, 43–44, 501. On Emerson's influence, see Holmes to Pollock, May 30, 1930, in Mark De Wolfe Howe, ed., *Holmes-Pollock Letters*.

20. James introduced the term in an address in 1898, "Philosophical Conceptions and Practical Results," delivered before the Philosophical Union of the University of California, Berkeley, August 26, 1898, first printed in the *University Chronicle*, September 1898, 1:287–310.

21. Flower and Murphey, *History of Philosophy in America*; 372, 536–53, 568–82; Kuklick, *Rise of American Philosophy*, 12–18, 33–35, 94–95. See Murray Murphey's summary of the intellectual/historical context of pragmatism in *C. I. Lewis: The Last Great Pragmatist*, 2–12.

club's possible influence on Holmes, or his influence on the club, but well before 1871 he wrote to James of having supplanted his focus on philosophy with "law—law—law."[22] He would take on the revision of the major legal encyclopedia Kent's *Commentaries on American Law* in December of 1869, and become coeditor of the *American Law Review* in 1870. The club had nothing to do with Holmes's inductive turn, as its first statement came in 1870.

However, something similar was involved: a round-robin of (mainly) one-on-one discussions with interested friends, including later members of the club. While the decade 1866–76 was crucial for the full emergence of Holmes's perspective, I look to the period 1866–70, *before* the Metaphysical Club, for the origin of the inductive turn, and the connection of his emerging legal thought with "philosophy," both as that term meant to him, and as it may mean to us today. As his appointed biographer Mark De Wolfe Howe observed, from the moment Holmes went from Harvard to war, he had become convinced that "the instruments of philosophy are to be found in the methods of science."[23]

Essential for evidence of this are Holmes's two pocket daily diary books of 1866–67, his lists of books read, and his first published theoretical essay on law written in August of 1870. Holmes's diary reveals readings on natural science, logic, and philosophy and conversations involving Peirce, James, Wright, John Chipman Gray, Francis Ellingwood Abbot, and others, following his meeting John Stuart Mill and Alexander Bain on a visit to London in 1866. Planning the voyage appears to have moved him to acquire the 1866 diary book, which then recorded his preparations and details of the trip itself, and was maintained afterward in Boston and Cambridge until December 22, 1867, to be succeeded by a spare (and not quite comprehensive) listing of books read until the end of his life. The later reading diary recorded only occasional personal comments (for example, on June 17, 1872: "*Married* [to Fanny Dixwell] sole editor of [American] Law Rev. July no. *et seq.*").[24]

22. Holmes to William James, December 15, 1867, Ignas K. Skrupskelis and Elizabeth M. Berkeley, eds., *The Correspondence of William James*, 4:237; this remark was followed by a lengthy critical reflection on Kant's *Critique of Pure Reason*.

23. Howe, *The Shaping Years*, 55; see also 17–18 (science as influencing his skepticism), 206–7 (legal education should be scientific), 256–58 (science in discussions with Wright and James); but see 221–22 (questioning Holmes's understanding of science).

24. Holmes, Daily Diaries, 1866–67, Harvard University Archives. That his reading lists were not comprehensive is indicated by certain works not listed but mentioned in correspondence as

In the brief period in which Holmes kept the daily pocket diaries we get a glimpse into his life, without which the nature and flow of informal associations, and especially Peirce's early thoughts on logic and his attendance at two of Peirce's 1866 Lowell Lectures on induction and scientific method, would be invisible. There is relatively little evidence of influence on his thought from the post-1871 meetings mentioned by Peirce, but there is much in the diaries from the earlier period.[25]

Regarding the two men who would later be identified with the founding of pragmatism, Peirce and William James, Holmes's correspondence was effusive in his respect and affection for James in the immediate post-war years, and the diaries note seeking him out to discuss both science and philosophy. He notes attending at least two of Peirce's remarkable 1866 lectures and receiving from Peirce a bound pamphlet of the latter's papers on logic in 1867. Nevertheless, Holmes never attributed any influence of either man to his own thought, and in late correspondence treated their signal accomplishments with near disdain.[26]

---

having been consulted (e.g., William Thomson, *An Outline of the Necessary Laws of Thought*, mentioned in Holmes to William James, December 15, 1867).

25. Although the original club may have died in late 1872, we know from correspondence that it was revived in 1876; Francis Ellingwood Abbot had a letter from William James in January of that year inviting him "to join a Club for reading and discussing philosophical authors, which meets once a week at present and is composed of C. C. Everett, N. St. John Green, O. W. Holmes, Jr., John Fiske, Thos. Davidson. J. B. Warner, Prof. Bowen, and one or two others [Peirce was in Europe until August]. We have begun with Hume's Treatise on Human Nature and the next meeting is at this house, next Sunday evening at ½ past seven promptly." Holmes's copious diary of his reading records Hume's *Treatise* in April of 1876, presumably in finishing it. See Little, "Early Reading of Justice Oliver Wendell Holmes," 192; Fisch, "Metaphysical Club," 7–8.

26. Holmes in 1908 commented to Pollock of James, "*I* think pragmatism an amusing humbug—like most of William James's speculations, as distinguished from his admirable and well written Irish perceptions of life." Holmes to Pollock, June 17, 1908, in Howe, ed., *Holmes-Pollock Letters*, 1:138–39. When Charles Hartshorne began preparing Peirce's *Collected Papers* in 1927, he wrote Justice Holmes, at eighty-six the only surviving member of the original Metaphysical Club, and received in reply: "I am afraid that I cannot help you much in the way of recollections of Charles Peirce. I think I remember his father saying to me, 'Charles is a genius,' and I remember the august tone in which, at one of the few meetings at which I was present, Charles prefaced his opinion with '*Other* philosophers have thought.' Once in a fertilizing way he challenged some assumption that I made, but alas I forget what. But in those days I was studying law and I soon dropped out of the band, although I should have liked to rejoin it when it was too late. I think I learned more from Chauncey Wright and St. John Green, as I saw Peirce very little." Fisch, "Was there a Metaphysical Club in Cambridge?," 10–11.

Only Wright, a solitary Cambridge bachelor who attended Harvard a decade earlier and welcomed Holmes and others to his rooms in Cambridge to discuss contemporary science and philosophy, received explicit recognition (with the exception of Emerson) in Holmes's later correspondence, as "a philosopher of real merit."[27] Wright is now identified as having occupied an influential role in the formation of pragmatism. Living mostly alone in Cambridge when Holmes returned from the Union Army to attend Harvard Law School, he was widely admired for his acuteness and depth of understanding, even by Charles Darwin with whom he corresponded. As a friend of the Peirce family, he had engaged in discussions of science and philosophy with the younger Charles since 1857. In that year Peirce would record that he talked about philosophy with Wright almost every day.[28]

An accomplished practitioner of science and mathematics, Wright grew interested in empirical philosophy from reading Francis Bacon's *Novum Organum* and other works after graduation from Harvard in 1857. Wright was energized by Bacon's mission to oppose uncritical axiomatic deduction, as having tended throughout history to control patterns of belief and discourage empirical investigation. Wright then became interested in the Scottish philosopher William Hamilton, as well as English followers of Bacon, especially Mill and William Whewell. Through Hamilton, Wright and other American intellectuals sought an accommodation between the "common sense" epistemology of Thomas Reid and the transcendentalism of Immanuel Kant.[29] Wright would draw from Whewell an extensive knowledge of the prior history of science, from which Whewell corroborated the enduring value of empiricism in a three-volume *History of the Inductive Sciences* (1840).[30]

Wright became a hub of influence reaching many younger (and some older) intellectuals, including Holmes and Peirce, the spokes of the wheel also extending to James and Abbot, variously encouraging them to engage with European writers including Reid, Kant, Hamilton, Mill, and Whewell—assuming Professor Bowen had not already reached them at

27. Holmes to Pollock, August 30, 1929, in Howe, ed., *Holmes-Pollock Letters* 2:252.

28. "Essays toward the Interpretation of Our Thoughts," 1909 MS 620, Charles S. Peirce Papers, Indiana University.

29. Kuklick, *Rise of American Philosophy*, 16–17; Flower and Murphey, *History of Philosophy in America*, 203–69.

30. Whewell is credited with having coined the term "scientist"; before him scientists were known in England as "natural philosophers." Laura J. Snyder, *The Philosophical Breakfast Club*, 3.

Harvard with his overlapping interests. Bowen had in 1864 published a treatise on logic reflecting the influence of these writers on philosophical thought in Cambridge.[31]

Wright is mentioned in Holmes's 1867 diary on April 22 in the following cursory notes: "Cambridge to see C. Wright on vis viva [a scientific controversy] he wasn't in so I went to H. James." On September 12 the diary reads: "Read Ch. Wright's article on Herb. Spencer—N. A. Rev. Apr/65", and the next day: "Debauch on Philosophy. Read Abbot's two articles Philosophy of Space & Time & The Conditioned & the Uncond. N. A. Review July & Oct 1864." Less than a month later on October 8: "Had some metaphysics with C. Wright—we agreed esp. on Abbot's view of Space." Then, on October 20 1867:

> Went out and had
> a long palaver with
> Chauncey Wright
> also with Wm James
> on philosophy—
> Kant.

Assessing the diary entries and the list of reading (assuming it to be roughly chronological), we find that sometime in 1865–66, his second year at Harvard Law School, Holmes turned to philosophy amidst law texts, first to histories of philosophy by Ritter and Lewes. He quickly added books on scientific subjects (Youmans on physics and chemistry) and then Herbert Spencer's then-influential *First Principles of a New System of Philosophy*, accompanied by a forceful essay by Wright criticizing Spencer for employing an axiomatic argument to reach his sweeping and later discredited conclusions on evolution. Wright's outlook has been characterized by twentieth-century commentators as a robust evolutionary naturalism, with a comprehensive opposition to all manner of axiomatic argument from teleological principles, such as the attribution of natural design to the universe.[32]

31. Francis Bowen, *A Treatise on Logic*. Holmes was reading Hamilton in 1866; Howe, *Shaping Years*, 203.

32. Kuklick, *Rise of American Philosophy*, 63–79; Flower and Murphey, *History of Philosophy in America*, 535–53; Edward H. Madden, *Chauncey Wright and the Foundations of Pragmatism*, passim; Cheryl Misak, *The American Pragmatists*, 14–25.

Holmes resigned from Harvard Law School in December 1865 to continue law studies as an apprentice to attorney Robert M. Morse in Boston. He was in and out of Cambridge, visiting James and Wright, and appears to have sharpened his focus on science from Wright's extended comments on scientific method in the essay on Spencer.[33] Immediately below their texts in his reading list he notes Whewell's *History of the Inductive Sciences* and "[John] Herschel's Review of same." Then, Morell's *History of European Philosophy* is followed by William Hamilton's *Metaphysics*, and by Mill's then-devastating[34] *Examination of Sir William Hamilton's Philosophy*. He notes more reading on the history of thought, as well as G. W. F. Hegel, before leaving for Europe on April 1866. He returned in late August with undiminished philosophical curiosity.

The 1867 note recording agreement with Wright "esp. on Abbot's view of space" (the agreement would most likely have been with Wright's *criticism* of Abbot) was entered on September 12.[35] The diary suggests perhaps a year or so of visits with Wright, and should indicate, to anyone who looks at Abbot's 1864 article "The Philosophy of Space and Time," the complexity of their discussions, which involved the philosophy of William Hamilton, the nature of fundamental abstractions like time and space, and the influence of Immanuel Kant regarding the nature and source of fundamental conceptions that had preoccupied the early modern philosophers.[36]

James, a student at Harvard since 1861, had returned from a field trip in Brazil to his studies of science when Holmes had mustered out of the army in August 1864 to attend law school, and the two engaged in regular

33. Wright, "The Philosophy of Herbert Spencer," in Charles Eliot Norton, ed., *Philosophical Discussions*; Little, "The Early Reading of Justice Oliver Wendell Holmes."

34. Kuklick, *Rise of American Philosophy*, 20–21.

35. In late 1864 Wright began a correspondence of several years with Francis E. Abbot, then a Unitarian clergyman and gifted metaphysician, on his article in the *North American Review* for July 1864, "The Philosophy of Space and Time." The nature of Wright's discussion with Holmes in 1867 is suggested by comments in the first letter, which included Wright's observation, "the intellectual form of Space through which we are necessitated to conceive of every thing as in relation to extension . . . is not in Hamilton's Philosophy an object of thought. It is a determinant, but not a constituent of knowledge. Indeed, a Form, in Kantian phraseology, is neither a knowledge nor a faculty of knowledge, but rather a determinant of the limits of knowledge, though regarded by Kant himself as something more than a negation of knowledge." Wright to Abbot, December 20, 1864, in James B. Thayer, ed., *Letters of Chauncey Wright, with Some Account of His Life*, 57–58.

36. Kuklick, *Rise of American Philosophy*, 93–103; Flower and Murphey, *History of Philosophy in America*, 549.

discussions until James's voyage to Europe in April 1866, corresponding by mail thereafter. This correspondence is replete with mutual affection and intellectual respect. (Both are strangely missing, on Holmes's side, from the latter's later comments in his lengthy correspondence with the English legal scholar Frederick Pollock.)[37]

James had earlier befriended Peirce at Harvard in 1861. The spokes of the wheel connecting all three to Wright were established by the end of 1865. Holmes's diary notes reflect discussions of epistemological issues emerging from the interaction of British empiricism and German idealism, as well as more recent British commentaries on the history and methods of science by Mill, Whewell, and Herschel. A rough indication of the framework of these discussions, at least with James, might be gleaned from James's 1909 Hibbert Lectures, which begins with a "look back into the sixties," several pages of reflection on the American reception during that period of British and German philosophical ideas.[38]

Regarding Holmes's mention of Kant on October 20, the diary also notes that while reading Thomas Reid's *Essays on the Intellectual Powers of Man* he borrowed Kant's *Critique of Pure Reason* on September 29 and finished it on November 13. The discussions with Wright in late October included abstractions like time, space, and causation, and Kant's complex perspective on the putatively innate categories of human thought. Holmes would write two letters to James in Europe assessing Kant's *Critique of Pure Reason* roughly a month later. His letters indicate, if not acceptance, comprehension of difficult issues. James apparently did not respond.[39]

Peirce in the latter 1860s was on a trajectory originating with a catalyzing impetus on his thought from Kant's *Critique of Pure Reason*. It led him intensively to reexamine the history of Western logic, analyzing the nature of induction and the varieties of the syllogism, and (likely with

37. See n. 26 above.

38. James, *Pluralistic Universe*, 4–5. This is discussed in chap. 10.

39. James's correspondence does not yet provide comparable evidence of interest in philosophy to that of Holmes, until he had passed through a long depression in early 1870 and began studying Kant, first through the work of Charles Renouvier. Kuklick, *Rise of American Philosophy*, 159–64. Holmes was already discussing Kant in the September 1867 meeting with Wright, and Abbot's view of space. In the letters to James in Germany on Kant's *Critique*, Holmes's reference to William Thomson (as well as to Henry Mansel in the diary) is evidence of the influence of Hamilton. An extended discussion of logic and philosophy in nineteenth-century New England is found in Flower and Murphey, *History of Philosophy in America*, 365–87.

Wright as a medium) intersected with Holmes at crucial points in both of their thinking. While Peirce had accepted Kant's notion of transcendent categories of human thought, and would adopt a revisionary approach to them, Holmes was rejecting Kant's basic approach in his correspondence with James in December 1867.[40]

In late 1866, after meetings with Mill and Bain in London, Holmes's interest in scientific method and the debates of Western philosophical logic was further stimulated by two lectures by Peirce, on deduction, induction, and scientific method. With this background I examine Holmes's attendance at the lectures and their bearing on his consequential "inductive turn."

40. Holmes to James, December 15, 1867: "Hoc nota as to what I conceive a fundamental error of Kant on his own principles (always protesting, as they say in pleading, his whole philosophy is unsound)." The letter continues with several objections to Kant's response to Hume regarding synthetic *a priori* judgments. Ignas K. Skrupskelis and Elizabeth M Berkeley, eds., *Correspondence of William James*, 4.236–40.

CHAPTER TWO

Logic

This chapter examines how Holmes's reading of Mill's A System of Logic, noting a passage dealing with the syllogism, was influenced by questions raised by Charles S. Peirce in lectures on logic and induction in late 1866.

* * *

Almost everyone knows Lord Mansfield's advice to a man of practical good sense, who, being appointed governor of a colony, has to preside in its courts of justice, without previous judicial practice or legal education. The advice was to give his decision boldly, for it would probably be right, but never to venture on assigning reasons, for they would almost infallibly be wrong.—John Stuart Mill, *A System of Logic*, 1843

The above passage, from John Stuart Mill's influential *A System of Logic*, is part of Mill's contribution to a nineteenth-century debate with Richard Whately (whose 1826 *Elements of Logic* captured Charles Peirce's interest at age twelve) over whether the logical syllogism "is, or is not, a process of inference; a progress from the known to the unknown: a means of coming to a knowledge of something which we did not know before." Mill there employs a story about the famous jurist William Murray, First Earl of Mansfield, to support his contention that "[a]ll inference is from particulars to particulars," and that "[n]ot one iota is added to the proof by interpolating a general proposition."[1] Mill continues:

> Since the individual cases are all the evidence we can possess, evidence which no logical form into which we choose to throw it can make greater than it is; and since that evidence is either sufficient in itself, or, if insufficient for the one purpose, cannot be sufficient for the other; I am unable to see why we should be for-

1. Mill, *A System of Logic*, 1:232.

> bidden to take the shortest cut from these sufficient premises to the conclusion, and constrained to travel the "high priori road," by the arbitrary fiat of logicians.[2]

As a disciple of Francis Bacon, Mill occupies a prominent place in the history of logic as an exponent of the empirical tradition, which would influence the thinking of Wright, James, and Peirce. While Mill was more engaged with the method of natural science, this example is drawn from law—specifically from judicial practice. It suggests the difficulty of applying syllogistic inference to unique disputes for the individual observer. Four years after reading through Mill's *Logic* in 1866, the young Oliver Wendell Holmes Jr., then editing James Kent's *Commentaries on American Law* and immersed in the records of actual cases, suggested another explanation: whereas the syllogism models how the idealized *individual* mind might operate to justify knowledge, judges are part of a *community* of inquiry. Influenced by his intellectual peers in Cambridge, perhaps also by his experience in the Civil War, Holmes looked to the effects of *society* on thought, and the question of how a *community* resolves doubt and reaches conclusions.

In late 1866, not long after returning from England where he had met Mill, Holmes attended at least two of Charles Peirce's twelve Lowell Lectures in Boston. The title of the series was "The Logic of Science; or, Induction and Hypothesis." The fourth lecture on November 3, three years before James would propose the idea of a philosophical discussion club in a letter to Holmes from Berlin, was an extended critique of Mill's logical views, and Holmes soon borrowed Mill's *System of Logic* from the Boston Athenaeum and despite a bad flu read large portions of it every day, finishing it in a week.[3] What did Peirce say that might have influenced this, and how did it fit into their thinking at this time? I will return to these questions, and Peirce's lectures, after glancing a few years ahead.

In 1870 we find Holmes, in an early essay on law, repeating the story of Lord Mansfield's comment, in a text that addresses the relationship of legal particulars and generals:

> It is the merit of the common law that it decides the case first and determines the principle afterwards. . . . In cases of first impression Lord Mansfield's

2. Ibid., 1:214.

3. Daily Diary, November 17–23, 1867, Oliver Wendell Holmes Jr. Papers, Harvard Law School Library, Cambridge, MA. The Boston Athenaeum served its members as a lending library, as it does today.

> often-quoted advice to the business man who was suddenly appointed judge, that he should state his conclusions and not give his reasons, as his judgment would probably be right and the reasons certainly wrong, is not without its application to more educated courts. It is only after a series of determinations on the same subject-matter, that it becomes necessary to "reconcile the cases," as it is called, that is, by a true induction to state the principle which has until then been obscurely felt. And this statement is often modified more than once by new decisions before the abstracted general rule takes its final shape. A well settled legal doctrine embodies the work of many minds, and has been tested in form as well as substance by trained critics whose practical interest is to resist it at every step.[4]

Here Holmes appears to have absorbed Mill's critique of the syllogism and his vision of "reasoning from particulars to particulars." But the relation of particulars and generals is different. Holmes adds an account of the *emergence* of generalization from particular judgments, entirely missing from Mill's account. Holmes's phrase "true induction" originates with Bacon and was repeatedly used by Whewell. It is an important addendum to Mill's "Not one iota is added to the proof by interpolating a general proposition." Focusing on the origin of the general itself, Holmes attributes it to a "series of determinations on the same subject." These are not already given, as assumed in the classic example "all men are mortal," but represent separate judgments in varying circumstances by a community of inquirers, namely, the disparate courts of law. And the "test" of settled doctrine includes "substance" as well as "form."[5]

The major premise of the basic syllogism (known as *Barbara*), "All men are mortal," refers to a set of conventionally comparable particulars. Mill observed that Socrates's mortality is already known to the syllogizing mind without having to detour (taking the "high priori road") to infer that Socrates is also mortal.[6] But what if the particulars are *not* all patently

4. "Codes, and the Arrangement of the Law," *American Law Review* 5 (October 1870): 1, reprinted in Frederic Kellogg, *The Formative Essays of Justice Holmes*, 77; *CW* 1:212.

5. The "substance" I will argue includes a key piece of what is required for entrenchment, which is adjusted *practice*. This is more than the traditional common law assumption of the adoption of custom, as Holmes here adds an element of broad social inquiry and practical adjustment, in accounting for the question of how general propositions emerge from particular judgments. See Matthew Hale, *The History of the Common Law of England*.

6. Mill, *A System of Logic*, 1:214. Peirce, in his notes on Mill for the fourth lecture (the second attended by Holmes), writes, "When we have said that Andrew Jackson is a man, and

comparable,[7] as in a set of *novel* situations or judgments? Then it is certainly not appropriate to "take the shortest cut from premises to conclusion." Holmes has raised, in relation to Mill's account, a distinct problem: that of social classification and the emergence of consensus. The "general" in question is yet unestablished, and the question of its development is raised.

Note first that the reflecting mind, in Holmes's version, is not attached to a single observer. Holmes's legal general is the work of "many minds, and has been tested by trained critics whose practical interest is to resist it at every step." Who are these many minds? Surely not just the judges, who while professionally skeptical are presumably not "resisting it at every step." There is also a succession of lawyers, bringing various practical considerations to bear, whether or not purely motivated. They bring the resisting interests of opposing parties, and through them participation of the community at large to bear (albeit divided and subject to partisan distortion). The eventual formula is being variously tweaked while passed from case to case and court to court. When the issue bears further scrutiny, critics and scholars may also weigh in.

Another thing absent in Mill is what John Dewey in his 1938 treatise on pragmatic logic would call the "continuum."[8] What, after all, is going on outside the courtroom between cases? Practices may adapt, as the particular decisions are followed and discussed, and have an increasing influence. Thus Holmes's comment implies a feedback loop of changing conduct and practical conditions influencing the ultimate formulation of the rule.[9] And there are further questions raised by this brief description: How is the "general" formulated? Does it just emerge, or must there be a creative

---

that all men are mortal we have already said indirectly that is have implied that Andrew Jackson is mortal." *Writings of Charles S. Peirce: A Chronological Edition* (hereafter *Writings*), 1:409.

7. By "comparable" here I mean that "men" share an obvious similarity in their *mortality*, an aspect that ignores their (also obvious) multiple *differences* as irrelevant to this particular syllogistic inquiry.

8. John Dewey, *Logic: The Theory of Inquiry*, 246–52. The continuum idea here refers to the progress of inquiry over a passage of time.

9. This adds the importance of practice to the concept of a rule. John Rawls analyzes the role of practice in rule formation in "Two Concepts of Rules," 1955, reprinted in Philippa Foot, *Theories of Ethics*. Rawls distinguishes the practice conception from the "summary view," in which rules are pictured as summaries of past decisions in particular cases, and hence "the decisions made on particular cases are logically prior to rules." Under the practice conception, practices are logically prior; and my claim is that Holmes's conception is closer to the practice than the summary view.

element? If science seeks understanding through the hypothesis, is there a *legal* analogy for the *scientific* hypothesis? The creative process of science was already occupying both Wright and Peirce when Holmes was visiting Wright and reading Spencer and Whewell, and had been touched on by Peirce in his earlier lectures and writings.[10]

The 1870 comment refers explicitly to common law decision making. It comes at the beginning of an essay for the *American Law Review* titled "Codes, and the Arrangement of the Law," exploring the merit of codification over the incremental, case-based method of the common law. The taxonomic question there was whether, in constructing a code, the overall structure should be based on "duties" rather than "rights," the latter notion having been favored by John Austin in his influential 1859 *Lectures on Jurisprudence*, which Holmes notes having already read and reread (the first after having just donned a Union uniform). This indicates an early concern with fundamental legal categories, to which I will return.

To us there might seem little reason to expect, at this stage in his work, that Holmes's observation about the common law would be applied to all aspects of nineteenth-century law. Yet Holmes is speaking in very broad terms: would it apply to interpreting statutes? He goes on to say that the tweaking process has "advantages the want of which cannot be supplied by any faculty of generalization, however brilliant." Underlying his point is that for *any* legal rule, no matter how well crafted (with "principles clearly enunciated"), the growing process will go on: "New cases will arise which will elude the most carefully constructed formula." The common law, he notes, "is prepared for this, and simply modifies the form of its rule." This he attributes to "successive approximations—by a continual reconciliation of cases."[11]

If the observation is applicable to specific provisions in a code, why then not to a statute, given the inevitable variety of unforeseen cases? Lawyers have long been looking up statutes accompanied by regularly updated annotations, to see whether there is a relevant doubt about their application. (Holmes would, indeed, apply it to statutes.)[12] Yet Holmes's comment is not readily squared with the ideal of law as unchanging, or the deductive presumption of legal interpretation, "strictly rule-governed, driven

10. See Max Fisch, introduction to vol. 1, *Writings*, xxiv, and Peirce's undelivered "Lecture on the Theories of Whewell, Mill, and Comte," 1:205–23.

11. Holmes, "Codes," 2; Kellogg, *Formative Essays of Justice Holmes*, 78; *CW*, 1:213.

12. *Northern Securities Co. v. United States*, 193 U.S. 197 (1904).

by the internal and ineluctible logic of the law."[13] It raises several questions. What exactly is a "case of first impression," and are there *truly* no applicable authorities to refer to? If there is *no* "general" yet articulated in the exploratory stage, on what grounds do the early cases get decided? Does the Mansfield story present a realistic example of legal uncertainty? What is the role of judicial reason, if any? What of the "continuum" of inquiry over time—do different standards apply depending on when (in the extended generalizing process) a given case occurs? And where in the continuum do the "approximations" come from?

The 1870 essay is a tantalizing exploration, with few answers, of legal uncertainty. Rather than focusing on the semantic elements of uncertainty in legal language (the vagueness of words in a legal proposition), it focuses on an uncertainty related to the underlying dispute, or better, to the underlying (and yet undefined) *problem*. It departs from the conventional understanding that a judge should decide each case from the "black letter" language of fixed authorities. Holmes may not have known in 1870 that he would become a judge, but if so, would he not have to drop this model or come up with some answers reassuring others that he had not abandoned a deductive understanding of applying the settled law? As it happens, far from dropping it, he would make it central to his judicial thinking about all manner of cases, reaching into constitutional law.

Further insights into his thinking arrive in another paper published three years later. Although still concerned in 1873 with the fundamental taxonomic issue of duties versus rights, Holmes (addressing personal injury law) returned to the continuum model with an important addendum. The uncertain case is no longer imagined in a vacuum with no applicable precedent, but rather as occurring between two opposing but already established precedents—one might say in a space of contested reasons. Holmes describes this process as follows:

> The growth of the law is very apt to take place in this way: two widely different cases suggest a general distinction, which is a clear one when stated broadly. But as new cases cluster around the opposite poles, and begin to approach each other, the distinction becomes more difficult to trace; the determinations are made one way or the other on a very slight preponderance of feeling, rather than articulate reason; and at last a mathematical line is arrived at by the contact

13. Postema, *Treatise of Legal Philosophy*, 7, describing legal formalism, which applies to both statute and common law.

> of contrary decisions, which is so far arbitrary that it might equally well have been drawn a little further to the one side or to the other.[14]

This graphic description suggests two precedential "poles," which we might mark A and B, each encompassing a cumulative formulation based on previous decisions, but now surrounded by new cases that "cluster" like marks on a graph, some nearer to one pole, some to the other, and still others in a space equidistant from both. The new cases are not decided independently as in 1870, but rather with an awareness of (if not explicit reference to) prior precedents that operate as the opposing "poles." New marks are being made on the graph, which we should visualize along a time line, with choices in the middle area occasioning explanation with regard to the earlier poles. As time progresses, the new cases are "marked" on either side of a "line" that defines agreement with one pole or the other.

Taken together with the gradual, retrospective "successive approximation" process outlined in the 1870 essay, the implication is that, as more cases are decided in the space of contested reasons, the meanings of both A and B, that is, the conceptual understanding of earlier discrete judicial experience (in the prior "clusters"), are subject to being retrospectively tweaked or refined to accommodate the new problem. Holmes has added the image of a time-dependent and possibly meandering "line," engaging the input of judges, lawyers, and affected potential litigants in the relevant environment; possibly also critics and scholars.[15]

This observation addresses the manner in which patterns of conduct are found, reinforced, and adjusted by legal decisions, as conflicts occur in society. It comes directly from his study of English and American cases while editing Kent's *Commentaries*. The case he cites for the remark, explaining his use of the term "mathematical" here, involves distance measurement, where eighteenth-century English courts settled on a formula to resolve continuing litigation over the competing rights of neighboring landowners concerning the height of structures near a boundary. In the absence of local building codes (a later development) a formula was eventually worked out. A comparable issue today might be the U.S. Supreme

14. Holmes, "The Theory of Torts," *American Law Review* 7 (July 1873): 652, 654; Kellogg, *Formative Essays of Justice Holmes*, 119; *CW*, 1:327.

15. Mill notes that Mansfield preferred a judge with "a mind stored with general propositions derived by legitimate induction." *Logic*, 1:218. This is discussed at greater length in chap. 6 below.

Court seeking an appropriate "buffer-zone" distance from abortion clinics to balance the rights of pro-life picketers against women seeking access to medical assistance.[16]

The diaries and letters reveal Holmes turning his focus in 1868 increasingly to law in place of science and philosophy. References to line drawing would recur throughout his career. He would apply it to a wide variety of judicial matters, including statutory and constitutional issues. In the introduction to this book, I proposed that Holmes brings an original contribution to the theory of logical induction by adding a "social dimension" to resolutions of uncertainty. That claim is grounded in his development of the line-drawing analogy into a theory of law, even to suggesting in 1899 its broader implications as a *general* theory of uncertainty.

The claim drives the entire argument of this book. To round it out, I will need to prioritize two things. One is to show the importance of the early line-drawing essay to his other, better-known positions, his 1881 treatise *The Common Law*, and his judicial opinions, especially his opposition (sometimes expressed in dissenting opinions) to axiomatic reasoning, in comments like "general propositions do not decide concrete cases." An important part of this argument will be contrasting his approach to the conventional view of legal uncertainty, which focuses heavily on the vagueness of legal language. The second important thing is to show how line drawing (and the underlying social induction) explains away an objection that has bedeviled his legacy, starting soon after his death and continuing to the present. This is the attitude that Holmes undermined the moral foundations of law, through his repeated warnings regarding the application of legal language with "moral overtones."[17]

16. The recent Supreme Court case is *McCullen v. Coakley*, 453 U.S. 199, 134 S. Ct. 2518 (2014), holding that Massachusetts's thirty-five-feet abortion buffer zones, established via amendments to that state's Reproductive Health Care Facilities Act, violated the First Amendment to the U.S. Constitution, because it limited free expression too broadly. In 1873 Holmes wrote, "To leave the question to the jury for ever is simply to leave the law uncertain. Accordingly, we read in a recent equity case that what was left at large to the jury fifty years ago has now become a mathematical rule; that a building cannot be complained of unless its height exceeds the distance of its base from the base of the ancient windows. This instance explains the meaning of the question ordinarily left to the jury in negligence case. They are not asked what was the condition of the defendant's consciousness." Citing *Beadel v. Perry*, L.R. 3 Eq. 465, 467 (1866).

17. Holmes gave a speech in 1897 (as the chief judge of the Massachusetts Supreme Judicial Court) to graduating law students at Boston University, which was published in the *Harvard Law Review* under the title "The Path of the Law." There he emphasized the importance for practicing lawyers to be wary of, and to deflate, the use of moral language in the law, and to

I will get to these points later; let's return to 1866, and Peirce's Lowell Lectures. Holmes first attended Peirce's second lecture on October 27, 1866, in the company of John Chipman Gray.[18] The subject was a survey of various forms of the syllogism; the diary records discussing "logic" with Gray immediately after the lecture. Besides Gray, Chauncey Wright may also have encouraged Holmes to attend (Wright "thought more of [Peirce's] ability than that of any one he knew"[19]). Perhaps James did so as well, as he accompanied Holmes to the fourth lecture on November 3. Soon after, in a letter to his sister Alice on November 14, James wrote that he had gone with Holmes "[t]o C. S. Peirce's Lecture of wh. I cd. not understand a word but rather enjoyed the sensation of listening to for an hour. I then turned in to OW Holmes's [family house in Boston] and wrangled with him for another hour." Holmes had planned to attend the third lecture, but wrote in the diary on that date (the thirtieth) that he "[h]ad to cut C. Peirce's lecture on logic to vote at Ward meeting. Soldier's bounty business wh. I am against."

On the thirtieth, Peirce, having diagrammed and analyzed various syllogistic forms in the first two lectures, had eventually produced a bag containing red balls and removed them one by one to demonstrate the experience of probable induction.

> I have here a bag of balls. I shake them up well; and draw out one. It is red. I draw out another. It is red. I shake them up again and draw out another. It is red, again. Another: red. Another; red. One more: still red.
>
> Now I suppose you have no doubt that almost all the balls in that bag are red. Why? Upon the correct answer to that question much depends. Our fate

---

draw meanings from "prediction" of court decisions: "The prophecies of what the courts will do in fact, and nothing more pretentious, are what I mean by the law." Largely from this source, Holmes soon after his death was branded as a "legal positivist," in the specific sense of advocating a rigorous separation of law and morals, as two separate spheres or entities. This has occurred despite a comment in the same address that "law is the witness and deposit of our moral life." What he intended was a *methodological* caution, rooted in the danger of thinking from axioms. Prediction would focus attention on the inductive method of inquiry, against incorporating moral overtones into interpretations of legal language. This is discussed in chap. 8.

18. Holmes's diary is blank for the entire week prior to date of the second lecture, except for the note, "This week has been spent mainly on the case of the indictment of Boston Water Power Co. for Church St. nuisance." Whether he attended Peirce's opening lecture on Wednesday evening is uncertain.

19. Ignas K. Skrupskelis and Elizabeth M Berkeley, eds., *Correspondence of William James*, 4:525

> hangs upon it. All difficult questions require an understanding of the reason of our faith in experience as a witness to the future and unexperienced [*sic*].

This lecture proceeded from the demonstration to a discussion, one that would continue through November 3 when Holmes returned to the lectures, on the grounds of inductive inference, with many critical references to Mill.[20]

That lecture began with Peirce again posing the question of when red balls successively removed from the bag would lead his audience to any inference that other balls in the bag were red; that is, when successive objects encountered in experience would presumably exhibit similar qualities. Here he turned to the other "common answer" (relied upon by Hume and Mill) to the problem of validating induction: the idea that its grounding (in similarity) is supported by a basic aspect of "nature," or the natural world, which appears to be filled with "natural" similarities (like red balls, for example, though of course they have been manufactured by humans and hence may only be presumed similar).

This idea is essential in Mill's *A System of Logic* (1843), and Peirce's fourth lecture was an extended critique of Mill, from his treatment of the syllogism to his thesis that inductive inference could be explained by "natural" uniformities. The matter of concern to Peirce was subtle. As one red ball after another was removed from the bag, Peirce raised questions regarding the process of recognition, by those observing the process, of a common nature in the experience of repeated events, which encompasses both similarity in quality but also in time, or regularity.[21] At what point in human experience is both *similarity*, and its corollary *regularity*, suggested, hypothesized, recognized, established, relied upon? And why? And *how*?

20. The leading and well-known skeptical objection to induction had famously come in the eighteenth century from David Hume (whose name does not seem from Peirce's notes to have been explicitly mentioned): that the only way to validate inductive inference was through a circular argument—through inductive inference *itself*. Hume, "Skeptical Doubts concerning the Operations of the Understanding," in *An Inquiry concerning Human Understanding*, 1748, secs. 4 and 5. Having devoted most of his time to an examination of the notion of validation through the concept of probability, Peirce announced his intention to devote his next lecture (which Holmes would attend) to "another common answer to our question." Peirce, *Writings*, 1:396.

21. Peirce, *Writings*, 1:404: "Suppose I were to open a book and look at seven pages, and were to find that the first letter upon each of these pages was a vowel. I should not conclude that every page of the book began with a vowel; because that would be even more extraordinary than that the first 7 pages that I lit upon began with vowels."

On November 14, after finishing other reading already underway, Holmes borrowed Mill's *Logic* from the Boston Athenaeum and immediately read it through. Only four months earlier, Holmes had privately dined in the Members of Parliament dining room with both Mill and Alexander Bain. Upon finishing the *Logic* he wrote in his diary "Logic—finished the book by tea time. This week I haven't felt very well and debauched on Mill acc'dingly, by way of removing an old incubus before endeavoring to immerse myself in law completely—wh, Shattuck says, a man must at some period of his career if he would be a first rate lawyer, though of being that I despair."

By "incubus" we can assume he meant *obsession*, and if so, his obsession was the interest in philosophy that drove his readings and meetings with Wright and James and his attendance at Peirce's lectures, and was still strong enough to motivate his 1876 letter to Ralph Waldo Emerson. That letter shows that he was still intent on showing that law "provides a path to philosophy" and hoped "to prove it before I die." Even a decade later, the incubus was still not "removed."

Given this, what was the impact of Peirce's comments, and the reading of Mill's *Logic*? Peirce's extended November 3 commentary on Mill's arguments in *A System of Logic* had addressed Mill's having left the problem of induction yet *unexplained*, in his idea that the inference to generality is automatic, and grounded in "natural" similarities. Holmes came four years later to emphasize a distinct view of legal induction, engaging the problem of similarity as it is encountered in the law. Though he never acknowledged the influence of Peirce, two clues might be taken from the two lectures recorded in Holmes's diary.

How does a legal case—before it is decided—compare to a colored ball? Both are particulars appearing in succession before the observer. A comment by Peirce in the first lecture attended by Holmes had one relevant warning against "abusing" the syllogistic form of argument, which utilizes general propositions that often take similarity for granted. According to his notes, Peirce had said: "[T]o say that If the wind is east the barometer rises, is equivalent to saying Every east wind makes the barometer rise. But such a transformation will not enable us to throw arguments into syllogistic form." The example he gave was

If the wind is east the barometer rises
The wind is east
The barometer rises.

The problem, Peirce noted, is that "we talk here of *occasions* instead of *things* as in ordinary propositions; and the objects which our terms denote are *bounded* by dates not by *positions*" (Peirce's italics). Legal disputes too are occasions bounded by dates, not things bounded by position, and gathering them together in legal analysis or interpretation might also not be (in Peirce's sense) an ordinary (that is, *thing*-like) proposition.

The second clue, in lecture four, is Peirce's extended commentary on Mill's insistence on thought moving exclusively "from particulars to particulars." Given that nature is not commonly prearranged, like colored balls in a bag, the question arises: Where, then, does the perception of similarity or likeness derive? Mill, claims Peirce, must rely heavily on a direct, somehow *immediate* sense of the existence of "natural" kinds, an implicit assumption of sheer prereflective uniformities in the natural world. Peirce expresses several doubts about this assumption, such as, "It must be admitted that there are exceptions, to almost any rule. Thus many of the characters which seem to belong to a class universally only belong to part of it. We do not know how far this limitation extends; it seems probable that there really are natural classes and that nearly everything belongs to one. But does this bare circumstance constitute any uniformity?"[22]

22. Ibid., 1:419; his extended commentary on Mill, the second lecture attended by Holmes and James, was on November 3, 1866. It opened with the following reference to the removal of red balls from a bag:

> Gentlemen and Ladies,
>
> At the last lecture we asked ourselves an important question. Having taken a bag of balls, we drew seven from it and found them all red; whereupon we judged that nearly all the balls in the bag were red. The question then arose *why* we know those balls we have not seen to be red? Before entering upon this question, we examined it to ascertain whether it had any meaning and if so what. We found it to mean, does this argument come under the general head of syllogistic arguments such as we have examined hitherto, and if so what is its specific difference from other syllogisms which only explicate knowledge and so not add to it; or does it differ from syllogistic argument, and if so what are the relations of the two modes of inference, and what are the common characters of inference in general? (1:407)

Peirce's Lowell Lectures, titled "The Logic of Science; or, Induction and Hypothesis," began on the evening of Wednesday, October 24, 1866, and continued on Wednesday and Saturday evenings until December 1. Holmes's diary entries suggest that he, John Gray, and James found other occupations on the successive evenings after November 3. Holmes's diary notes no further attendance at the lectures during the weeks following. On the date of the next (fifth) lecture, he notes attending a case in the Superior Court with Shattuck, and having "Begun Bowen's Polit. Econ. in horsecar going to Cambridge." He would finish Bowen on Tuesday,

Taken together, the two lectures focus the problem of finding similarity in *occasions*. Holmes's early texts address Mill's thesis in light of Peirce's doubts, examined in the context of the history of the common law. Legal precedents are the record of judgments from prior occasions. They are successions of judgments that, in Holmes's 1870 sense, have been decided from "particular to particular." As he notes in 1870, the notion of similarity follows as a *practical* matter: "It is only after a series of determinations on the same subject-matter, that it becomes necessary to 'reconcile the cases,' as it is called, that is, *by a true induction* [my italics] to state the principle which has until then been obscurely felt. And this statement is often modified more than once by new decisions before the abstracted general

---

November 13, and on Saturday the seventeenth borrowed Mill's *System of Logic* from the Boston Athenaeum.

On November 3, Holmes would have heard Peirce advance his own answer to the question of balls in the bag. "Finally we have seen to use the expression of Plato that syllogism never moves a step beyond its starting point—the conclusion is implicitly stated in the premisses—while scientific inference passes not a little but infinitely beyond the premisses." Thus Peirce went on to distinguish the three forms of inference, using the syllogistic form. Simplified (Peirce used a number of examples), these are as follows:

Deduction
The balls in the bag are red
These balls come from the bag
These balls are red
Induction
The balls drawn from this bag are red
These balls are red
These balls come from the bag
Hypothesis
These balls are red
The balls in the bag are red
These balls come from the bag

The scientific process employs all three. "Induction is the process by which we find the general characters of classes and establish natural classifications. . . . Hypothesis alone affords us any knowledge of causes or forces, and enables us to see the *why* of things." 1:428. It is uncertain but explanatory and "ampliative." Hypothesis introduces new ideas; deduction serves to explore its consequences; induction then serves for testing them. (Peirce's notes to a proposed 1865 lecture record his view that "Aristotle conceives of no other induction than that which is derived from the major premise of the first figure. Now, there is only one kind of induction which can be thrown into this form; and this is no other than induction by *simple enumeration* [Peirce's italics]. Bacon therefore was right when he said that Aristotle gave the rules for this form only" [1:265].)

rule takes its final shape." The phrase "true idea of induction" originates with Bacon and was repeatedly used by Whewell. Holmes's "true induction" is fully a *social* induction.

Where might this *social* deviation (or extrapolation) from Mill have come from? We may look to Holmes's readings on English science for a possible influence. Mill had wrestled with William Whewell over the operation of generalization in science, and their debate is amply reflected in Holmes's readings.[23] Whewell's view is summarized in his preface to the second edition of his *The Philosophy of the Inductive Sciences, Founded upon Their History* (1847, x–xi):

> On the subject of this doctrine of a Fundamental Analysis, which our knowledge always involves, I will venture here to add a remark, which looks beyond the domain of the physical sciences. This doctrine is suited to throw light upon Moral and Political Philosophy, no less than upon Physical. In Morality, in Legislation, in National Polity, we have still to do with the opposition and combination of two Elements; of Facts and Ideas; of History, and an Ideal Standard of Action; of actual character and position, and of the aims which are placed above the Actual. Each of these is in conflict with the other; each modifies and moulds the other. We can never escape the control of the first; we must ever cease to strive to extend the sway of the second. In these cases, indeed, the Ideal Element assumes a new form. It includes the Idea of Duty. The opposition, the action and re-action, the harmony at which we must ever aim, and can never reach, are between what is and what ought to be; between the past or present Fact, and the Supreme Idea. The Idea can never be independent of the Fact, but the Fact must ever be drawn towards the Idea.

Whewell's distinctive thesis envisions a reciprocal and research-centered growth of knowledge through a tension between the particular and the general: the opposition, interaction, and eventual "colligation" (a form of combination or negotiation) of the two critical elements, "facts and ideas." These tend to be seen as in "conflict" with each other, but over time "modify and mould" each other. The tension between them is itself transformative; as inquiry progresses, "the Ideal Element assumes a new form." Further, they progress toward a "harmony at which we must ever

23. See, e.g., William Whewell, *History of the Inductive Sciences* 1:3–16. Mill mentions Whewell throughout his *System of Logic*; his criticisms are discussed in chaps. 3 and 6 below. See also John Herschel, "Whewell on Inductive Sciences," 171–230.

aim, and can never reach. . . . The Idea can never be independent of the Fact, but the Fact must ever be drawn towards the Idea."

Here Whewell is "look[ing] beyond the domain of physical sciences"; his method applies to all knowledge. I can only suggest, from salient comparisons, whether and how Whewell influenced Holmes's inductive turn. The turn began in 1870, soon after the readings and discussions, amidst an exploration of legal structure. It was restated to account for conflicting legal positions in 1873, and eventually came to dominate his thought and judicial method. Chauncey Wright's article on Herbert Spencer, which Holmes read in 1866–67, had drawn upon Bacon and Whewell. Wright's discussion of scientific method includes the interaction of facts and ideas. Moreover (although Holmes may not have been aware of it) Peirce had commented extensively on Whewell in his writings in 1865, and would note in 1869 that Whewell "has shown with great elaboration that in every science two processes have taken place. One, the observation and grouping of facts. The other, *controversies* [Peirce's italics] which resulted in the establishment of clear conceptions."[24]

Especially in his later writings, Whewell's epistemic context implies a social component. The process involves an extended community of inquirers, both physically and chronologically. Holmes's eventual thesis, set forth in his own Lowell Lectures in 1880 (published in 1881 as *The Common Law*), envisions a gradual resolution of emergent disputes in the common law tradition, arising in the case-by-case operation of English and American courts of law. Depicted by implication is a process parallel to that of Peirce's communities of scientists engaged in the exploration of a common and ongoing, but specific, problem.

The law is plainly driven by controversy, and Holmes addresses this in the 1873 paper. Consistent with his 1870 text, conflicts among existing rights are not resolved at once, through interpretation and application of an antecedent underlying set of legal principles. Instead they are explored gradually, first by gathering new experience, and then by appropriately timed retrospective examinations of an array of specific prior decisions. New cases are seen as gradually filling a metaphorical space between the two or more precedents ("cluster[ing] around the opposite poles"). Judges eventually resolve the conflict by recognizing and describing a "line" between the opposing poles or principles.

24. Peirce, *Writings*, 1:340 (undelivered 1865 Harvard Lectures).

An early decision in an emergent controversy operates akin to a scientific experiment; it opens inquiry by creating a precedent for future similar cases.[25] Like the record of scientific inquiry, that of legal inquiry consists at first of carefully recorded observations of multiple concrete experiences. Connecting thought and action, preliminary judgments reflect the influence of both old and new patterns of conduct. Practice is a driving force behind competing precedents, to be reconciled within the developing system of classification. The "similarity" of legal occasions is not simply a "discovered" quality of prior judgments; it implies an element of coordination, of adaptation to prior experience, as well as cognitive comparison.[26]

After accumulation discloses a pattern (or suggests competing patterns), judges initiate the process of generalizing. Sufficient experience permits trained observers to "abstract" a "general rule." This is done by "reconciling the cases," distinguishing relevant from irrelevant detail in the articulation of a common rule or standard. Relevance, of evidence to ultimate conclusion, is an emergent property. As the notion of relevance emerges, so also does the perception of coherence, accompanied by the adaptation of practice. It will be helpful to think of this as a practical *convergence* toward resolution of opposing precedents.

This simplified and idealized account suggests a rough parallel between scientists and lawyers evaluating and generalizing within an established professional tradition from records of diverse but constructively related data. The nature of the data itself would appear radically distinct, but the forms of inquiry are comparable. Both are prompted by practical problems or doubts confronting the community at large, reflecting Peirce's doubt-belief model of inquiry.[27] Both are also distinctive aspects of the resolution of controversy and the ordering of human knowledge.

Holmes removes the problematic of the hard case from one of difficulty in comparison to existing doctrine to one of novelty in comparison to prior knowledge and practice. Holmes's view suggests aspects of Whewell's "consilience" and "colligation" (which Professor Bowen had discussed in his 1864

25. See Barry Barnes, David Bloor, and John Henry, *Scientific Knowledge: A Sociological Analysis*, 100–109.

26. This will be further discussed in chap. 6, in relation to John Rawls's practice conception of rules.

27. Peirce would recall in 1906 the importance for the Metaphysical Club of Bain's definition of belief as "that upon which a man is prepared to act," from which "pragmatism is scarce more than a corollary." Joseph Brent, *Charles S. Peirce: A Life*, 85; Cheryl Misak, ed., *The Cambridge Companion to Peirce*, 10.

book on logic).[28] The body of law is built up from legal categories and concepts in an often attenuated process of negotiation. The whole enterprise must be woven together while being adjusted to accommodate shifting standards guiding future conduct. Different cases, situations, parties, judges, and lawyers (and scholars) are all involved over a continuum, as diverse judgments are analyzed and interpreted to forge eventual settlements of multiple controversies.

Overall consistency is a dominant goal, but conceptual analysis is only partly an exercise in logical reconciliation. It is also one of negotiating each new requirement for conduct through the clash of conflicting patterns of conduct. Holmes stressed that the process of classification appears more analytical than it is, in the sense that consistency always *appears* to have been discovered, not made. In an essay written in 1879, just before *The Common Law*, Holmes wrote that consistency is by nature elusive:

> The truth is, that law hitherto has been, and it would seem by the necessity of its being is always approaching and never reaching consistency. It is for ever adopting new principles from life at one end, and it always retains old ones from history at the other which have not yet been absorbed or sloughed off. It will become entirely consistent only when it ceases to grow.[29]

This passage is repeated in *The Common Law*, and Holmes would soon become engaged with the question of *how* principles are formulated and reformulated. Chauncey Wright had closely followed the Whewell-Mill debate, which had drawn from Bacon's precept that "the human understanding is of its own nature prone to suppose the existence of more order and regularity in nature in the world than it finds." Peirce had been writing about Whewell at least since 1865, asking in 1866 how similarity is established, going beyond deduction and induction, eventually adopting the term "abduction" for the introduction of hypotheses.

Holmes would much later comment to Frederick Pollock in 1929 that Wright had taught him "while young that I must not say *necessary* about the universe, that we don't know whether anything is necessary or not. So that I describe myself as a *bet*abilitarian. I believe that we can *bet* on the behavior of the universe in its contract with us. We bet we can know what

28. Francis Bowen, *A Treatise on Logic*, 402–4.

29. Holmes, "Common Carriers and the Common Law," *American Law Review* 13 (July 1879): 609, 631; Kellogg, *Formative Essays*, 229; *CW*, 3:75–76.

it will be. That leaves a loophole for free will—in the miraculous sense—the creation of a new atom of force, although I don't in the least believe in it."[30]

In the interest of exploring what he may have meant by this "loophole," we might discount as a pose Holmes's final comment, "although I don't in the least believe in it." Having reached a view of law that would privilege (and ultimately defend) broad participation in legal inquiry through the feedback loop, the profession of disbelief should not be read as a withdrawal. Rooted perhaps in this notion of free will, Holmes leaves open the question of how change and creativity may enter the legal process from outside the legal profession. That he remained skeptical of the eventual outcome of experimentation may reflect the chastening experience of war. Change implies a degree of freedom, but it is a product of conflict. This presents questions about the "colligation" process, and Peirce's observations. How does retrospective generalizing operate, how does legal abduction work? How much, and what kind of, "free will" is there?

30. Holmes to Frederick Pollock, August 30, 1929, in Howe, ed., *Holmes-Pollock Letters*, 2:252.

CHAPTER THREE

Science

This chapter examines the influence on Holmes of writings on science by Mill, Whewell, and John Herschel (a distinguished astronomer and friend of Whewell), the debate between Mill and Whewell over the role of ideas in logical induction, and the importance, for that role, of the "continuum of inquiry."

* * *

What is the nature of general and of universal propositions? Are all true universal propositions necessary truths, or is any truth, or all truth, necessary? What is the act or series of acts of the mind in constructing general propositions, and when constructed, in what manner do we rest in them as expressive of truth?—Astronomer John Herschel, 1840

The above passage is from John Herschel's critical review of William Whewell's *History of the Inductive Sciences*. Both texts appear in Holmes's diary as having been read sometime in late 1865 or early 1866—roughly a year before he records attending Peirce's logic lectures. In regard to scientific concepts, Herschel seems ahead of his time in using the controversial word "construction," rather than the more conventional "discovery," asking whether general or universal truths are "necessary," and if so in what sense—and "What is the act or series of acts of the mind in constructing general propositions, and when constructed, in what manner do we rest in them as expressive of truth?" Herschel's use of such terminology in 1840 predates by more than a century the vigorous contemporary debates over "constructivism" and its implications.[1]

1. John F. W. Herschel, "Whewell on Inductive Sciences," Review of the *History* and the *Philosophy*, *Quarterly Review* 68 (1841): 177–238; see, e.g., Ian Hacking, *The Social Construction of What?*

Holmes's continuum of inquiry addresses, *for law*, the questions Herschel was asking about *scientific* method. Holmes's 1870 response to the Lord Mansfield passage in Mill's *Logic* reflects a concern comparable to Herschel's probing last question: how do "acts of the mind" lead to general propositions? But Holmes has amended the question by revising "acts of the mind" to "many minds." What, precisely, is involved in the human conceptualizing experience, with regard to law?

The continuum of inquiry would lead Holmes to a contingent view of the dualism, the "either-or," of inductive particularism versus deductive generalism: toward regarding them not as rival accounts of the thought process, but as perceptions of distinct stages of an extended process, toward eventual entrenchment of similarity. A continuum of *scientific* inquiry is apparent in Whewell's *History of the Inductive Sciences*; a rejection of the same dualism is implicit in Whewell's claim of a *temporary* division between truths that are experiential and those that are necessary.[2] Reasoning from particular experience characterizes an early stage of these continua; as inquiry proceeds, reasoning turns to comparison of generalizations until a "succeeding general proposition" may be articulated.[3]

If the 1870 comment on Mill, his tentative inductive turn, is the first important step Holmes took toward the goal expressed in 1876 to Ralph Waldo Emerson, "to prove that law provides a way to philosophy," what was the next one? The essay he sent to Emerson along with the note was titled "Primitive Notions in Modern Law No. I." It marks a turning point in his early legal research, decisively away from a fixed analytical perspective and toward a historical vision of the nature of law in transformation. It is also a turn away from the fixed fundamental ideas of right and duty, and toward *change* in fundamental ideas.

An important and often-overlooked record of Holmes's thought is the series of exploratory essays published in the *American Law Review* in the decade before the 1881 publication of *The Common Law*. Here there is a development; the essays cannot be taken as a set of consistent observations, forming constituent parts of a final viewpoint.[4] The essays began with a critical analysis of John Austin's 1859 *Lectures on Jurisprudence*,

2. Snyder, *Reforming Philosophy*, 84; see n. 38 below.

3. This may be compared to Whewell's account of "consilience," the means by which inquirers effect or "construct" the successive generalizations that advance science. Ibid., 175–76.

4. See Kellogg, *Formative Essays*, 3–74.

specifically Austin's organization of law under the rubric of rights.[5] In 1872, testing the concept of duty as an alternative classification, he set forth a table of law as a system of duties, but accompanied it with the comment, "it is obvious, however, that this scheme does not exhaust the whole body of the law." The ground for this statement is inductive; he cites cases of legal liability that do not fit comfortably under the concept of "duty."

> It is obvious, however, that this scheme does not exhaust the whole body of the law . . . [citing examples]. We have thus far only looked at a lateral section of the law,—at duties contemplated as existing a given instant of time; it remains to make a longitudinal section, that is, to show them as continuing in time.[6]

This observation would underlie his later critical—and often misinterpreted—comments on the concept of duty in "The Path of the Law" in 1897.[7]

Holmes apparently sensed that his move toward a longitudinal conception of law (or "diachronic" in contemporary terms)—although still developing—was significant enough to inform Emerson. It suggests a shift away from a legal theory focused on taxonomy, that is, away from asking (as with a traditional approach to the philosophy of science) what entities are *always* fundamental. Austin had tried defining law as always consisting of sovereign commands, habitually obeyed, and set forth in his *Lectures on Jurisprudence* a taxonomic system of legal rights.[8] Rather than

5. Ibid.; John Austin, *Lectures on Jurisprudence; or, The Philosophy of Positive Law*.

6. Holmes, "The Arrangement of the Law. Privity," *American Law Review* 7 (October 1872): 47; Kellogg, *Formative Essays*, 96; *CW*, 1:304.

7. "One of the many evil effects of the confusion between legal and moral ideas, about which I shall have something to say in a moment, is that theory is apt to get the cart before the horse, and consider the right or the duty as something existing apart from and independent of the consequences of its breach, to which certain sanctions are added afterward. But, as I shall try to show, a legal duty so called is nothing but a prediction that if a man does or omits certain things he will be made to suffer in this or that way by judgment of the court; and so of a legal right." Holmes, "The Path of the Law," *Harvard Law Review* 10 (1897): 457, 458–59. *CW*, 3:391.

8. Austin, *Lectures on Jurisprudence*; see Postema, "Legal Positivism: Early Foundations," 20: "Austin adds nothing to the command tradition that was not already securely established by Hobbes and elaborated by Bentham. Austin's innovation, which has had an enormous impact on Anglophone legal philosophy ever since, was to deploy this separation as a principle of jurisprudential method. . . . Opening Province [of Jurisprudence Determined], Austin wrote, 'The principle purpose or scope of the six ensuing lectures, is to distinguish positive laws (the

announcing to Emerson that he had discovered a better legal taxonomy, Holmes was in effect letting Emerson know that he had given up on that kind of inquiry. His subsequent analysis, of a transformative "longitudinal" perspective informed by history, would occupy his Lowell Lectures in 1880, published in 1881 as *The Common Law*.

Right and duty may both be said to be two of the "fundamental ideas" of law. When Holmes began his exploration of them in 1870, he was dubious of whether they could accommodate his own increasingly encyclopedic knowledge of Anglo-American cases. His 1872 observation that the abandoned project envisioned only a "lateral" and not a "longitudinal" section refers to its failure to accommodate time-dependent information—as he says, "show[ing] [duties] as continuing over time." The papers record what seemed to him an important insight: that legal philosophy should avoid synchronicity and account for conceptual change.[9]

In case you are wondering where this is going, here's an advance summary. The impact of the continuum of inquiry, and conceptual change, have (as I hope to show) profound effects on the nature of the conceptual space, what might be called the space of legal reasons, confronting courts and lawyers. They affect how Holmes will think about particular areas of law, like tort and contract, but also about more general legal doctrine, like the general theory of legal liability. Change affects various levels of generality. If there is one thing to keep in mind, it is that the "logical space of reasons" (which refers to the environment in which perception and cognition takes place)[10] is for Holmes a space of reasons *and action*, meaning that prior cognition (in the creation of legal precedents) is grounded in patterns of conduct, and conduct must be adjusted for disputes to be effectively resolved.

Regarding fundamental legal ideas, how about law as a system of *rules*, as Herbert Hart would argue in the next century? I will suggest below

---

appropriate matter of jurisprudence) from [a host of phenomena with which they are regularly confused] . . . they affect to describe the boundary which severs the province of jurisprudence from the regions lying on its confines.'"

9. By today's standards this would be considered a major theoretical claim, which should have been addressed in a volume, or at least a lengthy footnoted paper. But the record of Holmes's emerging thought suggests an intense man in a hurry to build on each insight and get quickly to the next one. See, e.g., Kellogg, *Holmes, Legal Theory, and Judicial Restraint*, 77.

10. The phrase is borrowed from Wilfrid Sellars, *Empiricism and the Philosophy of Mind*, 76, and John McDowell, *Mind and World*, 5. Holmes's approach is further compared to that of Sellars, McDowell, and Robert Brandom in the following chapters.

that the lesson of the feedback continuum is that Hart's concept of law is fundamentally incomplete in the same way that Holmes found Austin's to be, in failing to comprehend how a conception of law must fully encompass the process through which rules, as well as duties and rights, may still be inchoate, are constantly in formation, and relate to practices.[11] The notion that the law consists of the set of all legal rules (however defined), and of only that set, excludes actions by courts that are not properly definable as making or applying rules.[12] By 1876 Holmes had abandoned further consideration of a static system, what he called a "philosophical arrangement" of law, in favor of a search for a "philosophical series," through historical analysis of the forms of legal liability, encompassing the generation and revision of legal ideas, including the most fundamental ones.

What drove Holmes's historical turn? He begins the paper sent to Emerson with the following comment:

> In a former investigation in these pages [his 1873 paper on "The Theory of Torts," with the discussion of "the growth of the law," elucidating the continuum in contested matters], we endeavored to show, that, more generally than has been supposed, civil liability depends not on culpability as a state of the defendant's consciousness, . . . but upon his having failed to come up to a more or less accurately determined standard in his overt acts or omissions. . . .
>
> To lay the foundations for the discussion to which we have referred, we were led to glance incidentally at the historical origin of liability in some cases which Austin, following the jurists of the mature period of Roman law, had interpreted on grounds of culpability; and to point out that it sprung from the much more primitive notion, that liability attached directly to the thing doing the damage.[13]

11. See John Rawls's "Two Concepts of Rules," chap. 2, n. 9; and discussion, chap. 5, n. 5; and chap. 8 below.

12. Hence the tendency to interpret all particular decisions as creating rules; see Frederick Schauer, "Do Cases Make Bad Law?" See Dennis Patterson, "Can We Please Stop Doing This? By the Way, Postema Was Right," 49, approving Postema's criticism of the view that "[w]hile legal philosophy has its own unique set of questions and problems, one activity it shares with many other areas of philosophy is the urge to find the essence of 'law.'"

13. A footnote in the text refers here to Holmes's 1873 essay, "The Theory of Torts," as well as his related comment in Kent's *Commentaries on American Law*. Holmes, "Primitive Notions in Modern Law No. I," *American Law Review* 10 (April 1876): 422–23; Kellogg, *Formative Essays*, 129–30. *CW*, 3:4.

The next paper (titled "Primitive Notions in Modern Law No. II"), published in 1877, refers back to his 1872 comment questioning the taxonomy project:

> The object of the following investigation is to prove the historical truth of a general result, arrived at analytically in the pages of this *Review* five years ago.[14]

In this two-part essay he claims that modern forms of liability are rooted in vengeance. The law, he finds now, has undergone a gradual morphology of what Whewell might have called its "fundamental idea" of liability. There is extended discussion of this historical change in his 1881 *The Common Law*. It would lead to his controversial (particularly when taken out of context) theory of evolution from "moral" to "external" standards: his attempt, criticized in the twentieth century by Grant Gilmore and other scholars, to reduce the basis of all legal liability to a "philosophically continuous series." In 1877 he would comment (in "Primitive Notions in Modern Law No. II"):

> All special rights are legal consequences of a special group of facts. The law determines what facts must co-exist for special consequences to follow, as well as what the consequences shall be.[15]

In the period between 1873 and 1877, Holmes had added an historical evolutionary principle to the "growth of the law" continuum model. The entire legal system is now seen as a continuum, not unlike the individual continua driving the growth of the law to resolve particular conflicts. The overall continuum of legal inquiry is now viewed as extending backward in time, from the earlier legal response to injury rooted in the penchant for revenge. I suggest that, in his 1899 remark about law as a "great anthropological document," Holmes also extends it forward, suggesting that change is ongoing in the nature of legal inquiry, affecting even its fundamental form or structure.

The Common Law documents at length the gradual replacement of vengeance as the root principle of legal liability, even while vestiges of it remain: for example, the limit of liability in admiralty to damages no greater

14. A footnote in the text refers here to Holmes's 1872 essay, "The Arrangement of the Law. Privity", "Primitive Notions in Modern Law No. II," *American Law Review* 11 (July 1877): 641; Kellogg, *Formative Essays*, 147; *CW*, 3:21.

15. "Primitive Notions in Modern Law No. II," *American Law Review* 11 (July 1877): 641.

than the value of the burdened vessel, deriving from the ancient sanction of surrender.[16] But what precisely is the replacement for the principle of vengeance? His characterization in *The Common Law* is a move away from "moral" and toward "external" or "objective" standards of liability, a claim that has been puzzling in the context of debates over legal positivism. His use of the term "moral," to mean rooted in vengeance and its "feeling of blame," does not fit that context.

The notion of a grand historic transformation of law was hardly new. Sir Henry Maine's account of a historical transformation of legal relations from status to contract clearly played a role in the historical turn.[17] We might ask how the two authors were different in their approach. Here the influence on Holmes of Mill and Whewell is relevant, in the same manner as Chauncey Wright's: in their Baconian rejection of axiomatic thought. Holmes's comments on Maine apply that rejection to Maine's thesis, as an abstract plan lacking any empirical account of its operation.[18] Another significant difference is Maine's commitment to a paradigm of progress, as opposed to Holmes's contingent view of success or failure. Law in Holmes's account is not separate from society; he does not "describe a relationship between two spheres of life, the big sphere of society . . . and the smaller dependent sphere of the legal system."[19]

16. "I believe that it will be instructive to go back to the early forms of liability, and to start from them. It is commonly known that the early forms of legal procedure were grounded in vengeance." Holmes, *The Common Law*, *CW*, 3:116.

17. Mark De Wolfe Howe, *Justice Oliver Wendell Holmes: The Proving Years*, 137–53. Howe discusses the importance of Maine and of historical scholarship (140), and notes that "the earliest of Holmes's writings on law had been concerned more with the problems of scientific analysis than with those of historical explanation" (141), thereby separating the two aspects, scientific and historical, whereas they both appear to be related as reinforcing the earlier inductive turn. See also David M. Rabban, *Law's History: American Legal Thought and the Transatlantic Turn to History*, and "From Maine to Maitland via America."

18. Holmes commented in 1888 to Frederick Pollock that Maine "seems to have been impatient of investigation himself" and "I do not think will leave much mark on the actual structure of jurisprudence, although he helped many others to do so." Holmes to Pollock, March 4, 1988, in Howe, ed., *Holmes-Pollock Letters*, 1:31. In contrast he described Frederick Maitland's work as "of a truly scientific kind—accurate investigation of details in the interest of questions of philosophical importance." Ibid. Steven Utz details Maine's failure to meet exacting standards of evidentiary support, and compares Holmes's critique of inevitability in German legal theories as a "self-validating expression of the individual human will." Utz, "Maine's Ancient Law and Legal Theory."

19. Gordon, "Critical Legal Histories Revisited: A Response," 202. Holmes was not an "evolutionary functionalist" in the sense Gordon examined in 1984 in "Critical Legal His-

The comment in his paper sent to Emerson links the *historical* turn directly to what I have called Holmes's earlier *inductive* turn, in particular to the account of the "growth of the law" in the paper of 1873. The result of this connection, in the period leading to 1876, was to emphasize a Whewellian view of law itself as a continuum of inquiry, preferable to the analytical model of John Austin. Whewell and Herschel had themselves already moved away from an observation/discovery notion of scientific conceptualization, what Mary Hesse calls "[t]he deductive legacy of scientific structure . . . that saw science as a static, hierarchical ordering of statements resting on a firm base of observational truth."[20] As already noted, deduction was suspect in the works of Mill and Herschel as well as in Whewell, and the latter had moved toward a social theory of scientific knowledge, anticipating similar views advanced today.[21]

Holmes likewise advanced a view critical of law as another form of "static, hierarchical ordering of statements," one that Morton White later characterized as his contribution to a nineteenth-century "revolt against formalism." Yet White missed the influence of Whewell's research model, and the implicit comparison of scientific and legal induction.[22] Why would Holmes follow the Whewell model? There are several plausible motivators, from his early conviction that scientific progress held a key to philosophy, to the spirit of discovery in England and France, and perhaps also to the example of his famous father, Dr. Oliver Wendell Holmes Sr.

George Washington, leader of the American Revolution and first president of the United States, died of acute epiglottitis on December 14, 1799, after an unsuccessful eighty-two-ounce bloodletting that failed to reduce

---

tories." His perspective is consistent with the critical legal studies (CLS) view that law is an arena of social conflict and struggle, and (I think) also the view that "if the law were rooted in such structural contradictions, it could inherently be made functional to radically divergent forms of social ordering" (203). Holmes's convergence differs sharply from the CLS view that law is replete with incommensurable and never-reconcilable doctrine. His view is consistent with Gordon's closing comment, "All history can tell us is that opportunities for remaking law always exist and, if seized in a spirit of adventure and pragmatic experiment, may sometimes lead to better states of the world than those we have come to accept out of complacency and despair" (213).

20. Mary Hesse, *The Structure of Scientific Inference* 1–8, 89.

21. Ibid. 1–8; Barry Barnes, David Bloor, and John Henry, *Scientific Knowledge: A Sociological Analysis*; Steve Fuller, *Thomas Kuhn: A Philosophical History for Our Times*, 11 (placing Whewell in the tradition of "philosophical history").

22. Frederic R. Kellogg, "Holistic Pragmatism and Law: Morton White on Justice Oliver Wendell Holmes," with reply by White, "Holmes and Hart on Prediction and Legal Obligation."

the painful and ultimately fatal swelling in his throat. Bloodletting had been a mainstay of medical practice since antiquity, deduced axiomatically from Galen's principle of bodily "humors." Just thirty-two years after Washington's death, Holmes's father at age twenty-four crossed the Atlantic to attend the École de Médecine in Paris as a student of Dr. Pierre Charles Alexandre Louis, who had recently demonstrated, inductively, the ineffectiveness of bloodletting as a treatment for fevers and other disorders.[23]

Dr. Holmes received the MD degree from Harvard, where he later became Parkman Professor of Anatomy and Physiology. In 1843 he published *The Contagiousness of Puerperal Fever*, an essay demonstrating that the fatal disease attacking delivering mothers was carried from patient to patient by physicians and nurses; the washing of hands between visits was not a standard practice. The idea was not new; Dr. Holmes's influential paper drew its persuasiveness from an overwhelming documentation of cases.[24]

The progress of science in the early nineteenth century was revolutionizing the Western world, and the Holmes family was part of it even as their lawyer son was born in 1841. Advances arrived in anatomy, mathematics, organic and inorganic chemistry, photography, botany, psychology, astronomy, and other fields, a progress celebrated by Auguste Comte as the age of positivism ("to measure is to know"). The younger Holmes would write in the fall of 1859, at age eighteen, "It is only in these last days that anything like an all comprehending science has embraced the universe, showing unerring law prevailing in every department, generalizing and systematizing every phenomenon of physics and every vagary of the human mind."[25] Eleven years later he would author an anonymous criticism of Harvard Law School:

> The object of a law department is not precisely and only to educate young men to be practicing lawyers, though it will be largely used for that purpose. It is to furnish all students who desire it the same facilities to investigate the science of human law, theoretically, historically, and thoroughly, as they have to investigate mathematics, natural sciences, of any other branch of thought.[26]

23. Howe, *Shaping Years*, 17.

24. Henry R. Viets, MD, "A Mind Prepared: O. W. Holmes and 'The Contagiousness of Puerperal Fever,' 1843."

25. Howe, *Shaping Years*, 55.

26. Ibid., 206.

The scientific impetus from across the Atlantic was highly progressive and "meliorative," motivated to improve the condition of humankind. In England the century was one of reform in government and society, extending the franchise, softening legal discrimination against Catholics, and expanding educational opportunity. Both Mill and Whewell were energized by reformism and saw logical method as extending beyond natural science. Ideas could effect social and political change. Mill wrote in his autobiography that "economical and social changes, though among the greatest, are not the only forces which shape the course of our species, ideas are themselves a power in history." Both saw a need to redefine scientific method. Yet they conceived of it in different ways.[27]

Mill's autobiography records his intention in *A System of Logic* to challenge "the notion that truths external to the mind may be known by intuition or consciousness, independently of observation and experience," which was "the great intellectual support of false doctrines and bad institutions," and an "instrument for consecrating all deep seated prejudices." Hence his deflation of the syllogism: radical particularism was his philosophy of reform, clearing the air of "intuitionism" and making ample room for concrete reality. Ironically, one of the alleged "intuitionists" targeted by his criticism in *A System of Logic* was William Whewell.[28]

The debate between Mill and Whewell was recently illuminated by Laura J. Snyder in her book *Reforming Philosophy: A Victorian Debate on Science and Society*. In his aversion to intuitionism, Mill also challenged the notion of hypothesis formation, in favor of his view that abstraction came directly from the comparison of particulars. By contrast, Whewell was deeply concerned with hypothesis formation and examined it exhaustively in historical context. Meanwhile, he shared with Mill a Baconian mission against the tendency to assume "fixed and immovable truth" in "very general axioms," in order to "extract and prove inferior conclusions."[29]

Whewell, Herschel, and their circle at Cambridge University were committed no less than Mill to furthering Francis Bacon's mission to reform society through scientific and philosophical method. A principal target of the Cambridge circle was the economic theory of David Ricardo,

27. Mill, "De Tocqueville on Democracy in America (II)," *Collected Works* (hereafter *CW*), 18:197–98; see Snyder, *Reforming Philosophy*, 7–9 (spirit of reform), 62–82 (debate with Whewell).

28. Mill *Autobiography*, *CW* 1:233; Snyder, *Reforming Philosophy*, 4.

29. Snyder, *Reforming Philosophy*, 67–94.

incidentally a close family friend of the Mills, whose iron law of wages, deduced from the "desire to obtain as much wealth with as little effort as possible," would become a powerful influence on Karl Marx.[30]

Whewell studied discrete areas of scientific research and engaged in research himself, contributing to geology, astronomy, physics, mineralogy, mechanics, and dynamics, and winning the Royal Society gold medal for his work on ocean tides. As a young fellow at Cambridge his studies of mineralogy, influenced by the mathematical approach of the German Friedrich Mohs, convinced him of the need to combine empirical detail with abstract conceptualization. While opposing top-down rationalizing, he sought an epistemology subtly combining both empirical and rationalist elements, a project that he admitted to be inherently "antithetical."[31] Despite much hard thought and patient exposition, his work led others, including Mill and even his close friend Herschel, to misread him as an inconsistent empiricist.[32]

The views of Mill and Whewell clashed over one particular aspect of the progress of science: Johannes Kepler's discovery of the elliptical orbit of the planet Mars. While Whewell saw this as an example of the "colligation" of facts and ideas, Mill seized on it to insist that the conceptual element was a mere matter of observation and description. This will bear closer examination in chapter 6; I mention it now, as it will become central in my later analysis of Holmes's departure from Mill's understanding of the critical issue of finding similarity in logical induction.[33]

Whewell's attempt to combine both empirical and rational elements divided scientific processes into greater and lesser levels of abstraction. At the highest level were "fundamental ideas." "[M]ere Observation takes up an indiscriminate handful of them; Induction seizes some thread on which a portion of the heap are strung, and binds such threads together."[34] A general idea not directly given by phenomenal detail must be "superinduced"

30. Ibid. 276–77; Snyder, *The Philosophical Breakfast Club* 89, 120.

31. Whewell called this the "Fundamental Antithesis," or dual nature, of knowledge: all knowledge involves an ideal, or subjective, element as well as an empirical, or objective, element. Snyder, *Reforming Philosophy*, 37–38.

32. Ibid., 67, 80–82, 100, and n. 19.

33. This is discussed in Mill's *Logic* in the chapter "Abstraction, or the Formation of Conceptions," 2:191; it is important to Mill's account of how resemblance is recognized through the comparison of particulars, a process that I will claim in chap. 6 that Holmes reconceived as a social induction.

34. William Whewell, "Modern Science—Inductive Philosophy," quoted in Snyder, *Reforming Philosophy*, 38.

on the facts by the mind, drawing on a stock of established conceptions. This led Whewell to elaborate on the notion of "fundamental ideas" not derived from, but still governing, sensation. These provided general conceptual relations existing between objects and events, a mental structure for a disorganized multitude of sensations, and they included such notions as space, time, causation, and resemblance.

Whewell was acutely aware that accounting for such high level abstractions had led Immanuel Kant to posit that the human mind imposed them *a priori*.[35] Critics including Mill associated Whewell's speculative work with Kant's categories, but Whewell drew none of the intricate Kantian distinctions among precepts, categories, and transcendental ideas of reason, and insisted that his list of fundamental ideas was not a closed one; other fundamental ideas could and would emerge in the development of science. "By the very circumstance of classing many other ideas with those of space and time, I entirely removed myself from the Kantian point of view."[36]

Rather than identifying the forms of human conception as preternaturally innate, Whewell seems more concerned with a process through which conceptions become entrenched. Another point of distinction from Kant was Whewell's concern with how fundamental ideas emerge, not having been "self-evident at our first contemplation of them." He would introduce the concept of "germs" in the third edition of *Philosophy of the Inductive Sciences* (published in 1860) to describe the original form of these conceptions in our minds: "the Ideas, the germ of them at least, were in the human mind before [experience]; but by the progress of scientific thought they are unfolded into clearness and distinctness."[37] There was no fixed line between experiential and necessary truths.[38]

35. Snyder, *Reforming Philosophy*, 46, 55, 56, 57.

36. Whewell, "Remarks on the Review of the Philosophy of the Inductive Sciences," 4, quoted in Snyder, *Reforming Philosophy* at 45. Snyder identifies Dugald Stewart as at least as much an influence on Whewell's conceptual model. Ibid., 47.

37. Whewell, *On the Philosophy of Discovery: Chapters Historical and Critical* (London: John W. Parker, 1860), 373, quoted in Snyder, *Reforming Philosophy*, 55. Holmes uses the term "germ" in *The Common Law*, referring to retaliation as the "germ" of liability. *CW*, 3:132.

38. Snyder, *Reforming Philosophy*, 90: "Recall that this discussion began with the Fundamental Antithesis, according to which no fixed line divides experiential and necessary truths. We now see how it is that the line we draw between them, like that between fact and theory, is a relative one, based upon epistemic distinctions that change as our Ideas become more distinct. As we explicate our Ideas, we recognize empirical truths to be necessary consequences of these Ideas; and the truths are thus transferred from the empirical to the necessary side of the antithesis."

A dramatic difference between Mill and Whewell was the latter's view that the explication of conceptions is a process that occurs incrementally through discussion and debate among groups of scientists. Whewell's "discoverers' induction" was a process involving a "train of researches." Explication of scientific concepts was a social process, represented in a graphic design (on the cover pages of his published works) of a torch passing from one hand to another. Following Bacon, Whewell emphasized a gradual, successive process of generalization.[39]

Holmes applies a scientific model to a *normative* domain. It is easier to appreciate the hold of empiricism on inquiry into material objects, but law is a set of normative judgments. Yet, Whewell and Mill had applied their inductive empiricism to moral and political knowledge. Immersed in their work, Chauncey Wright had himself moved away from an epistemology of origin to one of verification.[40] He had graduated from Harvard in 1852; a classmate recalled after his death, "I think his interest in philosophy was not greatly aroused until after 1856. For in this year, while we roomed together, he was reading Whewell's 'History of the Inductive Sciences' and was deep in the Novum Organum of Bacon, whose aphorisms concerning the province of science and the interpretation of nature were constantly in his speech." A decade later, Holmes was meeting Wright and reading Mill and Whewell, as well as Herschel's provocative review. Their discussion in 1867 of Abbot's article on space and time suggests that Holmes was fully aware that Wright had a naturalistic, rather than transcendental Kantian, view of *a priori* forms of thought.

Wright's conversations with James, as a fellow scientist, would have at least touched on Whewell. Holmes and James had discussed in 1866–67 a famous scientific dilemma in the understanding of momentum, referred to as the "vis viva" problem, and Holmes wrestled alone with it over a period of several months.[41] Meanwhile, his relationship with his father, now detached from research and increasingly renowned as a poet and author, had become strained and competitive, and Holmes was remarking to friends

39. Ibid., 60–67. These ideas anticipate Peirce's "abduction" and "logical socialism." Fisch, introduction to vol. 2, *Writings*, xxviii, xxxv. They also plausibly anticipate Mary Hesse's network theory in *The Structure of Scientific Inference* and Larry Laudan's analysis of research traditions in *Progress and Its Problems*.

40. Flower and Murphey, *History of Philosophy in America*, 2:549–51; Madden, *Chauncey Wright and the Foundations of Pragmatism*, 107.

41. See Carolyn Iltis, "D'Alembert and the Vis Viva Controversy," *Studies in History and Philosophy of Science* 1, no. 2 (1970): 135.

that his father, in turning to literature, had failed to fulfill his own potential. He certainly knew that the essay on puerperal fever had been a powerful exercise in induction.

Peirce, whose philosophy would take on a distinctive architectonic structure deeply influenced by Kant, had been engaged since reading Whately's *Elements of Logic* at age twelve in a comprehensive study of logic and scientific method. Aware of the great debate, he had by 1866 adopted Whewell's side over Mill. The interests of Peirce and Wright intersected in multiple respects, and Holmes's inclination to attend Peirce's Lowell Lectures may have come from Wright, James, or just his own intense engagement with logic and science.

Possibly influenced by Wright's interest in all aspects of the scientific process, Holmes drew from Mill the deflation of the syllogism, and from Whewell and Herschel a keen interest in "the act or series of acts . . . in constructing the general proposition and how we rest in them." James was never much interested in formal logic, and Wright had treated it occasionally. Holmes's early focus on logic must have been reinforced, if not directly influenced, by Peirce. He may have drawn inspiration to examine logical method from Professor Bowen, and the idea of a research continuum from Whewell. His idea of a time line for conceptual creation and revision is consistent with Whewell's historical perspective.

What Holmes added to the conception of induction in 1873 is a distinct historical analysis of the social component, and its motivation in conflict, informed by his reading of generations of case law in the course of editing Chancellor Kent's *Commentaries on American Law*. Rather than the detached curiosity motivating the scientist, or even the urgency of technical problems, the engine driving the law was the constant and continuing imperative for resolution of conflicts, feeding and informing the process of intersubjective classification and expression. Legal knowledge, rather than formed through Peirce's formula of problematic doubt leading to inquiry and belief, is constantly driven by disputes needing, at the very least, a tentative resolution. Doctrine is thus embroiled in constant controversy. The conceptual content of rules must eventually be, not only believed, but acted upon, accepted in legal language, *entrenched*, even if not everywhere, nor all at once.

Further evidence of the scientific background to Holmes's perspective on legal theory may be found in his speech given in 1899 to the New York State Bar Association, "Law in Science and Science in Law." Now chief justice of the highest court in Massachusetts, by this time he had decided hundreds of cases and had recently dissented in the controversial 1895 workers' rights case of *Vegelahn v. Guntner*. In New York he would restate the line-drawing analogy, firmly establishing its centrality in his judicial thinking:

> In our approach towards exactness we constantly tend to work out definite lines or equators to mark distinctions which we first notice as a difference of poles. It is evident in the beginning that there must be differences in the legal position of infants and adults. In the end we establish twenty-one as the dividing point. There is a difference manifest at the outset between night and day. The statutes of Massachusetts fix the dividing points at one hour after sunset and one hour before sunrise, ascertained according to mean time.[42]

He suggests now that the line-drawing model is more than just a legal theory, it is a general theory of social uncertainty, of how an open society addresses and resolves doubt. The opening paragraph of this address implies that it relates to all forms of knowledge, including art and natural science:

> The law of fashion is a law of life. The crest of the wave of human interest is always moving, and it is enough to know that the depth was greatest in respect of a certain feature or style in literature or music or painting a hundred years ago to be sure that at that point it no longer is so profound. I should draw the conclusion that artists and poets, instead of troubling themselves about the eternal, had better be satisfied if they can stir the feelings of a generation, but that is not my theme. It is more to my point to mention that what I have said about art is true within the limits of the possible in matters of the intellect. What do we mean when we talk about explaining a thing? A hundred years ago men explained any part of the universe by showing its fitness for certain ends, and demonstrating what they conceived to be its final cause according to a providential scheme. In our less theological and more scientific day, we explain an object by tracing the order and process of its growth and development from a starting point assumed as given.[43]

Holmes's "given" was organic and embedded, born in a space of reasons *and action*, continuous but *real*, not an analytical "myth."[44] He had in mind

42. Holmes, "Law in Science and Science in Law," *CW*, 3:415–16.

43. Ibid., 406.

44. The "Myth of the Given" is of course the foundationalist empirical dogma challenged in Wilfrid Sellars's *Empiricism and the Philosophy of Mind*; see John McDowell, *Mind and*

an intimate connection of legal method with the rest of knowledge, and went on to explain uncertainty as rooted in differences of degree, resolved over time by consensual classification and reclassification:

> When he has discovered that a difference is a difference of degree, that distinguished extremes have between them a penumbra in which one gradually shades into the other, a tyro thinks to puzzle you by asking where you are going to draw the line, and an advocate of more experience will show the arbitrariness of the line proposed by putting cases very near to it on one side or the other. But the theory of the law is that such lines exist, because the theory of the law as to any possible conduct is that it is either lawful or unlawful. As that difference has no gradation about it, when applied to shades of conduct that are very near each other it has an arbitrary look. We like to disguise the arbitrariness, we like to save ourselves the trouble of nice and doubtful discriminations. In some regions of conduct of a special sort we have to be informed of facts which we do not know before we can draw our lines intelligently, and so, as we get near the dividing point, we call in the jury.[45]

Holmes is suggesting an important aspect of legal uncertainty distinct from the vagueness of reference in the terms in a rule (as in a sign reading "No Vehicles in the Park" that fails to direct attention to the precise class of forbidden object). The "tyro" asks a question suggesting the ancient paradox of semantic vagueness. This is the Sorites dilemma, of whether a "heap" of sand continues to exist when successive grains are removed. The tyro's impertinence suggests that the issue is indeterminate, but Holmes's reply is that, notwithstanding the appearance of "indeterminate" vagueness, the law *must* find an answer. Conflicts must be adjudicated; if the terrain is

---

World; and Maher, *The Pittsburgh School of Philosophy: Sellars, McDowell, Brandom*, 3: "[The] picture of knowledge—as a process of simply being 'given' something in the world—has recurred throughout the ages, lending some intuitive support to the idea of a foundation. For the Pittsburgh School, the idea of such a foundation is the idea of 'the Given,' which can take various forms. Despite its apparent appeal, they hold that there is no such thing. They hold that it is a mere myth."

"Given" in Holmes's account is the *assumed* starting point in the constructive process of "explain[ing] an object by tracing the order and process of its growth and development." Holmes's idea of a "starting point assumed as given" is discussed in chaps. 6 and 9.

45. Holmes, "Law in Science," *CW*, 3:416. Alexander Lian has suggested the plausibility of influence on Holmes's line drawing from Darwin's account of species formation and his radical undermining of the idea of species fixity.

unexplored, we "call in the jury." What that implies requires further discussion; for now I simply note the connection of this with Holmes's 1873 essay on how opposing precedents are resolved through particularized inquiry.

Holmes's 1899 essay is his only extended treatment of the topic of science. It came at the height of his judicial powers, between his two remarkable labor dissents defending the right of boycotting workers to picket a worksite, which led many people at the time to question his judgment, but which would also bring him to the attention of a progressive Republican president, Theodore Roosevelt, as a judge sensitive to the problems of the working class. The essay elucidates the relationship of *The Common Law* to the guiding insights of his early research, a complex topic, but integral to his thinking. And it provides an opportunity to consider his answer to questions of concern to Whewell and Herschel, quoted at the beginning of this chapter.

We should compare Holmes's language in 1899 with a comment of Herschel's, in his review of Whewell of 1840. First, the astronomer Herschel:

> Instead of barren and effete generalities of vague and verbal classifications of propositions promising everything to the ear, but performing nothing to the sense of maxims grounded on pure assumption, and argument dogmatically taking its stand on the appeal to our irremediable ignorance, we find that it has been practicable for human faculties to attain a knowledge of truths based on a foundation co-extensive with the universe, yet applicable to the closest realities. Science itself thus comes to be considered as an object not simply of philosophical interest, but of inductive inquiry.[46]

And then Holmes:

> I have given an example of what seems to me the uninstructive and indolent use of phrases to save the trouble of thinking closely. . . . Let me give one of over generalization, or rather of the danger of reasoning from generalizations unless you have the particulars which they embrace in mind. A generalization is empty in so far as it is general. Its value depends on the number of particulars which it calls up to the speaker and the hearer.[47]

46. John Herschel, "Whewell on Inductive Sciences," Review of the *History* and the *Philosophy*, *Quarterly Review* 68 (1841): 177–238.

47. Holmes, "Law in Science," *CW*, 3:419.

It remains to be shown how the shared commitment to induction of Mill, Whewell, Herschel, and Holmes would play out within the American judicial tradition. In developing that thought, there are larger issues, such as, What is the shape of legal theory? How does it impact on contemporary philosophy? How do Bacon's dicta play out in the contemporary world? What methods are favored as "inductive," and what are not? How might legal theory, opened to a broader critique, compare with current controversies in science?

CHAPTER FOUR

Induction

This chapter addresses past criticism of Holmes based on an erroneous view of his thought, and illustrates the application of his continuum of inquiry in social inductivism, extending to the appellate stage of litigation.

* * *

A distasteful man who, among other things, espoused social Darwinism, favored eugenics, and as he himself acknowledged, came devilish near to believing that might makes right . . . his pernicious legacy is evident, in much contemporary legal thought, from critical legal studies on the left to law and economics on the right. His legacy was not a revolt against excess formalism, it was a revolt against the objective concepts of right and wrong—against values.—Albert W. Alschuler, *Law without Values: The Life, Work and Legacy of Justice Oliver Wendell Holmes* (1999)

Justice and Mrs. Holmes, childless, left a gift of $25,000 to Harvard and their residual estate to the United States of America. Holmes's literary executor, John G. Palfrey, gave access to Holmes's papers to Harvard law professor Felix Frankfurter, who had selected a succession of Harvard law graduates to serve as Holmes's secretaries. Also given access was his colleague Mark De Wolfe Howe, who had served as a Holmes secretary. Frankfurter proposed that they work together on a biography, but Frankfurter was appointed to the U.S. Supreme Court in 1939 by Franklin Delano Roosevelt, and surrendered the project to Howe. In the twenty-seven years until his death in 1967, Howe organized the papers, published volumes of speeches and letters, and completed two volumes of a biography. These covered the "shaping" and "proving" years, through the year 1882 when Holmes was appointed to the Supreme Judicial Court of Massachusetts.[1]

1. See Sheldon M. Novick, introduction to *CW*, 1:3–7.

Next to take on the project was Yale law professor Grant Gilmore, a distinguished legal historian, who had published a critical analysis of the impact of Holmes's views on a unified theory of contract law. Already dubious of Holmes's outsized influence, Gilmore sat on the biography for fifteen years until his own death in 1982. In his Storrs Lecture at Yale of 1974, published as *The Ages of American Law*, he authored a judgment of Holmes's 1881 *The Common Law* that has since cast a shadow over Holmes's scholarship. Gilmore wrote:

> Holmes is a strange, enigmatic figure. Put out of your mind the picture of the tolerant aristocrat, the great liberal, the eloquent defender of our liberties, the Yankee from Olympus. All that was a myth, concocted principally by Harold Laski and Felix Frankfurter, about the time of World War I. The real Holmes was savage, harsh, and cruel, a bitter and lifelong pessimist who saw in the course of human life nothing but a continuing struggle in which the rich and powerful impose their will on the poor and the weak. Holmes had no use for the gentle optimism of Karl Marx who seems to have believed that after one more revolution the world would be a better place.

He then cited Holmes's comment in *The Common Law* that "[t]he *ultima ratio*, not only *regum*, but of private persons, is force, and that at the bottom of all private relations, however tempered by sympathy and all the social feelings, is a justifiable self-preference."[2]

Civil war was a catalyst for the views of both Holmes and Thomas Hobbes. Famously born into fear from the Spanish Armada, reinforced by the English Civil War, Hobbes in 1642 wrote, "The condition of man . . . is a condition of war of everyone against everyone," and "To this war of every man against every man, this also is consequent; that nothing can be unjust. The notions of right and wrong, justice and injustice have there no place. Where there is no common power, there is no law, where no law, no injustice. Force, and fraud, are in war the cardinal virtues." There followed his famous passage from the *Leviathan*:

> Whatsoever therefore is consequent to a time of war, where every man is enemy to every man, the same consequent to the time wherein men live without other security than what their own strength and their own invention shall furnish them

2. Grant Gilmore, *The Ages of American Law*, 48–49; citing Holmes, *The Common Law*, *CW*, 3.137.

> withal. In such condition there is no place for industry . . . no knowledge of the face of the earth; no account of time; no arts; no letters; no society; and which is worst of all, continual fear, and danger of violent death; and the life of man, solitary, poor, nasty, brutish, and short.[3]

Compared to Hobbes's description of the natural condition of humanity, Holmes's comments (many taken from private correspondence) seem restrained. Scholars do not denigrate Hobbes for his bleak view; from the premise of a natural state of war he derives the axiomatic necessity of a universal surrender of "natural liberties" to a sovereign state, thereby vindicating centralized secular authority as well as three centuries of political theory grounded upon social contract. Holmes departs from the Hobbes model of social order, replacing it with a contingent mechanism of dispute resolution in which convergence is possible but violence is always a prospect.[4]

Gilmore's criticism has informed other harsh reactions to Holmes, like Alan Bloom's *Closing of the American Mind*[5] and Albert Alschuler's defense of "values" in the passage quoted above. Part of the "pernicious legacy" of which Alschuler complains is that Holmes has been praised by contemporary scholars from "law and economics" to "critical legal studies."[6] Their shared theme, for Alschuler, is an acceptance of "moral relativism." Alschuler cites Holmes's famous speech in 1897 to the law students at Boston University, "The Path of the Law," where he commented (echoing his Lowell Lectures on the vestiges of the vengeance era), "I often doubt whether it would not be a gain if every word of moral significance could be banished from the law altogether."[7] It contains his famous remark that a lawyer should approach legal knowledge with the same calculation as the "bad man," and his notion (originating with the 1870 paper testing the concept of duty as an alternative legal classification) that the language of "duty" should be washed away with "cynical acid." The language seems designed to shock. Holmes's phrasing, just two years later, is more reflective, in his address on law and science to the members of the New York bar.

3. Thomas Hobbes, *Leviathan; or, The Matter, Forme and Power of a Commonwealth Ecclesiasticall and Civil*, 100.

4. Kellogg, "Hobbes, Holmes, and Dewey: Pragmatism and the Problem of Order."

5. Alan Bloom, *The Closing of the American Mind*.

6. Albert W. Alschuler, *Law without Values: The Life, Work and Legacy of Justice Holmes*, 7–8.

7. Ibid., 33.

While his 1897 address is fundamentally consistent with Holmes's overall perspective, Alschuler and other writers have removed its language from the overall context of his work. Alschuler's own view—he calls it "the opposite" of Holmes's "moral relativism"—is that law consists of "those societal settlements that a good person should regard as obligatory." In effect this is close to Holmes's own approach, if one exchanges "prudent" for "good," and adds his uniquely inductive account of the manner in which societal settlements are painstakingly reached.[8] How *are* they reached? What is the precise role of the judge in particular legal decisions? How does legal induction work?

Reassessment should begin with his early association with the scientific inductivism inherited from Francis Bacon, applicable, from Bacon on, to all branches of human knowledge. From Bacon to Mill and Whewell, inductivism has been associated with meliorism, the conviction that concrete knowledge brings power to reform and improve the condition of humanity.[9] Holmes's social dimension of induction extends to the problem of order, and hence should be contrasted with Hobbes. It was precisely Hobbes's deductive method (drawn from a reading of Euclid) that offended both Mill and Whewell. As Mill comments in his *Logic*: "One of the most notable specimens of reasoning in a circle is the doctrine of Hobbes, Rousseau, and others, which rests the obligations by which human beings are bound as members of society, on a supposed social compact."[10]

Holmes resisted the idea that the institution of sovereign government removes the threat of violent civil discord, as the year 1861 had amply shown. Constant contention is his root assumption. Certainly, Holmes recognized the inevitability of self-preference and the need to control violence through sovereign coercion, but he posits the alternative of adjustment engendered by the resolution of specific disputes. Turbulence is not removable, but it may be managed. The possibility of orderly adjustment illuminates the context of the particular case within the broader chronological inquiry into an underlying problem. Holmes's feedback loop provides a potentially therapeutic basis for analyzing legal litigation.

The notion of extralegal feedback, which can inform Alschuler's "societal settlements," suggests a difference in participatory scope: that is, whether courtroom rule making is done with extrajudicial input into the continuum,

8. Ibid., 161.

9. Snyder, *Reforming Philosophy*, 3–5, 7–32, 69–76.

10. Mill, *Logic*, 2:403.

or with premature finality imposed by judicial axiom, by "values" imposed directly by the judges. Unlike Alschuler, Grant Gilmore's assessment was based less on Holmes's later speeches and more directly on *The Common Law*, and turns on a confessed bafflement over putatively inconsistent views. On one hand, he notes, Holmes had written:

> The first requirement of a sound body of law is that it should correspond with the actual feelings and demands of the community whether right or wrong.[11]

While elsewhere he wrote:

> The general principle of our law is that loss from accident must lie where it falls, and this principle is not affected by the fact that a human being is the instrument of misfortune.[12]

Gilmore observes that "it is by no means clear what the link in Holmes's mind was between his hypothesis about the progress of the law toward externality and objectivity and his conclusion about the desirability of restricting or denying liability for the incidentally harmful consequences of socially useful activity." It clearly annoyed Gilmore that Holmes in the second passage appeared to approve a business-friendly axiom that "over the broadest possible range" liability for tort should be "kept to the absolute minimum."[13] This is a plain misreading.

Holmes's second remark was not a statement of approval. The confusion lies in the context of the two statements, both seeking to emphasize the role of jury judgments of prudence in forming standards of liability—the key element of his response to the puzzle of how Mansfield's magistrate should decide the case of first impression. Having given up by 1876 (as he reported to Emerson) his exploration of the "lateral" rights-duties taxonomy, and having by 1881 fully adopted the "longitudinal" view (in fancy words, having replaced a synchronic approach with a diachronic theory of law), the question remained of how this novel perspective would fit into mid-nineteenth-century jurisprudence. Drawing on history, Holmes proceeded to defend his perspective with case law in relevant areas, including criminal law, personal injury, and contract, in the process advancing his

11. Holmes, *The Common Law*, *CW*, 3:136, quoted in Gilmore, *Ages of American Law*, 49.
12. Ibid., 55.
13. Gilmore, *Ages of American Law*, 55.

own views for the unification of doctrine. In Whewellian terms, one might say he was "colligating." In Peircean terminology, I suggest that he was engaged in "abduction."

In the first of the two passages he was connecting foresight with criminal liability, making the point that it hinges on a jury finding that the defendant, under prevailing standards of conduct, should have *foreseen* that the victim would be killed or injured by his action, whether or not the defendant's intentions lay elsewhere. With perhaps excess hyperbole, Holmes insists that the applicable standard of prudence is what a jury concludes about the objective situation. This is clearly his meaning despite the comment "whether right or wrong"—in which he bypasses (I think excusably) the exacting question of subjective criminal intent.[14]

It is excusable if only because Holmes was emphasizing that judgments of foresight are the vehicle for importing new information—judgments that reflect actual standards of conduct—into the induction process. In the second passage, he was distinguishing the continuum in personal injury law (the process of conceptual entrenchment and revision) from two opposing views, one requiring personal deficiency (the defendant must always in some sense be morally "culpable" before having to pay for the consequences of an action) and the other strict liability (the defendant must pay regardless of intent if the otherwise innocent action "caused" injury). Holmes rejected both views.[15]

Far from approving minimal liability for tort, Holmes's comment that the "general principle . . . that loss from accident must lie where it falls" was designed to show how the 1870 induction method works in the flow of cases. When he alludes to "the general principle of law" here, he means (in a case not already governed by precedent) that *absent foreseeable harm* "loss from accident must lie where it falls." Thus a sheer "accident" for Holmes was an occurrence that a jury would determine to have been *un*foreseeable.

Given the continuing debate over subjective criminal intent since 1881, there are good reasons for contemporary bafflement over this position, but not that given by Gilmore. It is possible that he, like many scholars following

14. Holmes, *The Common Law*, 45; but see Nicola Lacey and Hanna Pickard, "From the Consulting Room to the Court Room? Taking the Clinical Model of Responsibility without Blame into the Legal Realm," *Oxford Journal Legal Studies* 33, no. 1 (2013): 1–29: "Within contemporary penal philosophy, the view that punishment can only be justified if the offender is a *moral agent* who is responsible and hence blameworthy for their offence is one of the few areas on which a consensus prevails."

15. Kellogg, *Holmes, Legal Theory and Judicial Restraint*, 89.

Howe, took the view that Holmes's early essays were mainly "drafts" for *The Common Law*, and thus missed the critical turning point of Holmes's 1870 response to Mill, advancing the continuum model as his research progressed. Gilmore and others have failed to see the subtle birth of Holmes's hypothesis of law as a continuum of social inquiry, drawn from natural science, sketchily portrayed but utterly original. Influenced by the experience of war, it encompassed the constant reality of conflict. Holmes envisions social life as continuously engaged in dialectical activity, constantly seeking consensual resolution through line drawing.

Occasionally expressed in raw language, this reeked of little "gentle optimism." Yet followed to its full implications, it admits of a hardy voluntarism. His remark quoted at the end of chapter 2, his willingness to bet on a "loophole for free will—in the miraculous sense—the creation of a new atom of force," allows a fragile and hardscrabble optimism, rooted in creative intelligence, working in a fresh hypothesis, "colligating" or "abducting" within the space of doubt. The system of order is malleable by increments, but the choices are always human, and all human enterprise is subject to failure.[16]

While the element of extralegal social input in Holmes's thinking is not explicit, it is not missing from *The Common Law*, even though roughly articulated and embedded in historical analysis. The "growth of the law" passage of 1873 is buried near the middle, at the end of the chapter on trespass and negligence. There is no mention in *The Common Law* of having decisively abandoned the "lateral" exploration of duties. Thus the 1872 comment telegraphing his decisive move toward a "longitudinal" analysis is absent.

Without this insight *The Common Law* is not clearly presented as an extended historical argument for the inductively grounded and socially guided transformation of legal ideas and ideals. Its history is truncated and selective. Much space is devoted to demonstrating an often haphazard and unhandsome transformation away from vestigial vengeance-based principles ("eye for an eye") toward gradual and piecemeal insertion by judges of policy reasons into inherited patterns of decision, along with Holmes's own views regarding the unification of diverse doctrine. Nevertheless, his

16. As noted in chap. 3, n. 19, Holmes's perspective seems consistent with the CLS view that law is an arena of social conflict and struggle, but (avoiding the law/society dualism) only because social life is such an arena. Hence it is also consistent with the view that "if the law were rooted in such structural contradictions, it could inherently be made functional to radically divergent forms of social ordering." Gordon, "Critical Legal Histories Revisited: A Response," 203.

account of the gradual emergence of external standards in English common law is not far removed from Milsom's conclusion in 2003, of the historical movement toward judicial abstraction from jury decisions.[17]

Gilmore's bafflement led him to ambivalence over Holmes as a theorist, at once awed by his brilliance and dismayed by the apparent incoherence of his grounds for proposing a unified theory of contract.

> The lectures [of *The Common Law*] have long since become unreadable unless the reader is prepared to put forward an almost superhuman effort of will to keep his attention from flagging and his interest from wandering. Our difficulty with the lectures may stem from the fact that they are not what they pretend to be. They pretend to be a historical survey of the development of a few fundamental common law principles which, according to Holmes, had recurrently manifested themselves in the several fields he chose to deal with—principally criminal law, torts, and contracts. In fact, the historical underpinning was patently absurd, even when it had not been deliberately distorted.[18]

Even annoyed by the perceived inconsistency, Gilmore sensed nevertheless that Holmes "was making a highly original, essentially philosophical statement about the nature of law."[19]

Alschuler, like Bloom, has very little positive to say and gathers evidence suggesting that Holmes grew increasingly bitter and nihilistic in old age.

17. S. F. C. Milsom, *A Natural History of the Common Law*, 16, 19, 45: "Ideas of right and wrong originated from the jurors and were formulated by judges into substantive rules of law. The rules were, so to speak, not so much made by judges as drafted by them; and the result had always to be acceptable to jurors, which is another way of saying that the law had to be acceptable to its lay subjects." (45). See Kellogg, *Formative Essays of Justice Holmes*, 42–57.

18. Gilmore, *Ages of American Law*, 52.

19. Ibid. Gilmore in *The Death of Contract* says that "Holmesian consideration theory [of contracts] had, as Holmes perfectly well knew, not so much as a leg to stand on if the matter is taken historically. Going back into the past, there was an indefinite number of cases which had imposed liability, in the name of consideration, where nothing like Holmes's 'reciprocal conventional inducement' was anywhere in sight. Holmes's point was that these were bad cases and that the range of contractual liability should be confined within narrower limits." *Death of Contract*, 63. Holmes's point actually fits into his overall scheme of external standards. In 1873 Holmes addresses the question of how deeds, or judgments, can take place within a preconceptual context. The starting point of action and inquiry takes place *in medias res*; it is essential to have the continuum in mind. Gilmore and Holmes may be closer than Gilmore suggests. Gilmore's critique of Holmes is doing what Holmes himself did: hypothesizing in regard to the emergent nature of contract law.

The experience of war, having blunted his early idealism, would reverberate in triumphalist comments and lectures (one of which, titled "The Soldier's Faith,"[20] with its stirring account of standing in formation before puffs of gunpowder and arriving shards from Confederate artillery, appealed to the Rough Rider president). Alschuler in 1999 contrived to blame Holmes for the "affinity between the nation's sullen mood and the ethical skepticism that now dominates the academy."[21]

While the "cynical acid" remark of his 1897 speech "The Path of the Law" seems to reinforce this view, the later address of 1899 offers important clues as to why it is off the mark. Given Holmes's opposition to judicial value-dictation as a form of axiomatic thinking, his view is more a therapy for the abuse of principle than an approval of value-nihilism. In any event, both Gilmore and Alschuler miss the critical question raised by Holmes's inductivism, still unaddressed amidst widespread misunderstanding: How, for Holmes, is the uncertain case decided, in a contested space among opposing precedents?

The 1899 speech to the New York State Bar Association refers in closing to an issue that roiled the industrial world at the turn of the century: labor organization and its methods, including picketing and boycotts. Holmes's dissenting role in support of the right to picket at an employer's worksite, in two cases before the Massachusetts Supreme Judicial Court, *Vegelahn v. Guntner* (1896) and *Plant v. Woods* (1900), brought the question of judicial method into a remarkably candid public conversation among the judges of his court.[22]

In *Vegelahn*, employees in a furniture factory had gone on strike and were picketing to persuade others not to do business with the plaintiff, Vegelahn. Fights ensued, and Vegelahn sought an injunction. Trial of the case having been assigned to Holmes in equity session, he enjoined violence and threats, but ruled that the picketing itself was lawful "so far as it confined itself to persuasion and giving notice of the strike." Vegelahn appealed, and the case was heard by the full seven-member court.

The majority held that picketing was "an unlawful interference with the rights both of employer and of employed," rights that were "secured by the Constitution itself," as employers had "a right to engage all persons who are

20. *CW*, 3:486.

21. Alschuler, *Law without Values*, 12.

22. *Vegelahn v. Guntner*, 167 Mass. 97, 105–6, 44 N.E. 1077, 1080 (1896) (Holmes, dissenting); *Plant v. Woods*, 176 Mass. 492, 504, 57 N.E. 1011, 1016 (1900) (Holmes, dissenting).

willing to work for [them] at such prices as may be mutually agreed upon," and "persons employed or seeking employment have a corresponding right to enter into or remain in the employment of any person or corporation willing to employ them." Note that the majority rested their ruling on a constitutional right of contractual freedom—the same ground on which the majority of the Supreme Court of the United States would overturn a state limitation of bakers' working hours, in the famous case of *Lochner v. New York* (1905).[23] A passage from Holmes's dissent in *Vegelahn* addresses the issue of uncertainty:

> [I]n numberless instances the law warrants the intentional infliction of temporal damage because it regards it as justified. It is on the question of what shall amount to a justification, and more especially on the nature of the considerations which really determine or ought to determine the answer to that question, that judicial reasoning seems to me often to be inadequate. The true grounds of decision are considerations of policy and of social advantage, and it is vain to suppose that solutions can be attained merely by logic and the general propositions of law which nobody disputes. Propositions as to public policy rarely are unanimously accepted, and still more rarely, if ever, are capable of unanswerable proof. They require a special training to enable anyone even to form an intelligent opinion about them. *In the early stages of law, at least, they generally are acted on rather as inarticulate instincts* [my italics] than as definite ideas for which a rational defense is ready.[24]

The salient point is Holmes's reference to "early stages of law." (He is not referring here to stages of legal history, but of specific judicial inquiry into the problem underlying a given uncertain case.) The inference is that it was premature for this court to assess in advance the complex policy answer to the lawfulness of emergent labor tactics. His reference to the issue being at an "early stage" clearly applies to this case. This comment alone should raise some eyebrows among contemporary appellate court justices: *Early stage* of law? Are *we* not the *final* stage? Not according to this account.[25]

23. *Lochner v. New York*, 198 U.S. 59 (1905).

24. *Vegelahn v. Guntner*, 106.

25. See generally Kellogg, *Holmes, Legal Theory and Judicial Restraint*, 118–36; Holmes's attribution of a "prerogative of choice" to judges, especially as it relates to the early case in the continuum, should be understood as a constrained choice, not extending too far beyond the facts of the particular case. Holmes compares it to the scope of decision by a jury: as "within our competence to decide without the aid of a jury." Ibid., 123.

Holmes's head, and this case, is firmly located in his 1873 model of "the growth of the law," where the uncertain case is situated not according to its place on the docket but rather in the continuum of inquiry into a broader problem. Though unionization had a long history in both Massachusetts and English common law, Holmes approached this case of picketing to discourage private business in 1896 as one, if not of "first impression," at least "early."[26] Holmes saw at once that there were opposing lines of precedent, one suggesting freedom to associate, the other suggesting interference with private business, with neither one clearly (to him) controlling.

As in the imagery of clusters discussed in chapter 2, Holmes pictured particular decisions as marks on a line between competing analogies, like the opposing "poles" referred to as A and B. The "poles" had themselves been the product of prior induction as described by Holmes in 1870, generated over time from particular cases. The poles, then, are "clusters" (Holmes's term), with their conceptual content derived from the factual nature of accumulated cases. Hence they have an implicit inductive boundary, such that (in 1896) neither pole could be assumed to extend to cover the matter of picketing in a labor boycott.

If the *Vegelahn* case was in the middle area, not covered by existing "clusters" of association or interference, what then of the majority argument that the case was covered by the employer's right of contractual freedom? Holmes removes this sweeping general principle from his spectrum of available precedents—he would do likewise in *Lochner v. United States*, soon after promotion to the Supreme Court. Why? Appealing to a general axiom short-circuits necessary inquiry into the question of whether and how particular instances of picketing in a boycott are consistent or inconsistent with applicable but contradictory poles of precedent. Moreover, a ruling of unconstitutionality would mean that the issue is closed, decided with finality from the outset, short of an arduous and unlikely constitutional amendment.

The opinions in the two cases record a conversation in which Holmes engaged with his colleagues after losing in *Vegelahn*, yet vying to keep

26. See Anthony Woodiwiss, *Right v. Conspiracy: A Sociological Essay on the History of Labour Law in the United States*. In the 1840 Massachusetts case of *Commonwealth v. Hunt*, Boston cordwainers were charged with conspiracy to form an unlawful club, conspiring not to work for masters who employed nonmembers, seeking to impoverish other masters and a worker by depriving them of work opportunities. Woodiwiss notes that use of state legal injunction against unions began in 1883 and increased rapidly and continuously until passage of the Norris-LaGuardia Act in 1932. Ibid., 77.

the issue open. He had written an article in 1894, "Privilege, Malice, and Intent," revisiting the notion of subjectivity in legal liability, touching in particular on English labor organization cases. The article tackled the problem of policy disputes, and criticized the resort to generalities by English judges in the 1898 case of *Allen v. Flood*.[27] Holmes had written that "[w]hen the question of policy is faced it will be seen to be one which cannot be answered by generalities, but must be determined by the particular character of the case." That he circulated this paper to his fellow justices is revealed by the majority opinion four years later in *Plant v. Woods*.

It may have helped that he had since been promoted to chief justice. The majority cited the article, and backed down on the free contract argument: "It is manifest," wrote Justice Hammond for the majority, "that not much progress is made by such general statements as those quoted above from *Allen v. Flood*, whatever may be their meaning. Still standing for solution is the question, Under what circumstances, including the motive of the actor, is the act complained of lawful, and to what extent?"

History may record no quicker Baconian conversion than this. It was more than a doff of the hat; it was an abandonment (at least for the moment) of axiomatic jurisprudence. Holmes's new dissent recognized this, with its own self-congratulatory passage: "Much to my satisfaction, if I may say so," he wrote, "the court has seen fit to adopt the mode of approaching the question which I believe to be the correct one, and to open an issue which otherwise I might have thought closed. The difference between my brethren and me now seems to be a difference of degree, and the line of reasoning followed makes it proper for me to explain where the difference lies."

What *was* the difference, and why was it so important to Holmes? In this dissent, Holmes defined the issue that now divided him from the majority as that of the legitimacy of the purpose of the threatened union action. For the majority, the purpose was somehow akin to extortion, like obtaining "a sum of money [from the employer] which he is under no legal obligation to pay." For Holmes the purpose of striking for a closed shop went no farther than, and indeed not as far as, the acceptable purpose of raising wages. For him the purpose of the union strike was to consolidate the union's organization in order to increase its effectiveness in the struggle for more pay:

27. Holmes, "Privilege, Malice and Intent," *Harvard Law Review* 8 (1894): 1, *CW*, 3:371. See Kellogg, *Holmes, Legal Theory and Judicial Restraint*, 118–32.

> I infer that a majority of my brethren would admit that a boycott or strike intended to raise wages directly might be lawful, if it did not embrace in its scheme or intent violence, breach of contract, or other conduct unlawful on grounds independent of the mere fact that the action of the defendants was combined. A sensible workingman would not contend that the courts should sanction a combination for the purpose of inflicting or threatening violence or the infraction of admitted rights. To come directly to the point, the issue is narrowed to the question whether, assuming that some purposes would be a justification, the purpose in this case of the threatened boycotts and strikes was such as to justify the threats. That purpose was not directly concerned with wages. It was one degree more remote. The immediate object and motive was to strengthen the defendants' society as a preliminary means to enable it to make a better fight on questions of wages or other matters of clashing interests.[28]

Why would another dissent, for what was now only a "difference of degree," be an occasion for "satisfaction"? It can only be that a critical battle over method had been won, leaving the issue still open to reconsideration. He had vindicated the importance of particular reasoning, and it seems evident that he believed, perhaps unrealistically, that the door was yet open for further consideration of particular instances that might illuminate whether labor tactics were closer to building a legitimate organization than to extortion.

With these two labor dissents, considered radical at the time, Holmes hardly improved his prospects for promotion to the Supreme Court of the United States.[29] The labor sympathies of the progressive Republican Theodore Roosevelt would not reach the White House but for President William McKinley's assassination in 1901. Without that, his labor dissents would have been among the more memorable judicial acts of a modest career. They stand nevertheless as a powerful rebuttal to charges of cynicism.

It should be clear from his early research, and from this look at the 1899 address and two dissents at the close of the century, that Holmes had developed a distinct perspective on legal logic, method, and conceptualization—a view guided by the early essays identifying a social dimension to induction. The labor cases serve as an example. The 1873 essay depicted the "growth of the law" through "line-drawing" in relation to opposing "poles," described as "clusters" of prior decided cases. The sometimes "arbitrary"

28. *Plant v. Woods*, 176 Mass. 492, 504, 57 N.E. 1011, 1016 (1900) (Holmes, dissenting).

29. G. Edward White, *Justice Oliver Wendell Holmes*, 289–92.

line was a reference to the context of reevaluation in light of new information. In the labor dissents, Holmes was seeking to place the new phenomenon of workplace picketing within its presumptive line-drawing context, comparing it to prior decisions defining "extortion" and those allowing organization or free association. These are established legal terms, but Holmes recognizes that meanings can change, and he has adopted an inductive rather than axiomatic model to account for change.

How then might we characterize his overall theoretical perspective? It does not neatly fit conventional models. Holmes was an engaged Baconian critic, simultaneously judge and theorist, combining an "internal" and "external" perspective. He could analyze his own account of the growth of legal generalization, even while engaged in the process. His view envisions novel cases constantly arising amidst an environment of ubiquitous controversy rather than settled authority. Conflicts are brought from the streets to the courts, and thence into the extension of usage of legal terms like "extortion," "malice," and "organization." Similarity and difference are constantly contested as new lines of meaning are drawn.

The overall conception is very different from that of analytic and conceptual jurisprudence, in the wake of Herbert Hart's *The Concept of Law*. Rather than a stable conceptual framework of primary and secondary rules (within which particular content may be changing, but not the basic system), the picture displays degrees of judgment, rules, and concepts, some stable and entrenched, others in formation or revision. The judge and lawyer must adapt to local conditions while navigating in particular areas, within a broader context of systemic understanding. Yet even fundamental system-wide assumptions may be in flux, such as the overall retreat from vengeance, leaving traces of ancient habits of thought and practice amidst contemporary doctrine.

This perspective is also distinct from the main strains of legal realism, examined in the next chapter. A conventional view holds that legal realism arose in reaction to "formalism," the notion that "lawyers and judges saw law as autonomous, comprehensive, logically ordered, and determinate and believed that judges engaged in pure mechanical deduction from this body of law to produce single correct outcomes." Realism argued that "judges decide according to their personal preferences and then construct the legal analysis to justify the desired outcome."[30] But the focus of realism

30. See Brian Tamanaha, *Beyond the Formalist-Realist Divide*, 1. See generally Postema, *Treatise of Legal Philosophy*, 124–25.

was on the relation of the judicial response to the individual case, not to larger problems.

This left out aspects of the continuum for which Holmes's "many minds"—and time for social feedback—were essential. Formalism is basically deductivism, assuming an amplitude of general propositions into which all disputed conduct might fit, as if governed by an overall syllogism: 1) the law covers all cases; 2) this new dispute is a case; 3) the law covers this case. Against this the realist model failed to propose an alternative other than anxiety. The succession of disputes was not akin to red balls being removed from a bag, or what Bacon and Peirce had called "enumerative induction." Nor could any other inductive practice attributable to the judge alone account for the imposition of ordered similarities. The judge was not simply the perceiver, but rather also part of the perceived experience to be ordered; hence the dual role as both internal and external.

One might rightly assume that there are cases arising in many areas in which novelty is not a pronounced factor, cases fitting more comfortably within the terms of statutes or settled precedents. This context may be presumed to be entirely deductive. These are cases in which line drawing is not involved, but in which other aspects of uncertainty arise, such as the meaning of a disputed phrase, like the famous example of the vehicle in the park.[31] Contemporary philosophy views uncertainty as primarily a semantic issue related to language. Holmes should be recognized for outlining a departure, in the direction later taken by John Dewey in his 1938 *Logic: A Theory of Inquiry*. Broadly speaking, this entails seeing classical logic and its view of uncertainty as insufficient to explain the process of growth and change.

Rather than a strictly judge-centric view of legal growth, his approach focused on the larger problem implied by the difficult case, its interpretation of legal uncertainty within a transformative continuum, and its focus on entrenchment amidst the inevitability of change in the conceptual structure of law. The following chapters compare Holmes to standard views that followed in his wake, legal realism, legal positivism, critical legal studies and, especially, the turn toward "principles" (a form of reasoning from general propositions) advanced by Herbert Wechsler and Ronald Dworkin. If Holmes's insights indeed lie outside the now-orthodox theories, can evidence of his basic claims about law have been invisible? I will show

31. H. L. A. Hart, *The Concept of Law*, 124; Frederick Schauer, "A Critical Guide to Vehicles in the Park."

that aspects of the transformative "continuum" are indeed identifiable in the literature, especially in classic works by Edward Levi, Karl Llewellyn, and Alexander Bickel.

Recognition of this is obscured by the fact that the actual inductive path of law is often circuitous, and clouded by technicalities, intricacies, and diversions. Judicial vision is frequently tempted toward premature generalizing. This too is understandable, given that new problems brought to law from society are rarely presented in a dispassionate, antiseptic environment.

CHAPTER FIVE

Realism

This chapter contends that Holmes is wrongly associated with legal realist concerns over "indeterminacy" in the difficult case. Uncertainty for Holmes was a feature of social life; for legal realism it was a problem within law and legal institutions.

* * *

I was much troubled in spirit, in my first years on the bench, to find how trackless was the ocean on which I had embarked. I sought for certainty. I was oppressed and disheartened when I found that the quest for it was futile. I was trying to reach land, the solid land of fixed and settled rules, the paradise of a justice that would declare itself by tokens plainer and more commanding than its pale and glimmering reflections in my own vacillating mind and conscience.—Judge Benjamin Nathan Cardozo, 1920 Storrs Lecture at Yale Law School, *The Nature of the Judicial Process*

This exclamation in the 1920 Storrs Lecture by New York Court of Appeals Judge Nathan Cardozo, who in 1930 would succeed Holmes on the Supreme Court of the United States, contrasts with the latter's upbeat attitude after twice losing to the majority in the Massachusetts labor cases. Cardozo had been navigating Holmes's often roiled, and often "trackless," ocean.[1]

Holmes's two labor dissents surprise us in three respects. First is his suggestion that any case arising before a final appellate court should be treated as an "early stage" in the judicial process. The second is that a broad constitutional protection should be set aside in deference to contrasting but specific analogies drawn from precedent. The third, and most surprising, is that Holmes could be gratified at having lost a second time to the majority. That was not a power trip; it was a teaching moment. Although Holmes did not convert his brethren on the Massachusetts Supreme Judicial Court

1. Benjamin N. Cardozo, *The Nature of the Judicial Process*, 166.

to card-carrying Baconians, he had lost a battle but won the greater war over judicial method. His approach was radical, and demands more careful explanation than Holmes ever gave it.

The three surprises have roots in Mill's *System of Logic*. Mill describes himself there as searching, like the legal realists, for "[w]hat really takes place" in human inquiry.[2] Like them, Mill questioned the assumption that correct inferences must be deductive;[3] his radical empiricism viewed abstraction as firmly grounded in particulars. Holmes's conception reflects that notion, in this way: because legal abstraction moves in and through particulars, for practical purposes it remains grounded in them. If precedents are cumulative of particular judgments retrospectively abstracted in "clusters," they are not controlling beyond where their extension is sufficiently entrenched—by which I suggest he means both *believed* and *acted upon*, inside and outside the legal profession. As he remarked to the New York lawyers in 1899, between his two labor dissents, in language reminiscent of Mill, "generalization is empty in so far as it is general. Its value depends on the number of particulars which it calls up to the speaker and the hearer."[4]

Mill's phrasing suggests something like a cumulative "container" theory of meaning, in which a concept consists in generalization only from its past experiential contents. Holmes adopts a more cautious, and forward-looking, characterization in saying that its "value" depends on the "particulars which it calls up to the speaker and the hearer." The "particulars" referred to here are, simplified, the accumulated judgments of prudence in the realm of known experience, "known" in the sense of being formally generalized into a "rule" at the closure of a prior continuum of inquiry.

That sort of general, he implies, is not empty, because of its grounding in adjusted practice.[5] That is his sense of "realism," or "what really takes

2. Mill, *Logic*, 2:196; see chap. 6, n. 10, and accompanying text.

3. Postema, *Treatise of Legal Philosophy*, 124; Mill, *Logic*, 1:245: "The real inference [in successive propositions] is always from particulars to particulars, from the observed instances to an unobserved one: but in drawing this inference, we conform to a formula which we have adopted for our guidance in such operations, and which is a record of the criteria by which we thought we had ascertained that we might distinguish when the inference could, and when it could not, be drawn. The real premises are the individual observations, even though they may have been forgotten, or, being the observations of others and not of ourselves, may, to us, never have been known: but we have before us proof that we or others once thought them sufficient for an induction, and we have marks to show whether any new case is one of those to which, if then known, the induction would have been deemed to extend."

4. Holmes, "Law in Science," *CW*, 3:419.

5. John Rawls in "Two Concepts of Rules" (chap. 4, n. 7) distinguishes the "summary" from the "practice" view of rules: the summary view "regards rules in the following way: one

place" in the growth of legal knowledge. His objection to deduction from the constitutional right of free contract in *Vegelahn* was due to its overbreadth; it would imply the unconstitutionality of many accepted laws, including economic regulation like the puritan laws against doing business on Sunday. For both Holmes and Mill, appeal to overbroad propositions is discredited as "axiomatic."

Discredited in favor of what? The uncertain or borderline case still has to be decided, presumably by a new judgment of prudence. What then is the role of abstract thought? Mill's rival inductivist, Whewell, contributed the notion that, while inquiry must be guided by the particulars of real experience, conflicts can only be resolved by creative engagement. Place must be found for the resolving hypothesis, a stage in inquiry where (in Whewell's phrase) "trains of hypotheses are called up and pass rapidly in review, and the judgment makes its choice from the varied group."[6]

This suggests that for Whewell scientific inquiry takes place in discrete stages. Holmes viewed the judicial role in the process of legal inquiry as differentiated according to different stages, as a problem is identified, explored, and resolved. I will return to this, and the tension between Mill and Whewell, after further examining Cardozo's anxiety.

Holmes's optimism even after twice dissenting in the labor cases focused on hope for the *problem*. This required time, experience, and the contribution of "many minds." Cardozo's complaint, seeing uncertainty as a "trackless ocean," focused on the troublesome *case*, on the demand for an immediate and definitive solution by the individual judge. This is not to suggest that Holmes ignored the immediate decision, but that he uniquely distinguished the problem according to its place in the continuum. Several

---

supposes that each person decides what he shall do in particular cases by applying the utilitarian principle; one supposes further that different people will decide the same particular case in the same way and that there will be recurrences of cases similar to those previously decided. Thus it will happen that in cases of certain kinds the same decision will be made either by the same person at different times or by different persons at the same time. If a case occurs frequently enough one supposes that a rule is formulated to cover that sort of case." In the practice conception, "rules are pictured as defining a practice," and they "are not generalizations from the decisions of individuals applying the utilitarian principle directly and independently to recurrent particular cases. On the contrary, rules define a practice and are themselves the subject of the utilitarian principle." Ibid., 158, 163. The relevance for this to Holmes's continuum is discussed in chap. 8.

6. Whewell, *Philosophy of the Inductive Sciences*, 2:42, quoted in Snyder, *Reforming Philosophy*, 63.

generations of scholars have placed the blame for Cardozo's anxiety on Holmes.

The above passage, from Cardozo's Storrs Lecture of 1920, was sympathetically cited by Grant Gilmore in his own Storrs Lecture of 1974, published as *The Ages of American Law*, in a chapter titled "The Age of Anxiety."[7] Columbia law professor Philip Bobbitt, in his own Storrs Lecture of 2014 (the fortieth anniversary of Gilmore's now-famous one) attributed Gilmore's "rueful writer's block" on not finishing the Holmes biography to "the conundrum into which Holmes and the legal realists had led American law."[8]

Why? Because, said Bobbitt, legal realism had presented an "antinomy": If law was simply what the judges did, then how could they ever be—from a legal point of view—wrong? Moreover, if the judges often contradicted and reversed each other and themselves—how could they ever be right? This unavoidably cast doubt on the legitimacy of the judicial process itself. Unless, as I have been proposing, we stop blaming Holmes for something he actually opposed, the judge-centric vision of legal realism, and accept the problem-centered fallibilism of his labor dissents, with their acceptance of experiment, along with the possibility of error and need of revision.

After his complaint about the trackless ocean, Cardozo continued thus:

> As the years have gone by, and as I have reflected more and more upon the nature of the judicial process, I have become reconciled to the uncertainty, because I have grown to see it as inevitable. I have grown to see that the process in its highest reaches is not discovery, but creation; and that the doubts and misgivings, the hopes and fears, are part of the travail of mind, the pangs of death and the pangs of birth, in which principles that have served their day expire, and new principles are born.[9]

The word "uncertainty" here is noteworthy, as is the word "creation." Cardozo sensed the importance of conceptual change, but its mechanism was invisible to him, submerged beneath the trackless ocean. Meanwhile, as Bobbitt observed in 2014, the notion of "inevitable uncertainty" has been increasingly displaced in recent decades by another term, "indeterminacy."

7. Gilmore, *Ages of American Law*, 76–77.
8. Philip Bobbitt, "The Age of Consent," *Yale Law Journal* 123 (May 2014): 2334, 2336.
9. Cardozo, *Nature of Judicial Process*, 166–67.

Indeterminacy has a hard edge to it, implying a concrete boundary around the settled law and its dictates, beyond which lies the deep. It conveys an image of a fixed and identifiable bounded entity of text and doctrine that may lack any extension to a particularly difficult case.

Analytical philosophers have in fact assumed such a conceptual extension in the very "concept" of law. When a case falls inside, there is an answer, but outside, it must be legally "indeterminate." Unless, now say most scholars, it is permissible to appeal to a hypothetical "background," which includes moral principles.[10] But hold on; this approach can also imply, as it has for the critical legal school, that law is *globally* indeterminate: the "background" is so replete with opposing broad directives and sweeping values that it cannot without arbitrariness be authoritative for *any* outcome. This "background" is the realm Holmes found in the 1870s to be heavily populated by axioms; it invites the kind of theorizing to which Chauncey Wright would certainly have objected.[11]

How did uncertainty become indeterminacy? The later legal realists adopted Holmes's occasional definition of law as "prophecies" or "prediction" of what the courts will do, an expression first coined after lectures by Holmes at Harvard Law School, described by him in an 1872 book notice.[12] Prediction had a broader and longer-term reference for him than immediate judicial conduct, and was connected with his conception of legal "growth"; but this connection has been overlooked. Hence, his use of "prediction" was interpreted by the realists, in particular Karl Llewellyn and Jerome Frank, as having an atomic behavioral reference, equating law with the sum total of conduct by legal officials.[13]

Holmes saw the available analogs in an uncertain case as rooted in particular judgments of foreseeability. When described as opposing clusters of prior decisions, these are subject to extension and refinement, even as are

10. See Jeremy Waldron, "Did Dworkin Ever Answer the Crits?," and Kellogg, "What Precisely Is a 'Hard' Case? Waldron, Dworkin, Critical Legal Studies, and Judicial Recourse to Principle."

11. Madden, *Chauncey Wright and the Founders of Pragmatism*, 73–90. I should note that the "background" as conceived by contemporary writers does not consist merely of empty axioms, but would include claims and arguments analogous to Whewell's colligation or Peirce's abduction; see, e.g., the discussion of Richard Epstein in chap. 6.

12. Holmes, "Book Notice," *American Law Review* 6 (July 1873): 723; Kellogg, *Formative Essays*, 91; *CW*, 1:294.

13. Karl N. Llewellyn, *The Bramble Bush: Our Law and Its Study*; Jerome Frank, *Law and the Modern Mind*. See also Frederick Schauer, "Legal Realism Untamed."

the patterns of conduct from which they are drawn. All of this affects "prediction." In thus describing the process, then and twenty-five years later in "The Path of the Law," Holmes was adopting an "external" perspective, as of a legal historian or sociologist observing judges and lawyers in operation. This attitude informed his "internal" perspective, acting as a judge in the courtroom. It explains his mental composure after the labor decisions.

A singular dimension of Holmes's vision, which helps elucidate the labor dissents, has to do with the distinction between trials and appeals. Conventional teaching holds that facts are determined in trials and that appeals are matters of pure law, arriving in a fixed context.[14] Only errors of strictly legal interpretation or legal application are supposed to be reviewable on appeal, with outcomes to be corrected accordingly. While never explicitly challenging that convention, Holmes clearly did not view the continuum of legal inquiry, with its ongoing openness to feedback from outside the adjudicatory system, as limited to trial courts. As with the labor cases, some disputes, even at the highest appellate level, and viewed in the broader context of an underlying social problem, could, like the organized boycott in 1896, represent an "early stage" of inquiry.

Later legal realism never recognized this aspect of Holmes's work and thought. The main legal realist analyses of doctrine, when focusing on the judicial role in appeals, perceived judges as confronted by an unguided deductive choice among opposing precedents relevant to the decision in a closely contested case.[15] Judicial interpretation of prior opinions was further aggravated by unclarity in the distinction between holding and dictum.[16] Having frozen the notion of the legal "rule" as fixed at the moment of appellate analysis, its status in a larger continuum of inquiry was obscured.

14. S. C. F. Milsom, *Historical Foundations of the Common Law*, 270; Roscoe Pound, *The Spirit of the Common Law*, 166–92.

15. E.g., Llewellyn, *The Bramble Bush*, 61–70; Twining, *Karl Llewellyn and the Realist Movement*, 70–83. Legal realism was not univocal, and took different views regarding both rational and causal determination of judicial decisions; Postema, *Treatise of Legal Philosophy*, 124–26. But diversity of approaches notwithstanding, there seems (with the exception of Edward Levi, discussed below) to have been no explicit recognition of the relation of appellate uncertainty to unresolved underlying social disputes, recognizing distinct phases or stages of judicial inquiry into such disputes as they matured. This is true even of realist analyses of the gradual emergence and refinement over time of rules and doctrines, as in Herman Oliphant's "A Return to Stare Decisis," 73–76; Postema, *Treatise of Legal Philosophy*, 125.

16. Andrew Altman, "Legal Realism, Critical Legal Studies, and Dworkin," and *Critical Legal Studies: A Liberal Critique*.

Holmes, in viewing all judicial decisions, even by the U.S. Supreme Court, as putatively located at some position (not necessarily at the end) along an ongoing time line, opened up the question of how a difficult case, *any* difficult case, stands in the generalizing process. One might say he "unfroze" the appeal, envisioning *all* decisions within the progression of social inquiry. Thus he also opened up, for the entire spectrum of adjudication, the question asked about science by John Herschel in his 1840 review of Whewell: What is the act or series of acts of the mind in constructing general propositions, and when constructed, in what manner do we rest in them as expressive of truth?

Cardozo in his Storrs Lecture noted the anxiety of his "first years on the bench"; he tried mightily in his lecture to account for every source of a judge's decision in a difficult case, and his reference to the judicial use of "background" material, like principles and policies, projects the "internal" assumption that the appellate court is always the final stage of decision.[17] Karl Llewellyn also took a largely internal view in *The Bramble Bush* and saw precedents as habits *of judges*—"in the large, precedent consists in an official doing over again under similar circumstances substantially what has been done by him or his predecessor before." Uncertainty for Holmes was a feature of social life; for Cardozo and Llewellyn (at least in this early writing) it was a feature of legal institutions.[18]

In his comprehensive study *American Legal Realism and Empirical Social Science*, John Henry Schlegel investigated the question, "Why did law not become a scientific study, in the twentieth century sense of science as an empirical inquiry into a world 'out there,' as did all the other disciplines in American life that formed in the late nineteenth and early twentieth centuries?" His answer addresses the varied responses of legal academics to the idea of empiricism in science, as well as to the emergent social sciences, and to leading pragmatic scholars like John Dewey. While space here cannot do full justice to Schlegel's analysis, it permits me to specify

17. Cardozo, *The Nature of the Judicial Process*, 40–41 (citing *Riggs v. Palmer*), 64–65, 90–92.

18. Llewellyn described the generalizing process in 1930 as follows:

> For [the judge] the logical ladder, or the several logical ladders, are ways of keeping himself in touch with the decision of the past. This, as a judge, he wishes to do. This as a judge, he would have to do even if he did not wish. This is the public's check upon his work. This is his own check on his own work. For while it is possible to build a number of divergent logical ladders up out of the same cases and down again to the same dispute, *there are not so many that can be built defensibly* [his italics]. (*The Bramble Bush*, 73)

the contribution Holmes had already made in moving to a social theory of induction.[19]

Schlegel focused on the question of why law did not become an empirical inquiry, in the sense of "fact" or "field" research, as distinguished from "library" research. "Such research," he observed, "was usually, but not exclusively, seen as research into present social, economic, or legal conditions or practices and as attempting to quantify relationships, though not to require hypothesis formation and testing. Thus, history was not a favored science." The rejection of history and its form of "library" research (though not rigidly followed even by empiricists like Walter Wheeler Cook) displaced Holmes's Whewellian perspective, of a comparative and diachronic inquiry into the relationship of particulars and generals over the sweep of relevant history. This was the insight that moved Holmes to send his 1876 paper to Emerson. Whewell's *History of the Inductive Sciences* had balanced Mill's radical but rigid empiricism, permitting Holmes to address Herschel's questions in their historical and social context.[20]

The pragmatic philosopher who influenced the realists was not Charles Peirce but John Dewey. As young faculty members at Columbia Law School, Cook, Underhill Moore, Thomas Reed Powell, and Herman Oliphant persuaded Dean Harlan Fiske Stone to invite Dewey to participate in a "Special Conference on Jurisprudence" in the summer of 1922, where he delivered an address titled "Some Problems in the Logic and Ethics of Law." Schlegel, reviewing Cook's extensive notes on the presentation, summarizes it as follows:

> Dewey offered no coherent social theory of ethics at all. He did offer three things: a quite interesting demonstration of the centrality of the many faceted concept of nature or naturalness in ethical theory; the suggestions that there were two kinds of ethical theories, those emphasizing right or correct behavior and those emphasizing good consequences; and a list of the interests to be taken into account in any consequentialist ethics, plainly the one he was selling. . . . The balance of the course only dealt with contemporary pragmatic logic in the interstices of a sustained criticism of Aristotelean deductive, and interestingly, J. S. Mill's inductive, logic. Central to this criticism was the assertion that people reason in response to the need to decide something, to deal with some trouble, and that in these circumstances people look not for rules to govern the case or instance at hand, but for solutions that will dispose of the matter to be decided,

19. John Henry Schlegel, *American Legal Realism and Empirical Social Science*, 1.
20. Ibid., 21.

> fix the trouble. The point of reasoning is thus to do or learn something. Doing or learning something new was, however, impossible under the formal logic of the syllogism, which could at most demonstrate the interrelatedness of propositions, or even through inductive logic, which smuggled in its conclusions with the assumption that the events being studied were similar.[21]

From this account Dewey appears to have focused on logical method for the observer faced with an immediate problem, which he associated with the particular difficult legal case, offering the basic pragmatic doctrine that the traditional logic of deduction and induction was insufficient to encompass the complex reality of problem solving, of "fix[ing] the trouble." However, the individual case and the larger problem, at least in this account, appear to have been conflated, rather than stressing Holmes's view that the uncertain case might represent an early stage of inquiry.

Dewey, then, simply failed to convey, at least in this presentation, Holmes's notion of the uncertain case as a stage of discovery of an emergent problem, and omitted reference to the complexity and duration of the process of inquiry. Dewey's vision was heavily influenced from the outset by analogies with biological development,[22] but he would later make explicit his recognition of the extended "continuum" in which a problematic situation may be passed from one cycle or generation of "fixing" to another, engaging multiple "fixers"—the fully *social* dimension of "fixing" that Holmes had seen in legal inquiry since 1870.[23] Dewey's own continuum was not fully articulated until later, in *Logic: The Theory of Inquiry*.[24] He would focus on it in *Experience and Nature*.[25]

In 1922 or soon thereafter, Dewey was preparing a paper titled "Logical Method and Law" for the *Cornell Law Review*, published in 1924. Refer-

21. Ibid., 57.

22. Dewey, *Logic*, 23–24.

23. Ibid., 168: "The position which holds that moral judgment is concerned with an objective unsettled situation and that ends-in-view are framed in and by judgments as methods of resolving operations is consistent with the fact that, because of recurrence of similar situations, generic ends-in-view, as ways of acting, are built up and have a certain prima facie claim to recognition in new situations. But these standardized 'prepared' propositions are not final; though highly valuable means, they are still means for examining the existing situation and appraising what mode of action it demands. The question of their weight with respect to it, may and often does lead to their being re-appraised and re-framed."

24. Ibid., 8–9, 11, chap. 13.

25. Dewey, *Experience and Nature*, 166–207; Ralph W. Sleeper, *The Necessity of Pragmatism*, 175–76.

ence to extended diachronic aspects of inquiry are absent there as well. The article refers to Holmes throughout, but its emphasis is again a critique of traditional logical forms that tend to obscure the vital logic of experiment, to effect immediate adaptation to new conditions. Emphasis on immediate adaptation discounts the relation of a complex problem to its relevant history, of a particular legal inquiry to its relevant conceptual background, the background of precedent.

This is the aspect of uncertainty that would confront Holmes in the labor cases. Dewey had apparently studied *The Common Law* and several of Holmes's later essays, though likely not the early essays. He appears overly optimistic, in this paper, about solving a legal problem in the short term, not recognizing the intractability of social and conceptual struggle that can occasionally accompany Holmes's feedback continuum.[26]

In the 1950s, Karl Llewellyn, responding to pervasive skepticism in the wake of realist writings including his own *Bramble Bush*, undertook a lengthy study of the appellate process to address what he saw as a crisis of confidence among practicing lawyers: "a new corrosiveness" over "whether there is any reckonability in the work of our appellate courts." Examining the development of case law and its relation to doctrine, he looked in particular at the question of what aspects of predictability might convince lawyers not to despair over the judicial process. His analysis produced various "stabilizing factors" in the profession as a whole, but more persuasive was his identification of a common element underlying and organizing the often confused mass of legal precedents, something he called the "situation sense."[27]

Searching a wide range of appellate opinions, Llewellyn noted that the better ones avoided a formal style of citation and analyzed "the differential impact of the facts of the individual case and the facts of the situation taken as a type." Within this situation sense lay, in Llewellyn's view, the key to better appellate decisions, increasingly replacing the formal style. In these opinions an "open willingness to recanvass a situation is present in an unusual degree, the result being now confirmation of the old, now the clearing up of divergent leads, now a new direction or position."[28]

26. Dewey, "Logical Method and Law."

27. Llewellyn, *The Common Law Tradition: Deciding Appeals*, 3, 121.

28. Ibid., 122, 148; Richard Posner's recent *Reflections on Judging* reaches a similar conclusion.

> We shall demonstrate that . . . sense and wisdom are thus used daily not only in application of doctrine or in choice among competing rules but in an area by no means frequently observed, to wit, in the on-going, careful readjustment of doctrine to needs by way of overt recourse to the sense which ought to control in the given type-situation. We shall show that this is not novel, but is old, is not occasional, but is standard, is not unsettling, but is stabilizing.[29]

The situation sense suggests an extended purpose within the appellate process: the finding of an underlying functional similarity among diverse particular judgments, indispensable to Holmes's diachronic continuum, coordinating legal predication with the external feedback from evolving practices. Llewellyn notes that this sense of similarity (he calls it "reckonability") is elusive, "sometimes far from evident, though given, and is often enough not given at all, but requires to be formed or forged from materials which are raw or rough and can be scanty." The situation sense interacts with the environment of conflict in a creative manner:

> The fact is that every opinion is in one aspect an argument, an argument prepared by a lawyer. It is an argument to the writer himself, is an argument to his brethren, it is an argument to bar or public or both. The fact is, moreover, that once a lawyer accepts an outcome, two things happen even though he may be stewing hard over how to shape the argument. The one of these things is that, without much work or thought, the facts reweigh, realign, recolor themselves, as has been noted above, into a familiar and therefore persuasive pattern or gestalt.[30]

As he examined this phenomenon in different jurisdictions, Llewellyn identified various intricately competing factors, including personal ones, of collegiality as well as competing commercial and private vision. Finding and describing the situation sense was a creative process:

> Beneath what looks on the page as "mere" following . . . , there swirls a constant current of creation. . . . this is the region in which the modern logician revels as he exposes the manipulation of the minor premise and watches the reasoned clamp some concept-label upon a still-amorphous mass of problem-facts and thereby haul "the case" in under a major premise which may have no particular need in either history or reason to apply.[31]

29. Llewellyn, *The Common Law Tradition*, 5, 149.
30. Ibid., 118.
31. Ibid., 116.

These are striking insights into the duration and difficulty of conceptualizing novelty amidst precedent. Even as he elucidated the judicial role, Llewellyn stopped short of Holmes's position on the often tentative and experimental status of general statements. In his assessment of the appeal, rules are described as complete, frozen; Llewellyn characterizes them as designed "not to control, but to guide decision."[32] "[T]he *rules of law, alone*, do not, because they cannot, decide any appealed case *which has been worth both an appeal and a response*" (Llewellyn's italics). He concludes that appellate courts should channel their focus into identifying the relevant situation, thence to discover the "immanent law" within it.[33]

> I doubt if the matter has ever been better put than by that amazing legal historian and commercial lawyer, Levin Goldschmidt: "Every fact pattern of common life, so far as the legal order can take it in, carries within itself its appropriate, natural rules, its right law. This is a natural law which is real, not imaginary; it is not a creature of mere reason, but rests on the solid foundation of what reason can recognize in the nature of man and of the life conditions of time and place; it is thus not eternal nor changeless nor everywhere the same, but is indwelling in the very circumstances of life. The highest task of law-giving consists in uncovering and implementing this immanent law."[34]

In suggesting that the law "within" the situation sense is always already "immanent," Llewellyn blocked from his own view any notion of an inchoate, emergent, or changing conceptual context, and thus of a coordinate judicial deference to the feedback loop. Missing from his analysis is Holmes's 1870 and 1873 recognition of stages in the continuum, where a problematic situation has first to be defined, and contingent and conflicting problems of policy sorted out, while the need to defer final resolution still remains. In Holmes's 1870 account, the legal general must be sought amidst an often still inarticulate succession of specific situations. Only gradually, in retrospective summaries of accumulated decisions, does it gain the foothold of predication and normative expression.

And yet, even while having missed Holmes's early essays, Llewellyn had untrammeled access to this insight from another source. In the course of his exposition of the "situation sense," he called attention to the 1949 analysis of judicial reasoning by Professor Edward Levi of the University of Chicago

32. Ibid., 179.
33. Ibid., 270.
34. Ibid., 122.

Law School in his *An Introduction to Legal Reasoning*. It included Levi's well-known essay on the history of the "inherently dangerous" rule, by which the original provider of a product found to be "inherently" injurious could be held liable for loss to a third party, absent any direct contractual relation between defendant and the injured party. Llewellyn had actually contributed to Levi's analysis, in a 1940 law review article.[35]

The hundred-year story of this circuitous path of legal conceptualization begins in 1816, with the famous case of *Dixon v. Bell*, where damages were recovered for injury from a loaded firearm; the court found liability without attempting an explanatory classification. It continues with *Langridge v. Levy*, the defective gun that exploded in the plaintiff's hand, where a distinction was offered between "inherent" dangerousness and faulty construction. Again urged in *Winterbottom v. Wright*, the case of a defective coach, the distinction was finally recognized in *Longmeid v. Holliday* involving an exploding lamp. The next stage involved diverse application, where the new concept was variously applied to cases of mislabeled poison, hair wash, a circular saw, exploding boiler, and painting scaffold. Courts struggled to make sense of it amidst considerations of due care, direct or indirect dealing, and other factors analyzed at length. The story famously ends with the liberalizing of liability (a foreseeability test for danger) by Judge Cardozo himself, in *MacPherson v. Buick* (1916), the car that collapsed with a defective wheel.

In Levi's portrayal the story is one of continuing intrusion of social influences in the construction (and, in this case, the ultimate failure) of a legal phrase, in a tentative and experimental process, drawn out over many years, as the meaning of "inherent" or "imminent" danger is applied in multiple contexts. Successive stages of inquiry are evident: "The first stage is the creation of the legal concept which is built up as cases are compared. The period is one in which the court fumbles for a phrase. Several phrases may be tried out; the misuse or misunderstanding of words itself may have an effect. The concept sounds like another, and the jump to the second is made. The second stage is the period when the concept is more or less fixed, although reasoning by example continues to classify items inside and out of the concept. The third stage is the breakdown of the concept, as reasoning by example has moved so far ahead as to make it clear that the suggestive influence of the word is no longer desired."[36]

35. Llewellyn, "The Status of the Rule of Judicial Precedent," cited in Levi, *Introduction to Legal Reasoning*, 9n.

36. Levi, *Introduction to Legal Reasoning*, 8–9.

Formalism, which assumes that general rules, once determined, remain fixed in application, is clearly inadequate here; Levi shows that rules change from case to case, and are remade with each case. "Yet," he writes, "this change in the rules is the indispensable dynamic quality of law. It occurs because the scope of a rule of law, and therefore its meaning, depends upon a determination of what facts will be considered similar to those present when the rule was first announced. The finding of similarity or difference is the key step in the legal process. . . . Yet it is a system of rules; the rules are discovered in the process of determining similarity or difference."[37]

Levi's account matches and illuminates Holmes's original 1870 model. Although he seems unaware of that essay and its importance for Holmes, Levi made explicit the implicit process of feedback from outside the legal profession, or even the adjudicatory system:

> [It] appears that the kind of reasoning involved in the legal process is one in which the classification changes as the classification is made. . . . in a sense all reasoning is of this type [citing Dewey's 1938 *Logic*], but here is an additional requirement which compels the legal process in this way. Not only do new situations arise but in addition peoples' wants change. The categories used in the legal process must be left ambiguous in order to permit the infusion of new ideas. And this is true even when legislation or a constitution is involved. The words used by the legislature or the constitutional convention must come to have new meanings. Furthermore, agreement on any other basis would be impossible.[38]

Holmes's 1873 notion of the drawing of lines between opposing poles is suggested by Levi's next reflection:

> The law forum is the most explicit demonstration of the mechanism required for a moving classification system. . . .
>
> What does the law forum require? It requires the presentation of competing examples. The forum protects the parties and the community by making sure that the competing analogies are before the court. The rule which will be created arises out of a process in which the differences have been urged. In this sense the parties as well as the court participate in the law-making. In this sense, also, lawyers represent more than the litigants.[39]

37. Ibid., 2–3. As Levi says on p. 2, "the determination of similarity or difference is the function of each judge."

38. Ibid., 3–4.

39. Ibid., 4–5.

A feedback mechanism is essential to the idea that the legal process responds, at least approximately over time, to the relevant community's idea of fairness:

> Reasoning by example in the law is the key to many things. It indicates in part the hold which the law process has over the litigants. They have participated in the law-making. They are bound by something they helped to make. Moreover, the examples or analogies urged by the parties bring into the law the common ideals of the society. The ideas have their day in court, and they will have their day again. This is what makes the hearing fair, rather than any idea that the judge is completely impartial, for of course he cannot be completely so. Moreover, the hearing in a sense compels at least vicarious participation by all the citizens, for the rule which is made, even though ambiguous, will be law as to them.[40]

This is distinct from the general drift of legal realism.[41] Jerome Frank had raised the problem of different judges seeing relevance differently in responding to the "stimulus of facts" in the concrete cases before them.[42] This was, however, relevance to the immediate case, not *emergent* relevance to the situation as it developed over time. Judges were seen by Frank as needing to exercise "behavior" or "habit control"; it is "a program of judicial self-discipline, not one of empirical science."

Felix Cohen opposed Frank's version of judicial behaviorism, writing that judicial decision making is a social phenomenon and cannot be treated as the action of an isolated individual. Decisions for Cohen are "social events," but he described them as a product of "social forces" and "social determinants" controlling the individual judge, rather than responding indirectly through the feedback loop. This distinction is important; rather than the operation of discrete "forces," what Levi describes is closer to the real world: "the examples or analogies urged by the parties bring into

40. Ibid., 5.

41. Legal realists shared opposition to a "formalist" model of judicial decision, that judges arrive at their decisions by applying law to facts, and the processes of finding the law and finding the facts are mutually independent. The decision was thought to follow deductively as in the syllogism. Realists criticized this model in two ways: as failing to recognize that the two findings are linked, and as reversing the end result and the beginning of the process. Instead, conflicting patterns suggest themselves, judges await an intuitive flash of understanding, and work back from the conclusion to the reasons. Postema, *Treatise of Legal Philosophy*, 118–19.

42. For Brian Leiter, this is the "Core Claim" of realism; "Rethinking Legal Realism: Toward a Naturalized Jurisprudence," 276.

the law the common ideas of the society. The ideas have their day in court, and they will have their day again."[43]

It is judicial recognition of the process of social induction that permits the adaptation of practices and convergence of opinion. If Holmes's concern with this process had been recognized, it might have made a difference in the jurisprudential debates since his death. Instead, new influences arrived to wrest the debate away from Levi's articulation of the common law continuum and toward a static perspective on the "essential nature" of law. The following chapters will follow those developments.

Llewellyn's own comment on Edward Levi is instructive as to why the feedback continuum has not been recognized:

> His [Levi's] interest centers more than, at this point, mine does on the manner of rationalizing the case results and on the manner of their integration into lines for future guidance, but his picture is directly relevant to the processes of actual deciding: the guiding, limiting, and suggestive power of a concept-label or slogan; the incursion of changing or changed community ideas and standards by way of shift in attitudes or in the language-meaning of such a label; the impact of life conditions and of learned categories and meanings via "reasoning by example" on the legal classification of a novel problem-situation or of a novel variant.[44]

Llewellyn's reference to "the manner of rationalizing the case results and on the manner of their integration into lines for future guidance" suggests that Levi was interested in the broader issues of the growth of knowledge, like those posed by the astronomer John Herschel. Llewelyn's focus was confined mainly to the difficult case, even while aware of the context in which it occurs. This has been true of the majority of legal literature. Writers in the prevalent traditions of jurisprudence have simply not been looking for a social continuum of inquiry in law.[45]

Charles Peirce, after his first four Lowell Lectures starting in late October of 1866, moved from an analysis of the syllogism and criticism of Mill to an exploration of the scientific hypothesis. Concerned, as Whewell had been, with the source of scientific discovery, he would eventually articulate a third logical category beyond deduction and induction, calling it

43. Levi, *Introduction to Legal Reasoning*, 5.

44. Llewellyn, *The Common Law Tradition*, 125.

45. Ibid., 125; see also Llewellyn, *Theory of Rules*.

abduction, the insertion of hypothetical explanation for which deduction and induction served as testing devices. There is no record that Holmes, Gray, or James attended any later lectures after the first four.

Holmes's attention had turned to Mill's *Logic*, finishing on November 17, 1866, writing in his diary, "Logic—finished the book by tea time. This week I haven't felt very well and debauched on Mill acc'dingly, by way of removing an old incubus before endeavoring to immerse myself in law completely—wh, Shattuck says, a man must at some period of his career if he would be a first rate lawyer, though of being that I despair." He would, however, continue to correspond regarding Kant's first critique in some detail with James in late 1867. He did not abandon philosophy completely, but was later regarded by Peirce as a contributing member of the Metaphysical Club.

By the time of his letter to Emerson in 1876, Holmes had indicated how he would move beyond the problem of simple deduction and induction. He had come to suggest another model for inquiry, accounting for new knowledge through contestation, and perhaps also a legal version of "abduction." His relation to later legal realism is a tenuous one, coming as it did from distinctly different sources, but it was no less determined to identify what (in Mill's phrase) was "really tak[ing] place." Mill, Whewell, Peirce, and Wright were the prime sources for Holmes's view of legal induction, drawn from English science, in which the individual decision is not the final product of logical inquiry, but rather a step toward the resolution of an underlying problem, in a process I have called convergence.

CHAPTER SIX

Dispute and Adjustment

This chapter addresses how social conflict affects the process of comparison of experience, through which generals are consensually developed and shared, comparing it with Mill's account of induction in his Logic.

* * *

All liability questions demand yes or no answers that are best obtained by bright-line rules. Was the ball fair or foul? Did the defendant drive his car across the middle of the road? Did the Kohler Act undo the original grant? If it did, then compensation follows to the extent of the loss. If not, then none is needed. Holmes's "too far" question turns a bright-line question into a matter of degree for no good reason.—Richard A. Epstein, *Supreme Neglect: How to Revive Constitutional Protection for Private Property* (2008)

In his 2008 book *Supreme Neglect*,[1] Richard Epstein criticizes Holmes for the right decision but the wrong reason, in a 1922 opinion involving the clause of the U.S. Constitution prohibiting government "taking" of private property without just compensation. Epstein approved that Holmes, writing for the majority in *Pennsylvania Coal Co. v. Mahon*, 260 U.S. 390 (1922), *extended* the constitutional right to reimbursement for a government taking of private property to government conduct *regulating* private land, rather than overtly *acquiring* it. But Epstein criticized Holmes for failing to ground his decision in timeless *principle*.

I cite this example to illustrate further the phenomenon that Holmes brought from William Whewell into his social inductivism, advanced in 1873 as line drawing, recasting the divide between particularism and generalism as stages of inquiry.[2] Keep in mind Holmes's position in the Massachusetts

1. Richard A. Epstein, *Supreme Neglect*, 105–6.

2. Laura Snyder comments of Whewell, "Recall that this discussion began with the Fundamental Antithesis, according to which no fixed line divides experiential and necessary truths. We

labor cases, another example of his aversion (in rationalizing a decision) to *principled finality*, when a *novel* problem was emerging.

Epstein (in the passage above) takes Holmes to task for couching his decision in the terms of the 1873 model: as a judgment of *degree*. Epstein continues:

> Justice Oliver Wendell Holmes got to a sound result but by the wrong path. He first noted, rightly, that the business of government could never go on if each change in the general law was treated as a compensable taking. He then switched gears to hold that the government had to pay compensation when its regulation went "too far," thus plunging the law of regulatory takings into intellectual incoherence, from which it has never escaped.[3]

The case involved the right of coal mining companies to tunnel under land owned and occupied by homeowners in Pennsylvania anthracite coal country. The right to dig underneath had been granted by lease (presumably fairly bargained), which in some cases conveyed (for extra money) the risk of collapse to the landowners or their successors in title. When actual collapses led to complaints, Pennsylvania passed the Kohler Act, which returned the risk to the miners without compensation. Writing for the majority, Holmes said:

> Government hardly could go on if, to some extent, values incident to property could not be diminished without paying for every such change in the general law. As long recognized, some values are enjoyed under an implied limitation, and must yield to the police power. But obviously the implied limitation must have its limits, or the contract and due process clauses are gone. One fact for consideration in determining such limits is the extent of the diminution. When it reaches a certain magnitude, in most if not in all cases, there must be an exercise of eminent domain and compensation to sustain the act. So the question depends upon the particular facts. The greatest weight is given to the judgment

---

now see how it is that the line we draw between them, like that between fact and theory, is a relative one, based upon epistemic distinctions that change as our Ideas become more distinct. As we explicate our Ideas, we recognize empirical truths to be necessary consequences of these Ideas; and the truths are thus transferred from the empirical to the necessary side of the antithesis." Snyder, *Reforming Philosophy*, 90. Here we find an echo of Holmes's position in *Plant v. Woods*, the second labor case, where he criticized the majority for doing in essence what Epstein favors in *Mahon*.

3. Ibid., 107.

of the legislature, but it always is open to interested parties to contend that the legislature has gone beyond its constitutional power.[4]

Holmes's survey of relevant Supreme Court decisions found just one, requiring a mining company to erect a "pillar of coal" as a safety device, holding it to be within the "police power" and thus not compensable. With little else to go on, Holmes concluded that a statute transferring the risk of collapse without compensation was, in effect, on the other side of that critical but hardly obvious "line" described in his 1873 essay. But the facts of this case, even before any emergent line, made it appear closer to an outright "taking" of private property for a public purpose, than to a typical safety regulation.

Epstein by 2008 had access to a vastly greater accumulation of experience, and many more court decisions, from which to offer his book-length justification for a "principled" rationale. His failure to find any "good reason" in Holmes's opinion seems inappropriate, as the *Mahon* case appears to have been the first finding in American history of a "regulatory taking," early enough that the term itself was yet uncoined and unimagined. Holmes's barely perceptible early line had as yet no extension, as there was no clear trail of decisions for comparison. From Epstein's perspective as an advocate (characterized by Robert Gordon as claiming an "absolute libertarian right to property secure from all private and public encroachments"[5]), Holmes's fame is a convenient vehicle for conveying umbrage. It is understandable as a rhetorical device, but Epstein's argument amply demonstrates how poorly understood is Holmes's approach. "Bright line" answers are not available to the nation when, in Lincoln's apt phrase, "our case is new."

Mahon is a classic early borderline case. Epstein complains, "By phrasing the question in this form, [Holmes] treats everything as a matter of degree, implicitly rejecting all principled distinctions in kind." Not so; Holmes only treated the *early borderline case* as a yet-to-be-rationalized matter of degree. If indeed the law of regulatory takings took a plunge "into intellectual incoherence, from which it has never escaped," this is hardly the fault of the long-deceased Holmes. It may rather be attributable to the kind of difficulty Edward Levi described in the century-long

4. *Pennsylvania Coal Co. v. Mahon*, 260 U.S. at 413.

5. Robert Gordon, "The Past as Authority and as Social Critic," in Terence McDonald, ed., *The Historic Turn in the Human Sciences*, 356.

rise and fall of the concept of "dangerous instrumentality"—the special nature of the dilemma, and the evolving situation itself.

Addressing Epstein's criticism provides an opportunity to clarify the role of principle in the borderline case, the role of dispute and conflict in Holmes's external view of law, and the social dimension of logical induction itself. It sharpens perspective—or rather divergent perspectives—on the continuum, and on the effect to different observers looking from different stages at an emergent and developing problem. Holmes was viewing "regulatory takings" at an early stage, and Epstein is advocating a principled solution some eighty-six years later. Given that Epstein's principles have taken a while to gain momentum, what should we make of their present legal status? Are they now part of the "background" to which judicial recourse may turn, when a judge concludes that the settled law has no clear answer? I should tread carefully here, as I do not wish to appear to take sides in an ideological or political debate, and I certainly do not want to portray Holmes as doing so.[6]

Epstein's principles may better be defined as "hypothetical," in the same sense as Holmes's controversial theory of contract, the failed concept of an "inherently dangerous" object, or the particle nature of light: they *may* (in the course of inquiry) supply an explanation. Holmes's contract theory eventually did, inherent danger did not, while the particle nature of light may still be in play. Epstein may eventually be proved right, wrong, or possibly neither. Such is the fate of observations and proposals from within a contested situation, both "internally" in the immediate context of a dispute, and "externally" in regard to the overall "situation" itself. Final principled answers lie unknown, somewhere down the road of experience. Epstein's comment is made from one side of the current competition; Epstein is an advocate. Holmes's approach shifts between within and without, both "internal" and "external."

Such texts as Epstein's play an important role in the development of legal knowledge, the role that competing "ideas" played in William Whewell's account of the growth of scientific knowledge, or that Peirce (draw-

6. To demonstrate the intimate connection of Holmes's *Mahon* opinion with his response to the *Beadel* case that influenced his 1873 model, I quote a letter he wrote on December 29, 1908, to Franklin Ford: "My own opinion often expressed through many years is that the only use of the phrase Police Power is to express the fact that you can't carry out constitutional provisions to their logical extremes. . . . A law forbidding the building of houses more than 80 feet high I presume might be good under the police power, one forbidding you to build more than one foot would be a taking and would have to be paid for." Holmes Papers, Harvard Law School.

ing on Whewell) gave to "abduction" in the process of all human inquiry. For Peirce, logic was tripartite, employing induction, abduction, and deductive testing of new hypotheses; then, unless belief was settled, induction demanded further experience. Legal inquiry has made the same use as science of all three elements, induction from early cases, timely abduction, deduction to clarify the entailment of a theory, and revision in light of further experience. Without fresh ideas the law cannot grow. The range of experience relevant to legal logic has a broad social component, but the formal elements remain.

This brings us to two questions. The first is, How does legal dispute and conflict affect the meaning and reference of legal terminology? What precisely is the role of social conflict in the domain of logic, and how does the social nature of inquiry bear on the question of logical validation? The other is a paraphrase of John Herschel (with Holmes's amendment): "What is the act or series of acts of the mind (or of many minds) in constructing general propositions"? Or, to turn to a phrase of John Stuart Mill (in a passage I am about to examine), What is "really tak[ing] place" in the inductive process?

The formation and function of principles exemplify the conceptual element of law, and can be illuminated by the model that Holmes set forth succinctly (perhaps too succinctly considering its failure to gain recognition) in the early 1870s. Holmes and Mill both used the term "principle" mainly in referring to accepted knowledge, as in the "principles of ethnology" or "principles of admiralty." Yet in *The Common Law* Holmes uses the term in observing, "the law is always approaching, and never reaching, consistency. It is forever adopting new principles from life at one end, and it always retains old ones from history at the other." He may have recalled that Mill in his *Logic* had also used the term in explaining the comment on Lord Mansfield's advice to the novice magistrate:

> Lord Mansfield knew that if any reason were assigned it would be necessarily an afterthought, the judge being in fact guided by impressions from past experience, without the circuitous process of *framing general principles* [my italics] from them, and that if he attempted to frame any such he would assuredly fail. Lord Mansfield, however, would not have doubted that a man of equal experience who had also a mind stored with general propositions derived by legitimate induction from that experience would have been greatly preferable as a judge, to one, however sagacious! who could not be trusted with the explanation and justification of his own judgments.[7]

7. Mill, *Logic*, 1:217–18.

Whether Mill would *join* Mansfield in viewing the second man, whose mind is already "stored with general propositions," as *preferable* to the first, is unclear, considering Mill's previous insistence that the novice should decide the case *without* giving reasons, as they would probably be wrong. Yet, he resists saying the second man would be right! Mill has put himself into a bit of a bind here; his radical mistrust of anything resembling "axiomatic" thinking hardly helps to understand how a new "particular" is affected by the abstract context of prior ideas into which it arrives. What I will now argue is that the resolution of this question depends on the nature and *timing* of the new particular, and how that governs the finding of its relative *similarity* to prior particulars.

Elsewhere in his *System of Logic* (book 4, "Operations Subsidiary to Induction," chapter 2, "On Abstraction, or the Formation of Conceptions"), Mill asks "what really takes place" in drawing concepts out of facts:

> There are, then, such things as general conceptions, or conceptions by means of which we can think generally; and when we form a set of phenomena into a class, that is, when we compare them with one another to ascertain in what they agree, some general conception is implied in this mental operation. And inasmuch as such a comparison is a necessary preliminary to induction, it is most true that Induction could not go on without general conceptions.[8]

Here he presents the tentative suggestion of (what I will call) a kitchen full of mental stuff in which to cook and digest new experience. Are they just ingredients, I wonder, or recipes? However, Mill quickly backs off from the suggestion of any *a priori* stuff at all in the following paragraph:

> But it does not therefore follow that these conceptions must have existed in the mind previously to the comparison. It is not a law of our intellect, that in comparing things with each other and taking note of their agreement we merely recognize as realized in the outward world something that we already had in our minds. The conception originally found its way to us as the *result* of such a comparison. It was obtained (in metaphysical phrase) by *abstraction* from individual things. These things may be things which we perceived or thought of on former occasions, but they may also be the things which we are perceiving or thinking of on the very occasion.[9]

8. Ibid., 2:192.
9. Ibid., 2:192–93.

This is about as spare an account as you can get of conceptual formation. We didn't need anything in the kitchen other than raw ingredients, no conceptual matter at all, whether partially or fully formed, as it derives directly from the process of comparison of the raw data. Mansfield's "second man" doesn't need to draw on his law school training, if indeed the comparison started from a discrete beginning point (the very notion of such a "given" starting point is a matter I will address). Now comes Mill's account of "what really takes place":

> The facts are not *connected* [Mill's italics], except in a merely metaphorically acceptation of the term. The *ideas* [again Mill's italics] of the facts may become connected, that is, we may be led to think of them together; but this consequence is no more than what may be produced by any casual association. What *really takes place* [my italics], is, I conceive, more philosophically expressed by the common word Comparison, than by the phrases "to connect" or "to superinduce." For, as the general conception is itself obtained by a comparison of particular phenomena, so when obtained, the mode in which we apply it to other phenomena is again by comparison. We compare phenomena with each other to get the conception, and we then compare those and other phenomena *with* [Mill's italics] the conception.[10]

Mill here says the conception is directly obtained from an early comparison, and applied to other phenomena by comparing them "*with* the conception." He gives no explanation of how the conception was first "obtained" in the process of comparison, even while implying a "beginning point" of conceptualization. He proceeds to illustrate this claim with reference to Johannes Kepler's discovery of the elliptical path of the planet Mars, a famous argument in his debate with Whewell. Mill's account of Kepler's simply connecting the dots, without what Whewell insisted was "ampliative inference," has not been readily accepted, any more than Peirce accepted his insistence on the uniformity of nature.[11]

10. Ibid., 2:196.

11. See Snyder, *Reforming Philosophy*, 101–2; Mill further explains his position:

> The conception is a conception *of* something; and that which it is a conception of, is really *in* the facts, and might, under some supposable circumstances, or by some supposable extension of the faculties which we actually possess, have been detected in them. And not only is this always itself possible, but it actually happens in almost all cases in which the obtaining of the right conception is a matter of any considerable

Peirce, influenced by Wright (who believed that we are overinclined to assume regularities in nature), adopted Whewell's side of the debate, and went on to analyze the process he would call "abduction" to supply the mental ingredients. His fourth Lowell Lecture chided Mill for ignoring the troublesome problem of similarity, which Mill either assumes as presenting itself directly in nature, or bypasses entirely in saying it is directly evident through "comparison." There is nothing self-explanatory to the finding of similarity, especially in law, as Edward Levi noted in 1947. The philosopher Hilary Putnam observed in 1981: "In fact, *everything is similar to everything else in infinitely many respects*."[12] Nelson Goodman finds the very notion of similarity elusive:

> Similarity, I submit, is insidious. And if the association here with invidious comparison is itself invidious, so much so the better. Similarity, ever ready to solve philosophical problems and overcome obstacles, is a pretender, an imposter, a quack. It has, indeed, its uses, but is more often found where it does not belong, professing powers that it does not possess.[13]

All this presents three problems for exploration: one, the nature of a "conception," two, the finding of "similarity," and, three, identifying whether there is (and if so what it might be) a "beginning point" of inquiry. Examining these problems will clarify where Holmes moves beyond Mill. (Recall that I noted in chapter 3 that Holmes's "given" was organic and embedded, born in a space of reasons *and action*.) The best way to address these problems is to examine Mill's consistent use of the pronoun "we," as in his observation above that "the mode in which *we* apply [a conception] to other phenomena is again by comparison."

> difficulty. . . . The honour, in Kepler's case, was that of the accurate, patient, and toilsome calculations by which he compared the results that followed from his different guesses, with the observations of Tycho Brahe; but the merit was very small of guessing an ellipse; the only wonder is that men had not guessed it before, nor could they have failed to do so is there had not existed an obstinate *a priori* prejudice that the heavenly bodies must move, if not in a circle, in some combination of circles. (*Logic*, 2:193–94)

N. R. Hanson in *Patterns of Discovery* characterizes Mill's position as "ludicrous." Snyder, *Reforming Philosophy*, 103; N. R. Hanson, *Patterns of Discovery: An Inquiry into the Conceptual Foundations of Science*, 84.

12. Hilary Putnam, *Reason, Truth and History*, 64.

13. Nelson Goodman, "Seven Strictures on Similarity," in *Problems and Prospects*, 437.

Put yourself now in the mind of Holmes in 1870, immersed in the detail of legal cases, testing Mill's approach as it might apply to common law legal disputes. Opposing sides are constantly contesting the very *comparison* that Mill says that "we" must make to "connect" facts in induction. Mill's "we" implies comparison by a single mind; but not so Holmes. As this point is crucial to my entire thesis, I will try to make it as clear as possible.

In addition to the three problems, I have now raised a fourth, the expository "we," as a possible key to understanding the others. What, after all, is "really tak[ing] place"? In the passages just quoted, it is obviously *Mill's mind* that is producing the words, and in seeking the reader's assent he uses the expository "we," an accepted and common practice in logical texts. That usage implies Mill's best guess for the train of thought of an ideal, rational, and universal mind, observing the inductive process—as it takes place *within that very same mind*. As a reader of the passage, I find it easy to accept his main point, that comparison is necessary in the inductive process, but with Peirce, Putnam, and Goodman in mind I have some questions: What is similarity, how is it found, and does it begin somewhere discrete and identifiable? Is there something identifiably "given" from which comparison and further inquiry commences?[14]

Holmes, with his early commitment to induction, must have had the same doubts and wondered how this element of comparison "really takes place" in law. Recall his attendance at the two 1866 lectures on induction by Peirce, who noted the difference between comparing "things" bounded by *positions* to "occasions" bounded by *dates*, and extensively criticizing Mill's account of similarity as something directly apprehended.

For Holmes, the comparison is actually accomplished, as he writes in 1870, by "many minds." In this early paper he does indeed posit a beginning point of inquiry (the "case of first impression," a traditional common law notion), but as noted above (in chapter 2) he goes beyond it in the 1873 paper, where the difficult case emerges not by itself but in a space surrounded by prior "clustered" and then articulated comparisons. This space consisted of logical reasons, to be sure, but also of action; those prior clusters were derived from practices, even while having found predication, that is, subject/object explanation, in language.

14. This term, the "given," indicating a universal epistemological starting point for all inquiry, became a leading issue in twentieth-century philosophy and remains so today. See chap. 3, n. 44.

What Holmes's first paper shows is that the process of comparison works differently from the one apparent to Mill. Comparison does not take place through immediate apprehension by a single "mind." Nor is it a purely *mental* operation, given that it arose from judgments regarding conduct, which must themselves have been influenced by prior judgments and prior conduct. Being a comparison of successive occasions, and of judgments regarding those occasions, emergent similarity must take into account a variety of factors influencing social conduct.

It is the 1873 paper that reveals the danger I have in mind about using the expository "we" in examining induction. The difficult or uncertain case arises in a space that is not empty (as Mill suggested) but is already filled with what I will tentatively call "conceptual matter"; perhaps a better phrase is conceptual "activity," consisting of statements reflecting an exchange of views among engaged observers. The 1870 essay describes how general terms and concepts got there—by cumulative judgments that Holmes describes in 1873 as "clusters." In an uncertain case, more than one of the clusters are similar *enough* to pull the new case in opposing directions. The two early Massachusetts cases involving picketing were pulled toward "extortion" for the majority of the Supreme Judicial Court, but (for Holmes) they were pulled instead toward the legal right of any legitimate enterprise to organize. Hence, Mill's image of comparison being accomplished by a universal "we" obscures the problem of contestation in *establishing* similarity.

As noted above in chapter 2, Holmes also outlined a process of *convergence* in the 1873 paper. His tantalizingly succinct outline can be filled in from his own judicial opinions or examples from historical or contemporary experience. As he writes in 1873:

> Two widely different cases suggest a general distinction, which is a clear one when stated broadly. But as new cases cluster around the opposite poles, and begin to approach each other, the distinction becomes more difficult to trace; the determinations are made one way or the other on a very slight preponderance of feeling, rather than articulate reason; and at last a mathematical line is arrived at by the contact of contrary decisions, which is so far arbitrary that it might equally well have been drawn a little further to the one side or to the other.[15]

15. Holmes, "The Theory of Torts," 654; Kellogg, *Formative Essays*, 119; *CW*, 1:327.

Another way to look at this is through Karl Llewellyn's apt phrase, the *situation sense*, which he used to explain those appellate opinions that seemed to him to have achieved "reckonability." An uncertain case is one that demands a *new* situation sense, having arrived in the space between clusters of cases that have already jelled around previous such senses. The phrase "situation sense" works nicely as a stand-in for Holmes's opposing "poles," because it shakes us loose from thinking of legal precedents as purely *cognitive* products of inquiry. A changing "situation" connotes interaction with practices.

Let's go back to the problem of defining "conception" for Holmes's model of inquiry, as opposed to Mill's. Mill talks in the above passages about how a conception emerges directly from the comparison of successive particulars. This reflects his radical Baconian empiricist distaste for thinking from axioms. Given that background, I infer that he views axioms as fully cognitive, and equates them as such with "conceptions," which, he is determined to insist, only arise from particular experience. That is, in showing how conceptions arise directly from particulars in order to discount their reliance on anything *a priori*, Mill is nevertheless isolating a purely mental substance of "conceptual matter." This assumption is then connected with the operation of an ideal universal mind, which is subtly at work through the expository "we," and is blocking out the messy interactive workings of a *community* of minds.

Holmes, on the other hand, describes the process of comparison with the imagery of "clusters" of legal judgments, and from 1873 on, he views conceptual development as constantly contested. He gives an account that does not oblige the observer to posit a separate realm of conceptual matter, but rather obliges it to inquire how the conceptual process is accomplished by multiple thinking, talking, *and acting* humans.

Holmes makes no clear distinction between the particulars of experience and the purely mental element of conception. The reason lies in the social nature of Holmes's model of legal knowledge. The legal principle and the legal precedent exist (that is to say, actually influence the law) only insofar as they gain belief, and consenting conduct, among a community. Recall his careful phrasing in the 1899 address to the New York lawyers, that "generalization is empty in so far as it is general. Its value depends on the number of particulars which it calls up to the speaker and hearer." Generalizing is always an intersubjective activity, a "calling up" of things, involving speakers and hearers, or (right now) a writer and a reader.

Holmes's process of convergence also implies more than a cognitive dimension to the analyzing and reconciling process. There must also be a convergence of communal *action*. Resolution of the uncertain case requires revising an *actual* context, not just a *sense* of context, because a larger problem is represented by the specific dispute. What "really takes place" involves a complex comparison of situations, and demands a wider perspective before it can be resolved. Defining the term "situation," John Dewey, in his own 1938 *Logic*, says "we never experience nor form judgments about objects or events in isolation, but only in connection with a contextual whole." Moreover, says Dewey, the "object of perception" cannot be "isolated from [its] place or function in promoting and directing a successful course of act[ion]."[16]

Mill in the above passages seized on the importance of "Comparison" (capitalizing *C* for emphasis) as an underappreciated function of the inductive process. He rightly identified, as a central aspect of induction, the finding of similarity among objects of inquiry. Indeed, the literature suggests that similarity, and by inference also regularity, is (as Wright was inclined to observe) all-too-commonly *presumed* among objects of inquiry in explanations of the inductive process. The similarity among red balls repeatedly drawn from a bag, leading to an induction that all the balls in the bag are red, discounts individual differences, presuming them minute or otherwise irrelevant.[17]

The presumption of similarity in induction was noted by David Hume: "all general ideas are nothing but particular ones, annexed to a certain term, which gives them a more extensive significance, and makes them recall upon occasion other individuals, which are similar to them."[18] Hume wrote, "[W]hen we have found a resemblance among several objects, we apply the same name to all of them, whatever differences we may observe in the degrees of their quantity and quality, and whatever other differences may appear among them."[19] The term "we," with which Hume, Mill, and other writers on induction have referred to the perceiver of a similarity, has by implication already found the resemblance and discriminated

16. Dewey, *Logic*, 66–67. The relation of this to John Rawls's practice conception of rules is discussed in chap. 5, n. 5.

17. Even the common notion of redness has to have become entrenched; as Mary Hesse has observed: "There are some predicates that are *better entrenched* than others, for instance, 'red' than 'ultra-violet,' 'lead' than 'pi-meson.' " Hesse, *Structure of Scientific Inference*, 22.

18. Bk. 1, pt. 1, sec. 7, para. 1, crediting Berkeley.

19. Bk. 1, pt. 1, sec. 7, para. 7, footnote omitted.

away the differences. In his 1866 Lowell Lectures, Peirce noted that this implies completion of an unexamined process. Mill's and Hume's expository reference of "we" may be a commonly accepted discursive practice, but its use obscures the possibility of disagreement over the purpose and consequences of a *disputed* resemblance. Who indeed is the "we" to whom Hume here refers, and how was the resemblance "found"?

The expository "we" represents an ideal observer of a paradigmatic situation; it obscures whether, in actual life, a general statement of resemblance applies to all possible communities of speakers. In this it obscures the social dimension of *establishing* similarity. The issue of similarity doesn't arise unless there is a practical uncertainty regarding the similarity in question. Such practical uncertainty arises constantly in the operation of contemporary legal adjudication. It may also be found in science and other branches of human inquiry.

What if the reach of application, the extension, of a particular "name" is disputed by opposing interests within the same linguistic community? Parties to legal disputes may seek to gain coverage of a legal term for their own interests, and to exclude other interests. This can be seen in minor disputes, or in major ones like the extension of the constitutional right of free expression to political campaign donations, of murder or homicide to doctor-assisted suicide, or of marriage to same-gender partners. With his famous aphorism "general propositions do not decide concrete cases," Holmes resisted responding to such disputes axiomatically, through premature deduction from a general statement about law or rights, rather than inductive exploration, a process informed by feedback into the legal process from society at large.

As I emphasized in chapter 4, this implies social resolution of borderline cases. The famous Sorites paradox questions at what point the addition or subtraction of an individual grain of sand governs defining it as a "heap." "Heap" has thus been accounted an inherently *vague* term, as are many other terms when removed from context; philosophers of law and language have commonly treated semantic vagueness as a natural quality of discourse.[20] This ignores that the *legal* extension of "heap," or any other disputed term, will in the process of litigation take on a specific social dimension: it will be subject to more precise determination through abstraction from particular decisions exploring the context of an emergent or

20. Timothy Williamson, *Vagueness*; Timothy Endicott, *Vagueness in Law*; G. Keil and R. Poscher, eds., *Vagueness in Law: Philosophical and Legal Approaches*.

ongoing practical dispute. Holmes suggested, to the New York lawyers in 1899, that not only law but other forms of knowledge develop through a similar process.

Thus, induction is not immediate; it is connected to conflict, the real instantiation of dialectical opposites, or conflicting opinions in general; its resolution is experimental and engages human creativity in the introduction of new ideas or hypotheses; and the enterprise of extending human knowledge is linked to the contentious nature of human social conduct. Nor does the actual inductive process have an identifiable starting point, as all induction takes place within a space of prior reasons and action.

Moreover, the process of legal inquiry is inadequately understood as an examination of authoritative texts or of judicial activity alone. Critical to the resolution of conflicting positions is the influence of opposing social standards and the patterns of conduct supporting them. It is not possible for detached individuals, no matter how great their expertise, to resolve a deeply rooted dispute at a single moment, or even a succession of such experts to do so over time, without input from and adjustments within society at large. Knowledge, conduct, language, and conflict are all actively interrelated. Inductive inquiry and inference is, to use a term later favored by John Dewey, socially transformative.

One issue that deserves emphasis is that the process of resolving uncertainty can be protracted, affecting the *appearance* of uncertainty. It is useful then to consider the process in terms of *stages of inquiry*. At the initial stage a comparison of factual situations with preexisting legal knowledge will appear at its most uncertain, indeed closest to a description as "indeterminate." At a later stage relevant factors will have been identified and addressed both within and outside the law, as, for example, medical practice, adjusted in response to disputes over medically assisted suicide. Uncertainty and resolution may eventually yield to description by "general principle," originating within *and outside* the legal arena.

There is, of course, an alternative and more conventional account of "what really takes place" in judicial decision making. That is the judge-centered account that was discussed in the previous chapter; it has a long history and is itself a multifaceted and contested account, with two primary explanatory positions known as formalism and realism, both of which have many distinct versions. All have in common that the mind of the judge is oriented toward the interpretation of legal materials as they apply to the case at hand, and the correct outcome is dependent upon that context. The legal realists proposed empirical versions of this as the real account, but I have argued here and in the preceding chapter that it is not an inductive account. Moreover it gives rise to the impression of indeterminacy, and (as Philip Bobbitt noted in his 2014 Storrs Lecture) does not have a satisfactory solution.

One of the questions I posed above still remains to be addressed: what about the matter of validation, or the justification of legal knowledge? Is this a form of conventionalism, when Holmes defers to input into the continuum from nonlegal resources? I mentioned that the extension of the inductive naming process is determined by a process of contested convergence. How might this compare to the contemporary understanding of the source of meaning and reference, an account of its relation to the "world?" This is the subject of my final chapter. My final point in the present chapter concerns the role of perspective in social inquiry. It began with Richard Epstein's comment on Holmes's decision in the *Mahon* case, and characterized it as an abductive contribution to the process of inquiry.

Epstein's book demonstrates that the problem of regulatory takings has taken on proportions unimaginable in 1922. It seems appropriate here to give voice to Epstein's motivation for writing *Supreme Neglect*, to his own sense in the opening pages of "appropriate[ness] to offer a short autobiographical account of why and how I became interested in the constitutional protection of private property under the takings clause." What follows are among the more revealing lines in the entire book.

> The explanation lies, in an odd sense, in the peculiar path of my own education, which began with my exposure to Roman law and the common law while I was a student at Oxford University in the mid-60s. The emphasis in an English education was on private law subjects. Private law covers only disputes between ordinary individuals, where the role of government is to adjudicate and enforce the rights of the future litigants and to lay down rules of more general application for future disputes.
>
> Private law dominated those studies because the English have no written constitution, and thus offer no explicit, but some customary, protection against governmental deprivation of private property. But the early study of common law rules convinced me that these rights had a utility, reach, and inner coherence that explained their wide acceptance not only in England but everywhere throughout the world, including the United States. . . . When I completed my legal studies in the United States, the study of American constitutional law loomed large. Immediately, I was struck with the major transformation from the property-protective regime that had been championed by the framers of

> our Constitution to the weak property regimes championed by the Progressive politics of the early twentieth century, which were turned into constitutional law during the New Deal.[21]

Epstein goes on to analyze this change in ways that reflect on how "private property is a sound institution, and not just an excuse for private selfishness and greed." Epstein examines this with care and attention to the path of history; I leave it to his text to make the case. My purpose here is to further examine his contribution to the process of inquiry.

At the initial stage of litigation of a new class of cases, such as existed in *Mahon* in 1922, there is a climate we may call indeterminacy. To individual judges, the close case may seem indeterminate. So also in the context of textual authority. But when the judicial system is seen as a problem solver and settler of disputes, indeterminacy is (was) a stage of inquiry. Ultimate resolution will be dependent on many factors leading to the realm of principle, where the eventual legal "lines" are drawn. Epstein's book illustrates that broad engagement with more profound questions before the constitutional law of regulatory takings will become anything close to settled. I dare say the same kind of appeal took place during the long campaign of NAACP lawyers to overturn separate racial education in America, in the process reconstituting the concept of equality.[22]

The purely judge-centered account of law misses the constant practical working out of the practical meaning of disputed terms. Instead it assumes that a vague term is inherently vague and must be dealt with as such, requiring judicial choice akin to legislation or "fiat." It gets hung up on indeterminacy through issues like vagueness of terms, not induction with relation to the underlying legal problem; nor does it direct itself to the questions that Holmes addressed in 1870 and 1873, prompted by Herschel as well as Mill: How does the conceptual element of the law emerge and influence conduct?

As Edward Levi recounts in his *Introduction to Legal Reasoning*, this will include adjusting practices and public perceptions, translated not only by lawyers into legal arguments for and against the prospect of liability, but by legal theorists including Epstein, to delineate the larger implications in

21. Epstein, *Supreme Neglect*, xv–xvi.

22. See Mark V. Tushnet, *Making Civil Rights Law: Thurgood Marshall and the Supreme Court, 1936–1961* and *Making Constitutional Law: Thurgood Marshall and the Supreme Court, 1961–1991*.

historical context for the nation's future. Here it is critical to note that a deep dive into philosophy and history is not required to decide the next case. It is not for the current justices to announce the regnant principles; they cannot know them. Some may indeed be persuaded by the arguments in Epstein's book. This is fair game, as long as they do not prematurely write them permanently into the Constitution. Epstein is as much a town crier for justice as the advocates of racial equality were before the middle of the twentieth century. It is not just with *new* ideas that the law must grow; it also cannot grow without *moral* ideas. Holmes unquestionably thought so, and said as much; the law is "the witness and deposit of our moral life."[23]

Ronald Dworkin has introduced the notion that the "right answer" in a controversial case requires a judicial mind of Herculean ability, drawing comprehensively on moral principles. This is the antithesis of Mansfield's story about the novice judge in the "case of first impression." The problem I have in mind is that of overgeneralizing from a discrete aspect of the continuum of inquiry, of building an inclusive theory around the limited perspectives of early "first case" uncertainty, "abductive" hypothesizing, or "deductive" testing of hypotheses, what Whewell called "colligation." It is important not to "colligate," or rather to privilege the idea of grand public reasoning and the abstract "balancing" of principles, before induction is complete and all relevant the facts are in.

Holmes implies that they are never completely in; "New cases will arise which will elude the most carefully constructed formula." Convergence, it must be kept in mind, is the successful outcome of the inductive project, and convergence cannot be achieved by cognitive and communicative activity alone. As Dewey wrote in 1943, the "object of perception" cannot be isolated from its place or function in promoting and directing a successful course of action.[24]

23. Debate over the extension of the meaning of unconstitutional property takings has taken place in several cases since it was renewed in the 1970s with *Penn Central Transportation Co. v. New York City*, 438 U.S. 104 (1978). See Suzanna Sherry, "Property Is the New Privacy: The Coming Constitutional Revolution." Brian Butler makes a strong case for the abuse of principle in conservative appeals to broader maxims than are required to fully assess the specific factors in each case. See Butler, *Law as a Democratic Means: Democratic Experimentalism and Constitutional Law*.

24. Dewey, *Logic*, 67. On precariousness in Dewey, see Melvin L. Rogers, *The Undiscovered Dewey*, 145–46, 191.

CHAPTER SEVEN

Principles

This chapter applies the lessons of the social continuum of inquiry to the operation and understanding of legal principles.

* * *

I put it to you that the main constituent of the judicial process is precisely that it must be genuinely principled, resting with respect to every step that is involved in reaching judgment on analysis and reasons quite transcending the immediate result that is achieved. To be sure, the courts decide, or should decide, only the case they have before them. But must they not decide on grounds of adequate neutrality and generality, tested not only by the instant application but by others that the principles imply? Is it not the very essence of judicial method to insist upon attending to such other cases, preferably those involving an opposing interest in evaluating any principle involved?—Herbert Wechsler, "Toward Neutral Principles of Constitutional Law," 1959 Oliver Wendell Holmes Lecture at Harvard Law School

An ironic legacy of legal realism, and the anxiety accompanying it, rather than a reformed induction, was a turn to "general principles." In the wake of this turn, it is now widely considered appropriate for judges to appeal to general principles as grounds for particular decisions, when it appears that a boundary of "indeterminacy," or the limit of clear settled legal authority, is crossed—a boundary whose precise location has been constantly contested by scholars, and must inevitably in real life be discovered within the mind of the deciding judge. So, reinforced by this understanding, judges often *do* appeal to general principles. I will address this turn, which began in the 1950s and continues today despite an emergent skepticism of "principlism" in philosophical ethics.[1]

1. E.g., Jonathan Dancy, *Ethics without Principles*; K. Danner Clouser and Bernard Gert, "A Critique of Principlism," *Journal of Medicine and Philosophy* 15 (1990): 219–23; Leslie Francis, "Applied Ethics: Misnomer for a Field?"; Amartya Sen, *The Idea of Justice*.

Legal principles might be viewed in two contrary ways. They might either be seen as free-standing, unrevisable, and frequently opposing one another in the context of a disputed matter; or they might be open-ended, tentative, and suggesting (though not supporting) alternative options for the matter at hand. In the first view, they can appear irreconcilable, while according to the second they are, in Edward Levi's words, part of a "moving classification system." In the first view, the conceptual space of principle is relatively fixed at the moment of decision, and the legal mind is free to roam among them, at risk always of a choice dictated more by subjective preference than logic. According to the second view the legal mind must always hesitate as to whether the matter at hand warrants a decision broader than the particular case, given the immediate complex of circumstances.

The two alternatives might be described as thinking and judging *from* principle or, as Alexander Bickel has shown, *toward* principle. The first is Bacon's model of axiomatic thought, while the second is consistent with induction. In the latter alternative, there is no naïveté about the availability of competing claims to principled objectivity,[2] as there are always competing *a priori* principles applicable to every conflict.

Richard Epstein, defending his 2008 *Supreme Neglect*, might concede my argument for the second view of principle, but still ask why he may not be free to choose the first. The second view, he might say, sounds like wise counsel to the cautious jurist who, like Mansfield's magistrate, is uncertain of the context and outcome. Nevertheless, his argument continues, a judge appointed to the Supreme Court, appointed by the president and approved by the Senate, *must* choose among permanent inflexible principles, lest the nation lose its way for timidity and lack of direction. The question raised by Holmes is, What difference will that choice make, if such matters, while drily legal in appearance, are intimately connected with unresolved social conflict?

Without that perspective, lost from view is the possibility that the structure of human thought, concerned with conceptual ordering, is contingent upon its own success in *human* ordering. Without the presence of ubiquitous conflict in sight, the possibility is invisible that the enterprise of intelligent action is precarious and can stupendously fail. As Peirce said of the importance of understanding the operation of deduction and induction in his third Lowell Lecture, "Our fate hangs upon it."

2. Brian Leiter, *Objectivity in Law and Morals*, 1.

The mid-twentieth-century turn to principles came as a reaction against two disparate views, first a doubt raised at Harvard in 1958 by Judge Learned Hand over Supreme Court "judicial review"—oversight of state and federal legislation under the sweeping but vague dispensation of the Constitution's Bill of Rights. The other was the abstract question now associated with legal positivism, and harking back to philosophies of law since ancient Greece, the question of whether law is inherently separate from morals, brought to Harvard the preceding year by Professor Herbert Hart of Oxford University. In arguing for a strict separation of law from morals, Hart prompted a response from Harvard law professor Lon Fuller, defending an "inner morality" of law.[3] More influential was the later response to Hart of Ronald Dworkin, which began with the assertion that judges, in hard cases where the "positive law" had no apparent answer, could, should, and *did* turn to "moral principles."[4]

With these dueling views, Harvard now pulled ahead of Yale in the great lecture race, as Hand and Hart delivered their thoughts at consecutive Oliver Wendell Holmes Lectures, followed by Columbia law professor Herbert Wechsler in 1959 with his appeal to principle, summarized in the passage heading this chapter. Even while his name was honored, Holmes continued to be misread. In the decade after his death, he had been defined as a legal positivist for his cautionary remarks on moral language in "The Path of the Law." Lon Fuller had written in 1940 that

> [c]ertainly it cannot be said that the positivism of his early essays was ever completely sloughed off during his career as a judge. . . . For him the notion that the law is something severable from one's notions of what it ought to be seems to have had a real and inhibitive meaning. We may admire his fidelity to a faith. But was it for the ultimate good of our law? I think there is reason to doubt it.[5]

In the wake of World War II, Fuller's criticism was joined by others and, taken with occasional "military" allusions extolling valor in Holmes's speeches and essays, led to the notion that Holmes was an authoritarian. In 1945 an article appeared in the *American Bar Association Journal* with the title "Holmes, Hobbes, and Hitler." Five years later Westbrook Pegler referred to him as a "cynical and senile brutalitarian." Holmes's dissents in

3. Lon Fuller, *The Morality of Law*.
4. Ronald Dworkin, *Taking Rights Seriously*, and *Justice in Robes*.
5. Lon Fuller, *The Law in Quest of Itself*, 62–63.

the *Lochner* and *Abrams* cases, that the U.S. Constitution is made for people of many faiths, carried almost no counterweight to these evaluations.[6]

The irony is more profound in view of an as-yet-unrecognized and deep congeniality between Fuller's and Holmes's views of the importance of understanding law in its social context. For Fuller, law to be effective must depend on informal and implicit social rules, as well as interaction between legal officials and those subject to legal rule making. The positivist view to which he objected was that law was ontologically and methodologically separate from morals, a view he saw carried forward by legal realism in equating law with the acts of judges and legal officials. Fuller believed that judges could only impose sanctions upon parties to legal disputes if social norms supported their doing so, norms that must be accepted and practiced in the community at large.

Holmes took a critical further step in a direction that Fuller could have approved, had he understood it. Both men recognized the role of law and lawyers in bringing the law into conformity with communal norms; Holmes saw that to accomplish this was to break away from the notion that judges should dominate the public debate over principle and control the outcome.

Meanwhile, Wechsler, in his 1959 Holmes Lecture, sought to refute Judge Hand's doubts about the controversial increase in substantive jurisdiction in the Supreme Court under the Fourteenth Amendment's "due process" clause. Seeing a growing trend, Hand in 1958 declared that he did not care to be governed "by a bevy of Platonic guardians, even if I knew how to choose them, which I assuredly do not."[7] His lectures set off a round of reassessment among legal scholars that has not died out, as debate continues over the enormous power wielded by the Supreme Court in "judicial review." Hand, the master guide and reliable illuminator of complicated litigation, left his mark as an oracle of misgivings. The Constitution was to be regarded primarily as the embodiment of historical compromise, not a set of durable principles or a resource from which to strengthen or modify the morals of society. The notion of a constitutional law of economic or personal rights knowable by judges, Hand maintained at the close of his career, was a fallacy.

In his response, Wechsler advanced the claim that Hand's doubts could be "transcended" if the Court would only follow "neutral principles" of

6. Kellogg, *Formative Essays*, 58–59.

7. Learned Hand, *The Bill of Rights*, 11.

constitutional law. Dworkin's path to principle would develop later, eventually worked out as an independent theory about the nature of legal interpretation. The two developments are close in the chronology of twentieth-century jurisprudence, and were matched by a new cycle of realist-inspired criticism: the claim of CLS that principles are not the solution, but rather the problem: legal doctrine, especially considering the diverse "background" of maxims and theories, includes so many diverse "principles" that any outcome can be given a principled defense by judges in a close case.

Legal realism had arisen in response to a perceived nineteenth-century deductive formalism, what Roscoe Pound called "mechanical jurisprudence." The social scientific component of legal realism had failed to light the way forward to an understanding of law, but its skeptical component would be taken up and deepened by CLS. Since his Harvard Lecture, H. L. A. Hart's rigorous analytical positivism has increasingly come to dominate Anglo-American jurisprudence, challenged mainly by Ronald Dworkin's argument that legal answers could be deduced from moral principles. As to the CLS claim of indeterminacy, Dworkin mostly ignored it.[8]

What exactly are "legal principles"? Where does the judiciary find them? Reference to principle can amply be found in the literature of jurisprudence, but there is no clear and agreed definition. How do principles compare in law and science? Can a "principle" change? Legal principles come in different guises: Wechsler's principles of constitutional law are "neutral," while Dworkin's are "moral" and cover law in general, as a therapy for legal indeterminacy. The very existence of legal principles has been questioned.[9] Their nature in legal theory has been more assumed than examined, as John Herschel sought to examine scientific principles with his questions in 1840. Paraphrasing Herschel, Are legal principles necessary truths? What is the act or series of acts of the mind (or "minds") in constructing legal principles, and when constructed, in what manner do we rest in them as expressive of truth?

Broad constitutional statements as found in our Bill of Rights may be read two ways, as a list of axioms, or, more consistent with induction, as

8. See Andrew Altman, *Critical Legal Studies: A Liberal Critique*; Jeremy Waldron, "Did Dworkin Ever Answer the Crits?"

9. Larry Alexander and Kenneth Kress, "Against Legal Principles." The contemporary moral particularist Jonathan Dancy writes: "Particularists think that moral judgement can get along perfectly well without any appeal to principles, indeed that there is no essential link between being a full moral agent and having principles." Dancy, *Ethics without Principles*, 1.

posing fundamental questions, posed always in a specific context. Wechsler's heading remark suggests a sweeping inclusion of anticipated but unexamined particulars. He concedes that courts should decide "only the case they have before them," but their reasoning must be "tested not only by the instant application but by others that the principles imply." To decide on principle is to decide on "grounds of adequate neutrality and generality," and "to insist upon attending to such other cases, preferably those involving an opposing interest in evaluating any principle involved." Wechsler's response to Hand was to abandon a gradual case-by-case approach.

How did Wechsler reach this broad license? He starts with the proposition that "the Court by rule has defined standards for the exercise of its discretion, standards framed in neutral terms, like the importance of the question or a conflict of decisions. Only the maintenance and the improvement of such standards and, of course, their faithful application can, I say with deference, protect the Court against the danger of imputation of a bias favoring claims of one kind or another in the granting or denial of review." Wechsler takes the Supreme Court's discretionary standards as models of neutrality, but it is difficult to see how either judicial "importance," or "conflict of decisions" among the lower courts, can provide any support for deploying general propositions in all controversial cases.

In his argument for neutral principle Wechsler condemned the unprincipled particular decision as "fiat." According to this claim, "neutral principle" provides the only alternative to an exercise of "naked power": "The man who simply lets his judgment turn on the immediate result may not, however, realize that his position implies that the courts are free to function as a naked power organ, that it is an empty affirmation to regard them, as ambivalently he so often does, as courts of law." Why is a concern with the "immediate result" equivalent to "fiat?" There appears here a profound confusion between principle and *transparency*. Holmes, in resisting the sweeping constitutional prohibition of picketing in his labor dissents, was not resisting explanatory *rationalization*; rather he sought to limit the court's method, as well as its explanation, to transparently specific reasons that would leave the matter open to further experience and revision.

In support of his claim of fiat, Wechsler cited Lon Fuller's 1946 article in the *Harvard Law Review*, "Reason and Fiat in Case Law." Originally delivered as a lecture in honor of Justice Cardozo, Fuller proposed that the distinction between reason and fiat is an "antinomy" embedded in the law, an inherent contradiction between two opposing conceptions:

> For Cardozo the law embraced many antinomies, but one of the greatest and most pervasive of these was that of reason and fiat. . . . Cardozo did not follow the example of those who make relativism itself an absolute. If the common law had not attained the perfection of reason, it could be understood only as an unremitting quest for that perfection. His view rejected neither branch of the antinomy of reason and fiat. For him law was by its limitations fiat, by its aspirations reason, and the whole view of it involved a recognition of both its limitations and its aspirations.[10]

Fuller held that "this antinomy is in fact inescapable," a "state of unresolved conflict" that "it is better to accept frankly" than "to purchase consistency at the cost of needed premises." To use the term "antinomy," denoting an immediate apprehension of final irreconcilability, is to conflate the stages of legal inquiry, placing them in opposition rather than succession. The effect of its use is to demonize one perspective as less desirable than the other, characterizing what is really an early stage as one of "fiat," not recognizing that there may yet in the quest for resolution come a later reconciliation with "reason."

Fuller and Cardozo both failed to appreciate, or at least to articulate, the manner in which reason itself is emergent from specific experience, but more important, from social conflict, and still more important, from its resolution in the adjustment of human conduct. "Fiat" suggests a prejudice against the necessity of choice in the context of unfamiliar experience. There is no antinomy between reason and fiat, so translated. To use the term is to stand upon a ground of unresolved cognitive conflict, and to do this is to obstruct the prospect of resolving *real* conflict.

The clash between Hand and Wechsler stirred another Hand-style conservative, Yale law professor Alexander Bickel, to take up Hand's doubts and seek to reconcile them with Wechsler's principles. Bickel began by recasting Hand's argument with a phrase that has changed the terms of the debate. Bickel characterized Hand's practical doubts into a democratic crisis: Supreme Court review under the due process clause raised a "counter-majoritarian difficulty," as to how it could be squared with democratically enacted legislation. Having refined the problem, Bickel added that the judicial process is "justified only if it injects into representative government something that is not already there: and that is principle, standards of action that derive their worth from a long view of society's spiritual and ma-

10. Lon Fuller, "Reason and Fiat in Case Law," 376–77.

terial needs and that command adherence whether or not the immediate outcome is expedient or agreeable."[11]

Bickel then set off on a different tack: principle is something less to be imposed than to be achieved. Examining a series of recent decisions, he asked whether they met Wechsler's neutrality test. He concluded that some had failed simply for lack of *coherence*: "A neutral principle is an intellectually coherent statement of the reason for a result which in like cases will produce a like result, whether or not it is immediately agreeable or expedient." But Bickel's analysis then posed a question ignored by Wechsler: can the "neutral principle" withstand the unknown future? "Now the demand for neutral principles is carried further. It is that the court rest judgment only on principles that will be capable of application across the board and without compromise, in all relevant cases in the foreseeable future: absolute application of absolute—even if sometimes flexible—principles. The flexibility, if any, must be built into the principle itself."[12] This future orientation led Bickel to a different conclusion on the Supreme Court's task.

How can we know the future? For this Bickel looked to the past. Instead of decrying the inevitable *ad hoc*, the raw "fiat," in law and politics, Bickel saw the problem as one of reconciling principled consistency with a realistic pragmatism. This he called the "Lincolnian tension," as where Lincoln had opposed all slavery in principle, while accepting the Missouri Compromise as "born of necessity":[13]

> Our democratic system of government exists in this Lincolnian tension between principle and expediency, and within it judicial review must play its role. Mr. Wechsler's dilemma is a false one. The constitutional function of the court is to define values and proclaim principles. But this is not a function to be exercised with respect to some exceedingly few matters, while society is left wholly to its devices of expediency in dealing with the great number of its other concerns. For, as with the segregation problem and slavery before it, we require principle and expediency at once. The rule of the neutral principles would excise the courts function of declaring principled goals.[14]

11. Alexander Bickel, *The Least Dangerous Branch*, 58.
12. Ibid., 59.
13. Ibid., 66.
14. Ibid., 68–69.

Our system, Bickel declared, calls for an *adaptation* of principle in novel circumstances. In this, "courts have certain capacities for dealing with matters of principle that legislatures and executives do not possess. Judges have, or should have, the leisure, the training, and the insulation to follow the ways of the scholar in pursuing ends of government. This is crucial in sorting out the enduring values of a society." The courts are always concerned with the "flesh and blood" of the actual case. "This tends to modify, perhaps to lengthen, everyone's view. It also provides an extremely salutary proving ground for all abstractions. It is conducive, in a phrase of Holmes, to thinking things, not words, and thus to the evolution of principle by a process that tests as it creates."[15]

In his description of a process "that tests as it creates," Bickel gave clarity to Holmes's admonition to "think things, not words." Bickel's account of principles is a Holmesian correction to Wechsler's hopeful but dubious ambition. It gives priority not to judicial autonomy, but to the experience felt by all participants in the process, through a continuum of inquiry. What does it mean to be thinking "things, not words"? It avoids the danger of runaway rule by principle, of its *abuse*:

> The Court—if Mr. Wechsler is right—either has set out to be a third legislative chamber or is imposing on the country an absolute rule of absolute principle. Thus it is either totally at war with the theory and practice of democracy or, far from being a stabilizing influence, it is leading the country to ruin by intractable, doctrinaire stages of irrepressible conflict. Or both, for the absolute rule of principle is also at war with a democratic system. But Mr. Wechsler, I believe, is not right.
>
> No society, certainly not a large and heterogeneous one, can fail to explode if it is deprived of the arts of compromise, if it knows no ways of muddling through. No good society can be unprincipled; and no viable society can be principle-ridden. But it is not true in our society that we are generally governed wholly by principle in some matters and indulge a rule of expediency exclusively in others. There is no such neat dividing line.[16]

Bickel is among very few writers to identify the problem of abusing principle through its own elevation. To avoid such abuse, his initial reflection was entirely in accord with Holmes: that "any first case is always a poor one

15. Ibid., 26.
16. Ibid., 64.

in which to pronounce new principles is no doubt an over-generalization. And yet it is not far wrong. A sound judicial instinct will generally favor deflecting the problem in one or more initial cases, for there is much to be gained from letting it simmer, so that a mounting number of instances exemplifying it may have a cumulative effect on the judicial minds as well as on public and professional opinion."[17]

But what about the *urgent* "first case," one that demands judgment when the courts are the only resort? It is Bickel's next suggestion that has failed to take hold as a realistic measure: he concluded that the Supreme Court should *avoid* deciding all "first cases." For this, he said, there is an "arsenal of techniques and devices . . . most of which are lumped roughly and often disingenuously together under the rubric of jurisdiction," like standing or ripeness, the political question doctrine allowing the court to recuse itself, or by simply denying review through the writ of certiorari. Bickel seems to have conceived that this answer was not a dodge, but rather a deferring to extralegal avenues for resolving controversy.

It was indeed a dodge, but Bickel sensed nevertheless that a continuum of inquiry existed, and that feedback from "political processes" was essential to it:

> When the Court, however, stays its hand, and makes clear that it is staying its hand and not legitimating, then the political processes are given relatively free play. . . . Most of [these techniques] are quite properly called techniques for eliciting answers, since so often they engage the court in a Socratic colloquy with the other institutions of government and with society as a whole concerning the necessity for this or that measure, for this or that compromise. All the while, the issue of principle remains in abeyance and ripens. "The most important thing we do," said Brandeis, "is not doing." He had in mind all the techniques, of which he was a past master, for staying the Court's hand. They are the most important thing, because they make possible performance of the court's grand function as proclaimer and protector of the goals. These are the techniques that allow leeway to expediency without abandoning principle. Therefore they make possible a principled government.[18]

17. Ibid., 176.

18. Ibid., 70–71. Bickel also noted: "It follows that the techniques and allied devices for staying the court's hand, as is avowedly true at least of certiorari, cannot themselves be principled in the sense in which we have a right to expect adjudications on the merits to be principled." Ibid., 132.

Bickel's turn to the techniques of avoidance failed to gain a scholarly consensus, largely from the urgency of controversies forced upon the federal courts and the reluctance of justices, perhaps not masters of avoidance like Brandeis, to exercise such an obviously evasive form of restraint.

Instead, according to Cass Sunstein, the Court has moved in a direction away from both Bickel and Wechsler: toward "incompletely theorized agreements." Sunstein claims that the contemporary Supreme Court (he wrote in 1999) has "embraced" judicial "minimalism."

> When the court ruled that the Virginia Military Institute could not exclude women, it refused to say much about the legitimacy of other single sex institutions, leaving the general question undecided. When it struck down the affirmative action program in Richmond, Virginia, it self-consciously refused to impose a broad ban on race-conscious programs. When it invalidated a Colorado law forbidding measures banning discrimination on the basis of sexual orientation, it said nothing about how the constitution bears on other issues involving homosexuality.[19]

In favoring "incompletely theorized agreements" Sunstein assumes that there is a time for exploration and a time for generalization, but he is unclear on the dynamics: in a move contrary to Lon Fuller, he eschews the language of "fiat" and defends particularizing as a universal method: a global particularism. "The Court's minimalist judges try to keep their judgments as narrow and as incompletely theorized as possible, consistent with the obligation to offer reasons." This is not Holmes's approach; there is no avenue forward to new legal knowledge.[20]

Sunstein advocates judicial minimalism for its "democracy enhancing" effect, by which I assume he believes that democratic pluralism does not need Holmes's resolution of social conflict, that of constant convergence. What then is to be done about the troublesome "first case"? Frederick Schauer has suggested that it is characteristic of all such cases that they tend to distort the process of making rules. He asks, in an article so titled, the question "Do Cases Make Bad Law?" There he insisted that "cases"—all cases—"make bad law."

19. Cass Sunstein, *One Case at a Time: Judicial Minimalism on the Supreme Court*, 3–4, citing *United States v. Virginia*, 518 U.S. 515 (1996), *Richmond v. Croson*, 488 U.S. 469 (1989), and *Romer v. Evans*, 517 U.S. 620 (1996).

20. Ibid., 262–63.

> [T]he distortion of the immediate case may systematically condemn common law law-making not only to suboptimal results, but also to results predictably worse than those that would be reached by making law in a less dispute-driven fashion. If this is so, then the entire "merit" of law-making in common law fashion may need to be reconsidered, and my goal here is to prompt just such wholesale reconsideration of the virtues of the common law method as a desirable way to create the rules and principles that constitute so much of our law.[21]

For Schauer, the focus returns to a primary concern over the "reason" side of Fuller's reason-or-fiat antinomy; and he writes that "Holmes may have ignored the extent to which even ordinary cases impress their facts on the judges who decide them, and scarcely less than great cases or hard cases appear to demand proper resolution purely by virtue of their very presence in the foreground of judicial phenomenology."[22]

Schauer's argument holds that the "vivid scenario" of a novel case has the effect of "framing" the judicial response in such a way as to have undesirable influence on the "rules and principles" of the law. This objection is addressed by the piece of Holmes's theory that is missing from Schauer's analysis: the continuum of inquiry, and the *retrospective* finding of rules and principles. For Holmes the vivid scenario is to be expected; but it must not be allowed to frame the issue until other and sufficient vivid scenarios are on record. Schauer invites generalizing too soon.

The notion that the novel case must be immediately decided by general principle is a view that has been extensively defended by Ronald Dworkin. Responding in 1967 to Hart's positivist separation of law and morals, Dworkin claimed evidence from two famous hard legal cases that judges *do* resort to principles.[23] One was *Riggs v. Palmer*, denying the right of a

21. Schauer "Do Cases Make Bad Law," 3. Robert Brandom recently asks the key question that underlay Holmes's shift to a social model of induction: "What is it about the actual cases that should be understood as privileging some of those aspects of similarity, as those that should be projected to govern assessments of novel cases? The trouble is that there will always be many ways of extending the prior practice to those future potential cases, many different ways of 'going on in the same way,' to use Wittgenstein's phrase." Brandom, "A Hegelian Model of Concept Determination," 25.

22. Schauer "Do Cases Make Bad Law," 2.

23. Ronald Dworkin, "The Model of Rules I," reprinted in *Taking Rights Seriously*, 22:

> I want to make a general attack on positivism, and I shall use H. L. A. Hart's version as a target, when a particular target is needed. My strategy will be organized around the fact that when lawyers reason or dispute about legal rights and obligations,

murderer to inherit from the will of his victim, by the bland assertion that "no one should profit from their own wrong." The other was *MacPherson v. Buick*, the case of the defective automobile decided by Judge Cardozo that (as Edward Levi wrote in 1949) ended the hundred-year history of the "inherently dangerous" rule. Cardozo appealed to another, clearly empty if not banal, rhetorical maxim: "Is there any principle which is more familiar or more firmly embedded in the history of Anglo American law than the basic doctrine that the courts will not permit themselves to be used as instruments of inequity and injustice?" This was only slightly improved by, "More specifically, the courts generally refuse to lend themselves to the enforcement of a bargain in which one party had unjustly taken advantage of the economic necessities of another."[24]

Neither of these cases conclusively shows, as Dworkin argued in opposition to Hart, that Hart's analytical positivist boundary between law and morals is pierced by the real existence of moral principles. What they show, indeed, is that judicial opinions, like legal arguments, can make effortless recourse to principled rationalization. But a showing of moral argument does not by itself demonstrate that Dworkin or Wechsler are right about the use or effectiveness of principles. The cases are more consistent with the alternative view, that I have associated with Levi, Bickel, and Holmes. In each case there is another countervailing principle that pulls in the opposite direction, and in neither case can it be said that particular facts (the long history of litigation over dangerous objects in *MacPherson*, and the size of the bequest to Elmer Riggs) did not shape and limit the principle announced.[25]

In the wake of Hart's positivism and Dworkin's challenge, it is now a commonplace in contemporary analytical jurisprudence that the so-called doubtful or hard case, appearing unresolved by any clear legal author-

---

> particularly in those hard cases when our problems with these concepts seem most acute, they make use of standards that do not function as rules, but operate differently as principles, policies, and other sorts of standards. Positivism, I shall argue, is a model of and for a system of rules, and its central notion of a single fundamental test for law forces us to miss the important roles of these standards that are not rules.

. . . Most often I shall use the term principle generically, to refer to the whole set of these standards other than rules.

24. Ibid., 111–19; *MacPherson v. Buick Motor Co.*, 217 N.Y. 382, 111 N.E. 1050 (1916).

25. See my "What Precisely Is a 'Hard' Case? Waldron, Dworkin and Judicial Recourse to Principle."

ity, is legally indeterminate and can be decided only through recourse to background principles.[26] As I have argued, there is an aspect of doubtfulness that militates strongly against such recourse: when viewed as representative of an early stage in the resolution of similar cases, perhaps the very first of a continuing class of disputes, then (especially in controversial cases of broad import) recourse to principles may lead to an improvident choice of reasons, and in any event violates fundamental democratic values. Principles incorporate moral views, which vary and conflict from judge to judge even as they vary and conflict in the society at large.

Importing Wechsler's and Dworkin's views to the European continent, the influential German jurist Robert Alexy has defended the notion that judges should appeal to principle in all cases where the law has an "open area." Open areas are created by "the vagaries of legal language, the possibility of norm conflicts, the absence of a norm on which to base a decision, and, in certain cases, the possibility of making a decision even contrary to the literal reading of a norm." Reinforced with Alexy's influence, it is now common abroad to refer to an "open area" of the positive law, existing in some degree in every legal system. This picture is rooted in the classical positivist position that since only the positive law is law, the judge must decide in open areas on the basis, we must conclude, of nonlegal or at least extralegal standards: "Accordingly," writes Alexy, "he is empowered to create new law essentially as a legislator does, on the basis of extra-legal standards."[27]

New cases may implicate emerging controversies; at an early stage, legal claims will not be fully representative of all relevant considerations, and public as well as expert attitudes have yet to form. Alexander Bickel's work suggests that principled resolution should await exposure to the variety of unseen aspects. The implication of Edward Levi's analysis is that public debate among legal, and nonlegal, scholars as well as citizens should play a role in the development of practical reasoning surrounding the broader controversy, as well as the transformation of relevant practices.

26. E.g., Robert Alexy, *The Argument from Injustice*, 169–70.

27. Ibid., 69. I have suggested that if this area is open, it is not *univocally* open, with all openness of a uniform quality, since different legal controversies are in different stages of classification and resolution at any one time. Thus, at the very least, different degrees of generality of reasoning are appropriate for different stages of judicial inquiry. Moreover, when the open area is viewed in the context of other influences in the feedback loop, it is not purely an open area in the law alone, but it is open also with regard to extralegal opinion, practices, and understanding. See my "The Abuse of Principle: Analytical Philosophy and the Doubtful Case," 218.

An obvious example is the controversy over medically assisted suicide. Cass Sunstein characterized the "right to die" as a "new dilemma," and applauded the fact that the U.S. Supreme Court had as yet refrained from a broadly defined resolution. The issue of physician-assisted suicide is even now engaging intense discussion. Sunstein claims that it is far too early for courts to preempt those discussions, certainly if there should be no systematic barrier to a fair hearing from any affected group.[28]

Difficult questions have arisen, like, When does life begin and end? What is personal autonomy and invasion of privacy? When is medical treatment criminally responsible for the death of a suffering and morbid patient? The questions cannot be answered in limbo. Arguments from principle are often framed in highly abstract and simplistic terms, such as, "Is there a right to die?" Practices affecting those answers are unsettled and inchoate, and opinions regarding them are unsettled as well. Particular claims are necessary to focus on relevant practices and, over time, to encourage their investigation, refinement, and transformation into the grounds for decision.

In effect, there is indeed a feedback loop from case to case, in which, as the name suggests, information about action and judgment is sent back, transforming the nature of opinion, understanding, and discourse of the overall situation. Argument from the "right to die" is least effectively advocated when there is little information concerning relevant circumstances. The phrase itself was unfamiliar before recent changes in both medical care and longevity. It took drastic instances, including the imprisonment of Dr. Jack Kevorkian, to overcome traditional attitudes.

The analytical model, suggesting that all doubtful cases can *already* have been decided according to *a priori* principles, can only further the polarization of discussion regarding the Supreme Court's powers over constitutionally enshrined "rights." There is a massive problem with this standard view: the notion that opposing principles can be "balanced." Alexy

28. In early litigation it is not necessary or typical for preliminary legal outcomes to prescribe practices; it is characteristic that they focus attention on them. Varying practices involving particular drugs and precautions, specific legal permissions, and designated medical and administrative procedures are influenced by the attention focused by litigation. Meanwhile, opinions and attitudes are influenced by the nature of cases made public through litigation. A literature of educated and expert opinion is part of the opinion-making process. E.g., Robert Young, *Medically Assisted Death*; Robert F. Weir, ed., *Physician Assisted Suicide*. Public and expert opinion affects, and is affected by, the refinement of practices.

writes that principles, as "optimizing" rather than "definitive" commands, must be "balanced" by the judge in a case where they appear to conflict:

> In undertaking to strike a balance, one necessarily appeals to principles for support. For it is necessary to strike a balance precisely when there are competing reasons, each of which is by itself a good reason for a decision and only fails to lead directly to a definitive decision because of the other reason, calling for another decision; reasons like this are either principles or supported by principles.[29]

What metric does the judge use to accomplish this? Girardeau Spann writes that principles so conceived are "incommensurable," and that balancing is inevitably a subjective act:

> Judges cannot balance interests without recourse to their subjective preferences. Even judges with the best intentions will balance competing interests according to their views about both the relative importance of those interests and the degree to which each interest will be advanced or frustrated by particular outcomes in the case before the court. Because this activity is essentially unconstrained, however, it is difficult to see how a judge could possibly engage in it without recourse to subjective values.[30]

It will take more than Alexy's bland assertion to overcome Spann's doubt that any clear logical path exists to resolve a difficult case by "balancing."

29. Alexy, *Argument from Injustice*, 72. See T. Alexander Aleinikoff, "Constitutional Law in the Age of Balancing," *Yale Law Journal* 96 (1987): 943, 945: "The customary way in which our contemporary legal system deals with competing interests is through balancing. The conflicting interests are identified, quantified, and compared, and the weightier interest prevails. The process of interest balancing, however, entails so many unconstrained judicial determinations that the subjective values of the judge are necessarily called into play on multiple occasions during the balancing process."

30. Girardeau A. Spann, in "Simple Justice": "When legal doctrine calls for interest balancing, therefore, it does something that is seemingly counterproductive. Because particular doctrinal applications are utterly dependent upon how the balance is struck, the subjective preferences that doctrine is designed to guard against necessarily drive application of the doctrinal rules. Once again, asking a judge to balance competing interests is a lot like asking a judge to prevent unjust discrimination." See also Mark Tushnet, "Anti-Formalism in Recent Constitutional Theory," and Stephen E. Gottlieb, "The Paradox of Balancing Significant Interests."

In my alternative account, where legal principles must await a comprehensive encounter with experience, context is critical. Context is also time-variant, and is changing with attitudes, practices, and technology. Competing principles are not in *collision* so much as in *transformation*; traditional principles are inapplicable due to the novelty of circumstances, and a new formulation must be found in engagement with the community and its sense of proportion. As in science, that engagement must be experimental. The metaphor of a balancing scale inaccurately portrays what takes place as judges draw on facts to decide cases, and as society responds to legal decisions. Balancing is a static metaphor, in which *a priori* principles are always already available. To draw on general propositions in a novel case is *abuse* of reasoning from principle.

The turn to principles, as exemplified by Herbert Wechsler and Ronald Dworkin in America, and by Robert Alexy in Europe, has been criticized here as a turn away from induction, and toward a tendency to think deductively from unrevisable "axioms." Holmes's own inductive turn has been characterized as grounded (via Wright, Mill, and Whewell) in the work of Francis Bacon, who in the interest of progress proposed, four centuries ago, his own revision of the inductive tradition:

> [G]oing by my method is to derive axioms gradually, in a connected succession, so as only at the end to arrive at the most general; however, when they do come forth they are not purely speculative but are well-defined, and such as nature would really recognize as better known to herself, and which lie at the very marrow of things.
>
> But far the greatest change I make is in the very form of induction, and the judgment made from it. For the induction of which the logicians talk, which proceeds from simple enumeration, is a childish affair, unsafe in its conclusions, in danger from a contradictory influence, taking account only of what is familiar, and leading to no result.
>
> Now what the sciences need is a form of induction that will analyze experience and take it apart, and through due exclusions and rejections necessarily come to a conclusion.[31]

The final sentence, Bacon's original contribution, implied a departure from Aristotle's assumption that similarities preexist in nature, turning attention

31. Francis Bacon, *Novum Organum*, 20–21.

instead to the process of "exclusions and rejections" whereby experience is fully examined and "taken apart."

Mill carried this emphasis further in his analysis of "comparison." It was left to Holmes to recognize how comparison really occurs in a contentious climate—how experience is "taken apart," but how it must then be reconstituted. Throughout its history, induction has been grounded in meliorist hope, the hope for human survival and progress. That hope is now conditioned by increasing evidence of precariousness, by an unabashed look at the reality of conflict, and by an association of logic with the real prospect of violence. It rightly presumes that convergence will depend on an ethical basis, the piecemeal, continuous, and sane adjustment of practice. As Peirce said of the study of logic in 1866, "Our fate hangs upon it."

CHAPTER EIGHT

Positivism

This chapter addresses the association of Holmes with the "positivist" separation of law and morals, and compares his perspective with that of H. L. A. Hart, Ronald Dworkin, and Lon L. Fuller.

* * *

In this [lecture] I shall discuss and attempt to defend a view which Mr. Justice Holmes, among others, held and for which they have been much criticized. But I wish first to say why I think that Holmes, whatever the vicissitudes of his American reputation may be, will always remain for Englishmen a heroic figure in jurisprudence. This will be so because he has magically combined two qualities: one of them is imaginative power, which English legal thinking has often lacked; the other is clarity which English legal thinking usually possesses. The English lawyer who turns to read Holmes is made to see that what he had taken to be settled and stable is always on the move.—H. L. A. Hart, "Positivism and the Separation of Law and Morals," the 1957 Oliver Wendell Holmes Lecture

On April 30, 1957, in Langdell Hall at Harvard Law School, Visiting Professor Herbert L. A. Hart of Oxford University opened his 1957 Holmes Lecture, "Positivism and the Separation of Law and Morals," with the above paragraph, claiming Holmes as a fellow "legal positivist," even while praising his "imaginative power" in recognizing the constant "move[ment]" of what is "taken to be settled." Legal positivism advances a conception of law as separate from morals, a notion with ancient roots that Hart brought to the center of interest and debate in the middle of the twentieth century.

Hart adopted Lon Fuller's 1940 assessment of Holmes, that his expression of law as "prophecies of what the courts will do," along with his caution to law students against confusing legal and moral language, defined him as also separating the two domains. The observant Hart was intrigued by (but not overly curious about) Holmes's perspective on "movement."

He concluded that Holmes really had no coherent theory, later describing his insights as a collection of diamonds, but connected only with a string.[1] For the many contemporary followers of Hart, Holmes now occupies a maverick catalyzing role, having stimulated behaviorist legal realism, which developed its own version of a positivist separation.[2]

In the wake of Hart's Harvard lecture, and his publication in 1960 of *The Concept of Law*, analytical positivism gained a foothold in America from which it rapidly advanced to control the agenda of legal philosophy. Two features of Hart's positivist view of law are of central concern in this chapter: its synchronicity, or nonextendedness in time, and its concrete and autonomous nature, which gives it an implicit boundary. My purpose is to show how radically different is Holmes's perspective, and to use that comparison to better situate Holmes in the context of contemporary theory. This exercise will cast further light on the controversial matter of judges' recourse to "principles."

Hart's praise of Holmes's sense of *movement* contrasts with his own perspective, which *doesn't* move in an important sense. Certainly it recognizes that legal content changes with both legislation and judicial decision. But Hart accounted for a system of law's continuity over time (as well as its validity) in terms of common origin or common recognition.[3] Understanding

1. H. L. A. Hart, "Diamonds and String: Holmes on the Common Law," in *Essays in Jurisprudence and Philosophy*, 278: "Holmes's famous book, *The Common Law*, admirably reintroduced to the general reader by Professor Mark Howe of Harvard, resembles a necklace of splendid diamonds surprisingly held together at certain points by nothing better than string. The diamonds are the marvelous insights into the genius of common law and the detailed explorations of the dynamic of its growth; they still flash their illuminating light on the dark areas beneath the clear and apparently stable forms of legal thought. The string is the sometimes obscure and hasty argument, the contemptuous dismissal of rival views, and the exaggerations with which Holmes sought to build up the tendencies which he found actually at work in the history of the law into a tough, collective philosophy of society."

2. I mean by this the identification of law by some realists as an autonomous entity consisting of the actions of legal officials. See Altman, "Legal Realism, Critical Legal Studies, and Dworkin."

3. Postema, "Law's System: The Necessity of System in Common Law," 77, 85. "[M]odern positivists offer a strictly formal account of law's system. They propose to explain not only the identity and unity of a legal system, but also its continuity over time, in terms of their doctrine of validity—the common origin or common recognition of all the constituent norms of the system. The common origin or common recognitional practice may explain the unity and identity (or at least the boundaries) of momentary legal systems (that is, time slices of a legal system), but the continuity of law is not merely a sequence of momentary legal systems. Momentary systems logically presuppose a temporally unified, continuous legal system.

Holmes requires a full appreciation of the *diachronic* nature of his own conception, its recognition of the source of continuity and validity in constant adjustments of practice, of change constantly taking place amidst what appears to be stable, and, finally, of law's fundamental unboundedness.

Hart criticized John Austin's command theory of law as reductionist, as Holmes had done in 1872,[4] but replaced it with a system based on rules: primary and secondary rules, including a governing "rule of recognition."[5] Influenced by his Oxford colleague, the ordinary language philosopher J. L. Austin (1911–60), Hart's conception was grounded in the contemporary meanings of legal language. In this view, "our common stock of words embodies all the distinctions men have found worth drawing, and the connexions they have found worth making, in the lifetimes of many generations: these surely are likely to be more sound, since they have stood up to the long test of the survival of the fittest, and more subtle, at least in all ordinary and reasonably practical matters, than any that you or I are likely to think up in our arm-chairs of an afternoon—the most favoured alternative method."[6] Thus the language of the present is the prime resource for

---

Something must bind momentary systems together into a single, continuous, albeit constantly changing, system. However, such legal systems persist through change in origins—whether sovereign law-makers, norms authorising law-making, or constitutions—so common origins cannot explain law's continuity. Hart sought to solve this problem by rooting laws in the recognitional practice of law-applying officials. But that practice, characterised by Hart as the convergence of behaviour and attitudes of officials, is just a present matter of fact. A change of those facts entails a change in the legal system, the appearance of a new legal system. So, Hart's rule of recognition cannot adequately explain law's continuity." Ibid., 85

Joseph Raz, in *The Concept of a Legal System*, 187: "The crux of the problem of the identity of (non-momentary) legal systems is the question of continuity, namely what events disrupt the continuous existence of a legal system, and bring about its disappearance, and, perhaps, result in the creation of a new legal system in its stead." This account leaves no room for disruption and change *within* a system.

4. Holmes reviewed Pollock's article of April 1872 and agreed with it, also objecting to reducing law to commands; he describes lectures he gave at Harvard College where he had already characterized the reduction as "a mere fiction to say that, either philosophically or legally, they [commands] necessarily emanated from the will of the sovereign *as law*." Book Notice, *American Law Review* 6: 723; Kellogg, *Formative Essays*, 91; *CW*, 1:294. The development of his thought through criticism of Austin is discussed in Kellogg, *Formative Essays*, 23–29. See Postema, *Treatise of Legal Philosophy*, 272.

5. Hart, *Concept of Law*, 77–107.

6. J. L. Austin, "A Plea for Excuses: The Presidential Address," in *Philosophical Papers*, 181–82; see also Nicola Lacey, *The Nightmare and the Noble Dream*, 133–46. Ordinary language philosophy was associated with conceptual analysis, which regarded philosophical prob-

philosophical understanding. Insofar as uncertainty exists, it is understood as present within the current set of available meanings.

The phenomenon of linguistic uncertainty had been previously addressed by Friedrich Waismann.[7] Hart took from Waismann the idea of a "core" of settled meaning, surrounded by a "penumbra" of doubtful application: whether, for example, riding a bicycle is prohibited by a rule against "vehicles" in the park. Uncertainty is attributed to the vagueness of words like "vehicle." Notwithstanding the existence of such penumbral uncertainty, lawyers and judges presumably can and do navigate fairly reliably from core to core.

This move by Hart dismissed as overstated a vast legal realist literature concerned with legal indeterminacy. When conceived as a system of rules, law can generally find a rule-based answer, appealing when necessary to Hart's guiding "rule of recognition." In setting forth the elements of his system, Hart did not direct much attention to the problems of adjudication in "hard" cases.[8] Earlier legal realist concerns were waved away, and law was seen as largely cognizable, not threatened by the tracklessness that troubled Cardozo. This left ample space for Ronald Dworkin's challenge to Hart's implicit boundary, arguing that it was not impervious to judges importing "moral principle."[9]

---

lems as conceptual and concepts as embodied in language. Hans-Johann Glock, *What Is Analytical Philosophy?*, and "The Influence of Wittgenstein on American Philosophy," 385–86.

7. Friedrich Waismann, "Verifiability": "Vagueness should be distinguished from open texture. A word which is actually used in a fluctuating way (such as 'heap' or 'pink') is said to be vague; a term like 'gold,' though its actual use may not be vague, is non-exhaustive or of an open texture in that we can never fill up all the possible gaps through which a doubt may seep in. Open texture, then, is something like possibility of vagueness. Vagueness can be remedied by giving more accurate rules, open texture cannot. An alternative way of stating this would be to say that definitions of open terms are always corrigible or emendable." See also Waismann, *The Principles of Linguistic Philosophy*, 3–14, 21–22, 69–86.

8. Geoffrey Shaw, "H. L. A. Hart's Lost Essay," 674: "Hart's relative silence on legal reasoning is a shortcoming of his legacy—one that left him vulnerable to attack in his debates with Fuller and Dworkin, in which legal reasoning was a primary axis of controversy."

9. Realist uncertainty could thereby be managed and "domesticated" by Hart, albeit significantly altered from the actual realist accounts. Altman, "Legal Realism, Critical Legal Studies, and Dworkin." Altman did not have access to the long-missing and recently published paper entitled "Discretion" that Hart presented at Harvard Law School in 1956, his closest text to an examination of legal uncertainty, "where arguments in favour of one decision or another may be rational without being conclusive," 665. Hart chose not to elaborate on this in his response to Dworkin; Nicola Lacey concluded that "Hart seemed unwilling in his later work to explain how the broader constraining criteria that rebut the rule of law objection to

In chapter 4, I compared Holmes's perspective on legal inquiry with navigating a "roiled ocean." If law is seen as a dynamic process, legal terms like rights, duties, and rules refer to phenomena that are not merely "moving," but constantly emerging, and subject to revision. If the ocean metaphor suggests a body, it is one in a constant state of local "movement," disturbed by novel and recalcitrant experience, continually challenging any putative conceptual order in piecemeal fashion, not all at once. New experience leads to novel cases, creating localized doubt, which for Peirce is the engine that drives scientific inquiry. Peirce did not see natural science as a solid and static body of knowledge; in later years he would describe it as a like a "bog": it is "not standing upon a bedrock of fact. It is walking upon a bog, and [I] can only say, this ground seems to hold for the present. Here I will stay till it begins to give way."[10]

Like the bog, the ocean metaphor is not perfect; liquidity undermines the importance of sustained inquiry in *hardening* and *stabilizing* its results. But deferring that, how did "positivism" get its association with Hart's strict separation of law and morals? The association with the term "positivism" comes from Auguste Comte, and it gained currency in law with the influence of John Austin. Wolfgang Friedmann of Columbia University has connected legal positivism to a more recent context, "[t]he conflict between those thinkers who construct the world from a priori concepts and ideas, and those who

---

discretion could be accommodated within the identifying criteria of his rule of recognition." Lacey, "The Path Not Taken: H. L. A. Hart's Harvard Essay on Discretion," 644.

10. Charles Hartshorne and Paul Weiss, eds., *Collected Papers of Charles Sanders Peirce*, 5:589. The ocean image suggests a region with constant but localized change, like "weather," a metaphor favored by Chauncey Wright in describing the cosmos. The weather metaphor will serve (cautiously) to avoid positing any distinct Holmesian boundary around law suggesting an autonomous, coherent, or static entity. Nancy Cartwright proposes a vision of scientific theory (which she calls "metaphysical nomological pluralism"; *The Dappled World*, 31) that resembles the roiling ocean of Holmes's law:

> [W]e live in a dappled world, a world rich in different things, with different natures, behaving in different ways. The laws that describe this world are a patchwork, not a pyramid. They do not take after the simple, elegant and abstract structure of a system of axioms and theorems. Rather they look like—and steadfastly stick to looking like—science as we know it: apportioned into disciplines, apparently arbitrarily grown up; governing different sets of properties at different levels of abstraction; pockets of great precision; large parcels of qualitative maxims resisting precise formulation; erratic overlaps; here and there, once in a while, corners that line up, but mostly ragged edges; and always the cover of law just loosely attached to the jumbled world of material things. (Ibid., 1)

regard matter as prior to ideas," thus reflecting both "the scope and heightened importance of science on one hand, and—in political philosophy and legal theory—the rise of the modern state on the other hand."[11]

As noted earlier, Holmes's supposed positivism derives in the literature largely from his 1897 address to Boston University law students, "The Path of the Law" (or "Path"). There he repeatedly associated law with "prediction" and said "the prophecies of what the courts will do in fact, and nothing more pretentious, are what I mean by the law." This address has consistently been misinterpreted as expressing a view comparable to that of his friend John Chipman Gray (who in 1909 defined law as judicial conduct in *The Nature and Sources of the Law*) and later Jerome Frank, writing in *Law and the Modern Mind* that law is *equivalent* to the set of all judicial decisions, to the cumulative behavior of legal officials.[12]

Holmes had first used the word "prophecies" in July of 1872 (in between writing his two papers on legal induction) in a book review responding to John Austin's definition of law as a set of sovereign commands; he wrote there that the practicing lawyer (like the law student, but not necessarily the legal *theorist*) is concerned with prediction in this sense. This brief early comment assessed the various influences on judging as not limited to authoritative legal texts, thereby denying a discrete global textual realm. It was quickly followed by his essay in October rejecting the "latitudinal" perspective in favor of a "longitudinal" one, which then led to the historical turn, developed in the April 1876 essay that he sent to Emerson. The next four years were spent rounding out the historical context of induction, finalized in 1880 by his Lowell Lectures, published as *The Common Law*.[13] This background supports a reading of the 1897 "Path" that is quite distinct from Hart's positivism.

The essay opens with the observation, "The first thing for a business-like understanding of the matter is to understand its limits, and therefore I think it desirable at once to point out and dispel a confusion between morality and law." As explained in chapter 5, his use of the term "confusion" is easily misunderstood; Holmes meant this in a context where particular

11. Wolfgang Friedmann, *Legal Theory*, 253.

12. John Chipman Gray, *The Nature and Sources of the Law*; Jerome Frank, *Law and the Modern Mind*.

13. Anthony d'Amato disputes the "standard interpretation" of Holmes's prediction theory as focused on the judge, rather than what he calls the "quantum interpretation" focused on the attorney. Anthony d'Amato, "A New (and Better) Interpretation of Holmes's Prediction Theory of Law."

judgments of prudence or foreseeability may converge toward an accepted community standard to become embodied in a rule. The confusion refers to words that suggest moral judgment, like "malice." That theme was repeated throughout *The Common Law*: "malice" in criminal law is simply a heightened standard of imprudent conduct; "[d]eceit is a notion drawn from the moral world, and in its popular sense distinctly imports wickedness" but "consists in uttering certain words" in a context of foreseeable consequences.[14]

Unfortunately, Holmes restated this point in "Path" as follows:

> The law is full of phraseology drawn from morals, and by the mere force of language continually invites us to pass from one domain to the other, without perceiving it, as we are sure to do unless we have the boundary constantly before our minds. The law talks about rights, and duties, and malice, and intent, and negligence, and so forth, and nothing is easier, or, I may say more common in legal reasoning, than to take these words in their moral sense, at some state of the argument, and so to drop into a fallacy.[15]

Holmes's use of the notion of a "boundary" here refers not to separate worlds of law and morals, but to verbal meanings. But his language appears to have increased concern among the law faculty at Harvard in the years after Fuller's 1940 attack, aimed not just at Holmes but at the positivist separation in general.

In the decade before Hart's 1957 Holmes Lecture, the issue of Holmes's supposed positivism was already being debated, with Holmes's biographer, Professor Mark De Wolfe Howe, writing in the 1951 *Harvard Law Review* an extended response to Fuller's 1940 criticism. Fuller had characterized Holmes as "the American father of legal positivism." Howe cited in mitigation the comment (early on in "Path") that law is "the witness and external deposit of our moral life." But Howe made an unfortunate concession; addressing what he called "the considerations which led Holmes to *accept* [my italics] the positivist theory of law," Howe explained that Holmes had "shaken off" religious faith and "learned from the War that personal taste in morals does not establish universal or objective truth in ethics." His war experience shook what Howe assumed to be the "stagnant compla-

14. Holmes, *Common Law*, 52, 106; *CW*, 3:146–47, 182

15. Holmes, "The Path of the Law," *CW*, 3:392.

cency" of the intellectual climate in Cambridge and Boston, particularly the "world of legal theory."[16]

Howe vastly overstated the "complacency" of the post–Civil War intellectual climate as one of residual Calvinist doctrine. The discussions of Holmes and his friends had some bearing on religion, but were anything but complacent. Inferring too much from an 1860 disciplinary reprimand of Holmes by Professor Bowen,[17] Howe associated Bowen (later recognized by Bruce Kuklick as having laid the foundation for academic philosophy at Harvard) with this religion-based "complacency," connecting it with "Harvard's stubborn assurance that reason and morality, religion and piety had discovered the final answers to the mysteries of the universe."[18]

Also overconstrued by Howe was a much later Memorial Day speech by Holmes in 1895, in which he said (in the context of war and conflict), "I do not know what is true. I do not know the meaning of the universe." This echoed Chauncey Wright's denial of any privileged teleological perspective on the cosmos.[19] In fairness, Howe did not have the advantage of later scholarship on Wright and Peirce, including publication of the early volumes of the chronological edition of the massive papers of Peirce, accompanied by steadily increasing interest in American pragmatism as it had emerged through Wright, Peirce, James, and the Metaphysical Club. Thus the debate over Holmes at Harvard Law School was blind to their intense and formative engagement with early modern philosophy, sharpened as it was by Darwin's evolution, in the same city, just eighty-five years earlier.

As a result, Howe interpreted Holmes's later attitude as "not to be found in the maturing process of the intervening years" but "in the drama of the civil war itself." Howe concluded:

> Professor Fuller, with others, treats Holmes' definition of law—the prediction of what the courts will do in fact—as another aspect of the positivists' refusal to let conceptions of morality play their *appropriate* [my italics] part in the legal process.[20]

16. Howe, "The Positivism of Mr. Justice Holmes," 537–38.

17. Ibid., 534; Howe, *Shaping Years*, 62.

18. Howe, "The Positivism of Mr. Justice Holmes," 534; Kuklick, *The Rise of American Philosophy*, xv–xvi, 28–45.

19. Edward Madden, *Chauncey Wright and the Foundations of Pragmatism*, 88.

20. Howe, "The Positivism of Mr. Justice Holmes," 542. Another statement by Howe shows how the argument over separation presents a false imagery dominating the entire debate:

The idea here is that moral conceptions must cross a *real* boundary. Talk of boundaries dominated the Harvard conversation, thereby reifying the two areas as distinct. This made it harder to see Holmes's unconventional view of the "appropriate" role of moral conceptions, because even in *denying* any separation there crept in a tacit admission of distinctness. For both sides, the question was whether and how moral conceptions might cross the line into the separate world of law. For Holmes, however, moral conceptions develop in a coordinate relationship with legal inquiry, in a society in which they are constantly contested, and where final choices among them are not the sole province of the judiciary. Hence Holmes's caution in "Path" against viewing moral language as inviting moral choices by the profession. This will become clearer below, when I get to Ronald Dworkin's advocacy, in uncertain cases, of judges' drawing upon moral principles.

Fuller's attack on Holmes had come from a very different place than that of Albert Alschuler in 1999. In accusing Holmes of a "law without values," Alschuler blamed Holmes for banishing values from interpretation of legal meaning, and so setting a *bad example*. Alschuler's book gives little clarity to his own alternative view, other than decrying the "slide" from moral realism to moral relativism (which he associates with "pragmatism") in the late nineteenth century. The symptoms of this slide include "skepticism of the academy," the "nation's sullen mood," the "politics of resentment," "selfish consumerism," "homelessness," and "juvenile homicide," although he concedes, "One cannot blame teen pregnancies on Oliver Wendell Holmes." Alschuler continues, "The intellectual revolution that Holmes helped to spark has affected nearly every field of knowledge, and this revolution surely would have happened without him." Alschuler's hyperbole aside (and I am hardly innocent of that practice), how does, or might, some other view of law correct any such slide, or have a cogent effect on "morals"? The only causal link that Alschuler suggests is that if the decider of the uncertain case doesn't have unrestricted access to moral propositions, morals will then be unavailable to the law in general.[21]

> If my efforts thus far have met with any success, I trust that I have demonstrated that Holmes did not deny that a primary source of law is the realm of moral standards in which society has its being, and that he considered the first responsibility of the lawyer and judge to be that of bringing the law into conformity with those moral standards. (Ibid., 544)

This assumes, of course, that the relevant moral standards are uncontested.

21. Alschuler, *Law without Values*, 132–80, 187–94. See Brian Leiter, *Objectivity in Law and Morals*.

Mark Howe had addressed this type of claim when he wrote in 1951:

> Those persons whose articles of faith include the conviction that the Law of Nature has real existence and that virtue as we conceive it lies at the heart of reality, are compelled, of course, to believe that *when Holmes repudiated the absolute in morals, he destroyed the ethical foundations of the law* [my italics]. For those of us, however, who doubt the cosmic significance of human values, I wonder whether the rejection of the absolute necessarily entails such destructive consequences. May not the value which is merely human have an influence on law as decisive as that which is gloriously absolute?[22]

This raises questions concerning *foundations*: does Holmes's theory close off *any* objective grounding for law, any ascent through legal inquiry to larger questions, and does his conception contemplate room for moral progress and validation?

I hope to show by the end of this book that Holmes did not (as Howe says) "doubt the cosmic significance of human values." Howe's defense of Holmes took the position that he did not have, or even need, *any* foundational view: that he was basically agnostic, but that this was harmless when considering that "human values" can be just as "constructive" as "absolutes." On whether he "repudiated the absolute in morals," there is no suggestion that Holmes was not a moral individual; it was unclear at Harvard precisely in what way he was perceived to *repudiate* the absolute, rather than (as I will claim in chapter 10) *reconceive* it.

As an advance on this, I suggest we examine how his overall view compares in practical effect to that of his chief moral critic, Lon Fuller. As Robert Gordon writes, careful attention to legal history can have the effect of "recovering suppressed alternatives."[23] In addressing the questions raised by the debate over Holmes and positivism, the most surprising conclusion will be how close Lon Fuller's theory of law, considered as a whole, actually was to Holmes's implicit social perspective, despite Fuller's harsh criticism and continuing negative influence on Holmes's legacy.

Kenneth Winston has demonstrated how Fuller offered a richer account of the multiple relations of law and morality than many other jurisprudential writers. His account is based upon Fuller's conception "that law is the work of its everyday participants, a continuous effort to construct

22. Howe, "The Positivism of Mr. Justice Holmes," 544.
23. Gordon, "The Past as Authority and as Social Critic," 364.

and sustain a common institutional framework to meet the exigencies of a shared existence, to resolve current conflicts, and in general to realize the aspiration of just and harmonious relations among citizens."[24] Lawyers should be willing to be, if not social activists, constant workers for better citizenship.

Both Fuller and Holmes shared a common resistance to the strong thetic posture of an ontological and methodological separation of the two realms, law and morals; both held that there is no sharp boundary around law.[25] Yet in addition to misreading Holmes's terms like "prediction" and "prophecies," Fuller felt strongly that the lawyer's role was poorly delineated in Holmes's advice to the Boston University law students. Telling them to "see the law as the 'bad man' sees it" was antithetical to Fuller's meliorist vision. I suggest that if Fuller had appreciated Holmes's revised Millian inductivism, he might have been more sympathetic.[26]

Fuller's overriding concern was for lawyers to promote patterns of reciprocal expectations and actions; this purpose is fulfilled in the function Holmes gave not to the legal profession alone, but to the social continuum of inquiry, which is promoted by their participation in the inductive common law method. Fuller saw meliorism as a volunteered element, while Holmes viewed it as necessarily generated and maintained with the aid of legal inquiry, in conjunction with cognate processes of inquiry outside the legal process.[27] The difference is an empirical one: how much of the

24. Kenneth Winston, ed., *The Principles of Social Order: Selected Essays of Lon L. Fuller*, 1, 3.

25. Ibid., 232. Opposing the idea of strict separation was Fuller's "interactive" view of the relation between law and society, developed from insights dating back to the 1940 *Law in Quest of Itself*. See also Fuller, "American Legal Philosophy at Mid-Century," 457–85 (whether a social arrangement counts as legal is matter of degree). See generally Postema, *Treatise of Legal Philosophy*, 141–62.

26. Fuller emphasized reciprocity with lawmakers in a community-wide custom of obedience not just of courts and officials. Winston, *The Principles of Social Order: Selected Essays of Lon Fuller*, 188. He did not accept the "momentary legal system" of analytical theory; "law is not a datum, but an achievement that ever needs to be renewed." "American Legal Philosophy at Mid-Century," 467. In replying to analytical critics in 1969, Fuller criticized the positivist position for "recogniz[ing] in the functioning of a legal system nothing that can truly be called a *social dimension*. The positivist sees the law at the point of its dispatch by the lawgiver and again at the point of its impact on the legal subject. He does not see the lawgiver and the citizen in interaction with one another, and by virtue of that failure he fails to see that the creation of an effective interaction between them is an essential ingredient of the law itself." *Morality of Law*, 193.

27. Both Fuller and Holmes recognized the influence of law upon operations in society; meliorist patterns do not always arise "tacitly" out of human interaction, and in cases of legal

necessary coordination, and advancement of human purposes, depends on the legal profession?

The difference boils down to the precise role of the lawyer. Fuller recommended a much more activist role for the practicing lawyer than Holmes. The private practice of law had greatly changed by Fuller's time, after the vast growth of bureaucratic government following mobilization for two world wars, urbanization, and the complexity and diversity of community life. Fuller's passionate opposition to legal positivism was driven in large part by his desire for engagement by lawyers with the social concerns on which a good legal order depends.

Fuller's vision was concisely stated in an untitled paper discovered and published by Winston:

> In recommending a philosophic approach for legal education, I do not mean that we should increase our pretensions to cosmic understanding. I mean merely that we need to become aware of, and reflective about, the ends of law and government. . . .
>
> We need a philosophic awakening that will put law in its proper place in the human struggle to achieve order and justice and will see it as a part of the eternal quest for those principles that will enable us to live and work together in harmony. This philosophic quest should I believe, dominate the law school curriculum from the beginning to the end.[28]

This attitude is not so radically opposed to that of the unsigned note regarding Harvard Law School that Holmes cowrote in 1870 with Arthur Sedgwick, five years after leaving Harvard to study law as an apprentice under attorney Robert Morse:

> The object of a law department is not precisely and only to educate young men to be practicing lawyers, though it will be largely used for that purpose. It is to furnish all students who desire it the same facilities to investigate the science of human law, theoretically, historically, and thoroughly, as they have to investigate mathematics, natural sciences, or any other branch of thought.[29]

---

conflict the process must engage them and assure that anticipations congeal into behavior. Both saw law as adjusting reciprocal interactive expectations.

28. Kenneth Winston, *The Principles of Social Order: Selected Essays of Lon Fuller*, 305.

29. Howe, *The Shaping Years*, 206.

Holmes, I submit, also urged a "philosophical awakening" in legal education. If he could have transformed it to suit his own interests in 1870, he might have begun with the problematic of early modern philosophy and the methods of science, Mill's Baconian meliorist induction, and the controversy over conceptualization between Mill and Whewell. He would obviously have emphasized legal history, interpreted through his own recent experience of conflict; this would have addressed Fuller's goal to "put law in its proper place in the human struggle to achieve order and justice." To be sure, he would have added what has always looked to many like "skepticism" from his experience with a conflict that had afflicted all of society. But sixty years later, when asked about this famous skepticism, Holmes told Morris Cohen that it came from *science*.[30]

Throughout *The Common Law* as well as in "Path," Holmes reminds the reader of his main point: "Moral predilections must not be allowed to influence our minds in *settling legal distinctions* [my italics]." This is a reference to the inductive line-drawing method of determining the meaning and reference of a disputed term, rather than of importing content from general normative propositions.[31] To illustrate, recall the sources of Holmes's legal inductivism. The motivation that drove Mill to write his ("ostensibly apolitical"[32]) *System of Logic* was induction, with a Baconian aversion to thinking from axioms, against which he stressed and radically privileged the importance of particular experience. As Mill wrote in his 1873 *Autobiography*:

> The notion that truths external to the mind may be known by intuition or consciousness, independently of observation and experience, is, I am persuaded, in these times, the great intellectual support of false doctrines and bad institutions.

30. Ibid., 17–18; It came from "the scientific way of looking at the world. . . . My father was brought up scientifically . . . and I was not. Yet there was with him, as with the rest of his generation, a certain softness of attitude toward the interstitial miracle—the phenomenon without phenomenal antecedents, that I did not feel. . . . probably a skeptical temperament that I got from my mother and something to do with my way of thinking. . . . But I think science was at the bottom."

31. Toward the end of *The Common Law*, Holmes summarized, "[A]s has been said before in these Lectures, although the law starts from the distinctions and uses the language of morality, it necessarily ends in external standards not dependent on the actual consciousness of the individual." *CW*, 3:280–81. Although Holmes referred to law and morals as "two domains," he meant a critique of "moral terminology"—*not* a global separation of law and morals.

32. See Snyder, *Reforming Philosophy*, 2.

> By the aid of this theory, every inveterate belief and every intense feeling, of which the origin is not remembered, is enabled to dispense with the obligation of justifying itself by reason, and is erected into its own self-sufficient voucher and justification. There never was such an instrument devised for consecrating all deep-seated prejudices.[33]

"Intuitionism" was the view that Mill associated with Samuel Taylor Coleridge, that there are certain truths known to the mind whose source was *not* experience, and which could only erroneously be recognized as necessary truths. Mill held that intuitionism wrongly validated taking what is *deeply believed* to be *true*, and thus was an impediment to reform. This led Mill to radicalize induction, denying any *a priori* contribution of the mind, lest the door be opened to intuitionism and its reactionary consequences.[34]

Mill's radical induction introduced a lean mental picture of induction itself, with its minimal vision of the *conceptual* element, conceived as a set of virtual containers (my term, not his) of particulars, expressed in his view that "individual cases are all the evidence we can possess."[35] This was the ground of his opposition to Whewell; Mill's *Autobiography* reports that Whewell's publication in 1837 of the *History of the Inductive Sciences* (which Holmes would read in 1866) had motivated him to overcome a five-year impasse over the problem of induction and finally to finish his influential *Logic*.[36]

I noted earlier that Mill's view was too spare for Peirce, who preferred Whewell's account of the contested relation of facts and ideas, and who later came to describe the introduction of concepts as "abduction." Mill's view was too minimal also for Holmes, who, while suggesting something akin to the virtual container in his remark (in the 1899 address to New York lawyers), "we must think things not words," nevertheless created

33. Mill, *Autobiography*, 96.

34. Snyder, *Reforming Philosophy*, 2, 100, 127, 134, 156. Mill thought intuitionism supported slavery: "I have long felt that the prevailing tendency to regard all the marked distinctions of human character as innate, and in the main indelible, and to ignore the irresistible proofs that by far the greater part of those differences, whether between individuals, races, or sexes, are such as not only might but naturally would be produced by differences in circumstances, is one of the chief hindrances to the rational treatment of great social questions, and one of its greatest stumbling blocks to human improvement. This tendency has its source in the intuitional metaphysics." Mill, *Autobiography*, *CW*, 1:270.

35. Mill, *Logic* 2:215.

36. Mill, *Autobiography*, 124; Snyder, *Reforming Philosophy*, 98.

room for the general concept as a product of dispute, emergent and revisable within the space of contested reasons, the latter conceived (and "naturalized") as "clusters" of judgments.

How then does Holmes's aversion to "general propositions" compare to Mill's opposition to intuitionism? Recall Holmes's comment in the 1899 essay that law embodies the ideas and ideals of society that "have been strong enough to reach that final form of expression." I have suggested that this implies a theory of entrenchment. His attitude toward general propositions depends upon where they lie in the social continuum of inquiry. Where the case represents a new controversy, the general proposition does not decide it, as "hollow deductions from empty general propositions"[37] will throw the judges off the inductive trail, as in the Massachusetts labor cases. Holmes seems not to have denied "intuition" entirely, recognizing entrenched ideas and ideals without which society could not function, appearing in the garb of "final form." The question is, what "final form" do they take?[38]

With this in mind let me turn to an issue crucial not just to legal theory but also to the contemporary problem of polarization on the nation's courts. How are general principles conceived to operate in the wake of Hart's positivism? Ronald Dworkin famously argued, in his early essays critical of Hart's positivism, that lawyers and judges do (and by inference therefore properly *should*) bring principles to bear in cases that are uncertain, in roughly the way that they were seen at Harvard in the 1950s: bringing them across a boundary, wherever the settled core meaning of the contemporary set of understandings has presumably expired, and where a controversial case appears to sit outside that imagined conceptual boundary.[39]

Two remarkable things happened in the wake of Dworkin's challenge to Hart. One is that Holmes's well-known resistance to general propositions was entirely ignored (as was the root question of induction in legal logic[40]), and the other is that Dworkin's claim not only went largely unchallenged

37. Holmes, "Privilege, Malice and Intent," *CW*, 373.

38. It would seem from Holmes's treatment that principles cannot take final form as general propositions; Holmes opposed this in the labor dissents, *Lochner v. New York*, and *Abrams v. United States*.

39. Postema, *Treatise of Legal Philosophy*, 404–6.

40. The dominant mode of analysis has been the dualism of legal formalism and legal realism. This will be addressed in the following chapter. See, e.g., Richard Posner, *Reflections on Judging*.

but was adopted as a "datum." Hart's followers, despite their disagreements with Dworkin, largely accepted his claim of judicial recourse to principle. Hart himself, followed by other positivists, accepted Dworkin's account of the binding force of principle in uncertain cases, even while holding firm to the positivist belief that this did not require morals to be carried across the boundary. While Dworkin's argument left the faith of most positivists unshaken, it also led to a division in the positivist camp between "hard" positivists, who considered principles to be within the source-based boundary around law, and "soft" positivists, who accepted their distinctly moral nature.[41]

As we have seen, for Holmes uncertainty was not purely a function of the reach of authoritative texts, but came from the novelty of the case in comparison with prior classifications. In that regard, the novel or "first" case (as Alexander Bickel calls it in *The Least Dangerous Branch*) was precisely where reaching for general principle is least appropriate, given the respect the Supreme Court should have for democratic values. A similar view of the early case was the factor motivating Holmes to dissent in the Massachusetts labor cases, where he opposed reliance upon the "contract" clause of the Massachusetts constitution because it foreclosed inquiry into the emergent issues of labor organizing. He dissented later on the same ground in *Lochner v. New York*, where the majority of the Supreme Court sought to block democratically enacted labor reform legislation, as inconsistent with the contract clause of the U.S. Constitution.[42]

In his *Lochner* dissent, Holmes made a point that should help understand his conception of entrenchment:

> It is settled by various decisions of this Court that State constitutions and State laws may regulate life in any ways which we as legislators might think as injudicious or, if you like, as tyrannical as this, and which equally with this interfere with the liberty to contract. Sunday laws and usury laws are ancient examples.

41. Postema, *Treatise of Legal Philosophy*, 408, 457–82 (on the "Incorporation Debate"). Critics rarely disputed the main premise that principles play a pervasive role in legal reasoning. As a "hard" positivist, Joseph Raz, defending the positivist "pedigree" thesis, claimed it is one thing for a principle to be binding on a judge, and another thing to be binding by virtue of being part of the law. Ibid., 407. See also Jeremy Waldron, "The Irrelevance of Moral Objectivity," questioning whether incorporation *vel non* made any difference, 158.

42. But see Anthony Woodiwiss, *Rights v. Conspiracy: A Sociological Essay on the History of Labour Law in the United States*, on the prior history of decisions regarding organized labor cases.

> A more modern one is the prohibition of lotteries. The liberty of the citizen to do as he likes so long as he does not interfere with the liberty of others to do the same, which has been a shibboleth for some well-known writers, is interfered with by school laws, by the Post Office, by every State or municipal institution which takes his money for purposes thought desirable, whether he likes it or not. The Fourteenth Amendment does not enact Mr. Herbert Spencer's *Social Statics*.[43]

In effect, the more general the terms of a proposition, the farther it extends, and the more particulars it will encompass, thereby "containing" cases well beyond the scope of known experience. On their face, the general propositions of the Bill of Rights are too general to be employed deductively, as the certain premise of a syllogism.[44]

We might ask how, precisely, Dworkin's own method of principle is conceived to operate. Dworkin claimed that it takes place in three stages, consisting of identification, justification, and reform. In the first (or pre-interpretive) stage, the judge identifies "the relevant rules and standards taken to provide the tentative content of the practice." The second (interpretive) stage is one of constructing a theory of "why a practice of that general shape is worth pursuing, if it is"; the judge must "settle on some general justification for the main elements of the practice." Note here that Dworkin ignores the possibility that competing or conflicting practices might be involved in a lawsuit; he says the judge must "see himself as interpreting that [singular] practice, not inventing a new one." The third stage is "reforming" and "post-interpretive"; the judge "adjusts his sense of what *the* [my italics] practice 'really' requires, so as better to serve the justification he accepts at the interpretive stage." Here the judge puts "the practice," and the scheme of values or principles "the" practice can be said to serve, in its "best light." The practice is what the best interpretive theory says it is.[45]

Dworkin emphasizes the need for achieving "consensus" to resolve the "inevitable controversy, even among contemporaries" over the "exact

43. *Lochner v. New York* 198 U.S. 45, 74 (1905).

44. This recognizes a distinction between entrenched principles and their general expression in a constitutional document. How propositions expressing constitutional rights are applied is discussed in the final chapter.

45. Dworkin, *Law's Empire*, 66–67; Postema, *Treatise of Legal Philosophy*, 430. It is not clear from Dworkin's account what standard he assumes for that which is "best," and how different standards privileging distinct purposes are to be reconciled.

dimensions of the practice they all interpret." This barely gives even lip service to the prospect that the "controversy" in a legal case has arisen from (often bitterly) opposed plural practices, suggesting that these can be "interpreted" in a courtroom, all at once, as a judicial redescription of a *singular* practice. If that practice is what the best interpretive theory says it is, then Dworkin obliges the judge to settle any controversy by simply imposing a "theory."[46]

Dworkin's stages of interpretation are comparable to what might, under favorable conditions, take place *over time* in the hoped-for convergence of Holmes's continuum of inquiry. Llewellyn described the best appellate decisions as successfully honing in on the appropriate "situation sense." This sounds similar to Dworkin's description of the first stage, in which the judge determines what those informed and active participants *say* is paradigmatic of a practice. But Dworkin makes this sound plausible for articulation by an individual judge, in defining the situation as a *singular* practice, rather than presented in a contested account recognizing the clash of *alternative practices*. His second or interpretive stage sounds like a further exploration of Llewellyn's "situation," putting the practice in its "best light." This stage includes assessing the competing eligible theories to see which "fits the data" and has a unique quality Dworkin calls "moral appeal." But here two distinct problems are elided. If the sense of the situation is itself contested, then (as Edward Levi and Alexander Bickel sought to demonstrate) further experience and choices have to be encountered before it is "identified in its best light."

The critical difference between Dworkin's "stages," in *one* judge's (or court's) inquiry, and the successive stages of Holmes, is that, although Dworkin describes them as stages, they are part of an immediate judgment. There can be, sometimes, instances where the larger problem can be resolved at

46. Rawls's practice conception of rules was mentioned in chap. 2, n. 9; chap. 3, n. 7; and chap. 5, n. 5; and distinguished from the "summary" view that in cases of certain kinds the same decision will be made, either by the same person at different times or by different persons at the same time (such that if a case occurs frequently enough one supposes that a rule is formulated to cover that sort of case). In the practice conception, rules are pictured as defining a practice, not as summary generalizations from the decisions of individuals applying instrumental or utilitarian principles directly and independently to recurrent particular cases. Where rules define a practice and are themselves the subject of utilitarian principles, no accommodation between competing rules is possible by simply making exceptions. A new practice must be articulated and accepted by the community as a whole. Rawls, "Two Concepts of Rules," 162–67.

once;[47] but there are many more that require time and wider experience, both of which are foreclosed even to the most omniscient judge. Dworkin overrelies on the opposition of legal arguments, which he presumes can bring every relevant consideration to bear, ignoring underlying conflicts that remain intransigeant. Dworkin's conceived resolution through opposing arguments of counsel is less than fully participatory. Even if the arguments somehow included all relevant considerations, reasoning would still rely on the supremely unnatural powers of his mythical judge "Hercules," capable not just of seeing any situation in its "best light," but of articulating its consistency with the governing idea of integrity.

Dworkin's argument from principle has yet to encounter any strong resistance from the standpoint of the empirical tradition of Bacon and Mill. It runs counter to the recent current of particularism in ethical theory, a philosophical critique of principle that will be discussed in the next chapter. The overwhelming acceptance of his view among legal theorists, of recourse to principle as a "datum" of law, reflects an ill-articulated rhetorical form of realism; that "principles" (ill defined though they may be) have a present and causal existence, simply because the legal profession deploys them in legal advocacy.

The view assumes that any difficult judgment, underlying the determination of whether the law applies to an uncertain case, is always in some important degree deductive, open to comparison of propositional content (the "black letter" law, authoritative texts, or the background of legal and moral principles) to the facts at hand. Dworkin does not escape the fundamental deductivism of an analytical positivist model, but depends upon it for his assumption that clear law in a hard case may simply "run out," giving lawyers and judges access to principles. This underlies his notion of constructive interpretation, and his theory of law as grounded in "integrity."[48]

47. What I have described as the continuum of inquiry was helpfully discussed in 2013 by the Legal Theory Research Group at the Edinburgh Law School, where several "knotty" problems of its precise nature and definition were raised that are not addressed here. Legal problems that take place within a broader social continuum of inquiry are diverse, and while the duration may be seen as extended, as in Levi's example of the inherently dangerous rule, it may also be short in matters resolvable by the judiciary at an early instance. Kellogg, "What Precisely Is a 'Hard' Case?," 28.

48. Dworkin, *Law's Empire*, 225–75. In *Law's Empire* Dworkin widened the scope of his criticism of Hart and proposed an alternative "third conception" of law, stressing as a distinction from positivism that the law is fundamentally argumentative (the "argument from con-

Dworkin's view of law as enabling critical, justice-focused politics, and providing a "forum of principle" for deciding the most important issues of justice, translates into turning responsibility for public reason over to the courts.

> Hard cases arise, for any judge, when his threshold test does not discriminate between two or more interpretations of some statue or line of cases. Then he must choose between eligible interpretations by asking which shows the community's structure of institutions and decisions—its public standards as a whole—in a better light from the standpoint of political morality. His own moral and political convictions are now directly engaged. But the political judgment he must make is itself complex and will sometimes set one department of his political morality against another: his decision will reflect not only his opinions about justice and fairness but his higher order convictions about how these ideals should be compromised when they compete.[49]

The social networks of judges and lawyers will always be somewhat insulated from the concerns of much of the population. Tradition and practice prevent having a representative from every minority, much less every major economic or social interest group, represented in the federal circuit courts of appeal, much less on a nine-member Supreme Court. Even the ability to monitor the debate over principle is diminished by rules against television cameras in the courtroom. Dworkin extends the rule of judicial

troversy") affecting all aspects of law including Hart's rule of recognition. While positivism held that law could be described by criterial semantics, Dworkin held that disagreement is common among lawyers about the ground rules—the very rules that are supposed to establish the grounds of propositions of law. Positivism could accommodate principle by emphasizing method, or methodological positivism, based as it was on the rule of recognition, and also the distinction positivists made between neutral analytic jurisprudence and engaged moral inquiry and argument. Dworkin countered that argument was pervasive and theoretical (in "justificatory ascent" from particular cases and issues): "[N]o firm line divides jurisprudence from adjudication," which is the "silent prologue to any decision at law." Throughout its history judges in the American legal system treated the techniques they use "for interpreting statutes and measuring precedent—even those no one challenges—not simply as tools handed down by the traditions of their ancient craft but as principles they assume can be justified in some deeper political theory, and when they come to doubt this, for whatever reason, they construct theories that seem to them better." *Law's Empire*, 139.

49. Ibid., 255–56.

reason to its absolute limit, incorporating moral and political theory into the realm of adjudication.[50]

Writing before the politicization of judging had reached its current scale, Herbert Hart believed deeply that there existed articulable standards constraining the exercise of judicial discretion, and that they were part of the law. An early essay in defense of his position at Harvard, addressed to scholars of the American legal process school, conceived of constraints on judicial discretion as institutional, grounded in the history of legal inquiry, and controlled by an understanding of the specific purposes in view. This approach Hart later largely downplayed, and in any event it was not capable of withstanding Dworkin's assault.[51] It is mentioned in his 1973 essay "American Jurisprudence through English Eyes: The Nightmare and the Noble Dream," where Hart divided American jurisprudence into two camps: those who see the hard case as legally indeterminate, so that judges must "legislate" (the "nightmare"), and those like Dworkin who deny the notion of judicial legislation but "dream" that there is always a right answer to be found in the background realm of moral principles. Viewing the history of American legal theory, as seesawing from deductive "formalism" to "realism" and back again, Hart suggested that we are stuck in a never-ending "oscillation" between extremes. Dworkin, he concluded, is "the noblest dreamer of them all."[52]

50. Dworkin's judiciary virtually takes over the role of public reason found in the work of John Rawls, *A Theory of Justice*, and public discourse in Jürgen Habermas, *Between Facts and Norms*.

51. Process theorists used the study of "comparative institutional analysis" to infer normative requirements binding legal officials. Cases like the desegregation decision in *Brown v. Board of Education* suggested a much more potent role for courts than the process theorists had envisioned; Dworkin claimed that this could only be guided by principle. Hart's 1956 view of discretion addressed the problem of indeterminacy with the assumption that experts in legal traditions and institutional design could somehow resolve it through "insights into judicial behavior, institutional design, and social reality," because "society's ability to regulate the future is inherently limited by imperfect information and an imperfect understanding of aims." Geoffrey Shaw, "H. L. A. Hart's Lost Essay," 669, 677, 681. For Holmes, "aims" and "social realities" were emergent, and not accessible to experts where genuine novelty was involved and the outcome was contested.

52. Hart, *Essays in Jurisprudence and Philosophy*, 144, 137.

CHAPTER NINE

Logical Theory

This chapter traces the development of Holmes's social inductivism to elucidate what Hart saw as an "oscillation" between the "Nightmare" of realism versus the "Noble Dream" of formalism in American jurisprudence, and to clarify its import for logical theory.

* * *

[T]he gradual revolution that is taking place in society and institutions has, thus far, been decidedly favourable to the development of new opinions, and has procured for them a much more unprejudiced hearing than they previously met with. But this is a feature belonging to periods of transition, when old notions and feelings have been unsettled, and no new doctrines have yet succeeded to their ascendancy. At such times people of any mental activity, having given up their old beliefs, and not feeling quite sure that those they still retain can stand unmodified, listen eagerly to new opinions. But this state of things is necessarily transitory: some particular body of doctrine in time rallies the majority round it, organizes social institutions and modes of action conformably to itself, education impresses this new creed upon the new generations without the mental processes that have led to it, and by degrees it acquires the very same power of compression, so long exercised by the creeds of which it had taken the place.—John Stuart Mill, *Autobiography*

The above quote, from Mill's *Autobiography*, serves nicely to put Holmes's theory in historical perspective, as it, too (along with Whewell's history and philosophy of science), contains a "germ" of the continuum of social inquiry that became crucial to Holmes's theory of logical induction. But before considering it, recall the problem that Professor Hart of Oxford identified at the end of the last chapter. American jurisprudence, he wrote in 1973, has "oscillated between two extremes with many intermediate stopping-places. For reasons which I hope will become plain, I shall call these two extremes, respectively, the Nightmare and the Noble Dream." Hart meant by "oscillation" that there is an unstable dichotomy or dualism between seeing the difficult legal case either (1) as if all relevant authoritative legal materials do not extend to it and provide an answer, so it is legally *indeterminate* (the nightmare), or (2) as if the law consists of ample background principles such that the case is somehow always already deductively *covered* (the noble dream).

In this chapter I will review the sources of Holmes's social continuum of inquiry, starting with Mill; but first I want to address a relationship between the real-world operation of the continuum (which Hart could not recognize due to his commitment to a static theoretical perspective on law) and the appearance of *oscillation* that he identified as endemic in American legal theory. The transformative nature of the continuum of inquiry, which operates both on a small scale on particular problems as well as on a long-term historical one, provides an alternative to this oscillation, a way of understanding, if not resolving, the seesawing standoff between two extreme views, which have often characterized the two perspectives commonly known as legal "realism" and "formalism."[1]

You may already have guessed my explanation for Hart's "oscillation": the nightmare is an unyielding commitment to the perspective that appears to the observer of the "early case," the yet *unclassified* particular dispute; hence the illusion of its being "outside" legal authorities and legally indeterminate. This was often the perception of legal realism and critical legal studies, and it is unstable because (as a stage of inquiry) the ground underneath new cases in a continuum of inquiry is constantly shifting. The noble dream is a commitment to an opposite illusion, in which all particular cases already fall under an existing system of normative rules or principles, and are always "preclassified." This was the implication of legal formalism, and underlay the theory of Ronald Dworkin, although he raises the ante: his solution to the problem of the hard case is to see it as a really tough law school exam question, one that only the smartest students can solve, assuming they are totally conversant with the entire range of principles from every relevant field of law, on up to the root principles of Western political philosophy and the founding principles of the American republic.[2]

1. Conventional legal theory is committed to a dualism between formalism and realism, which structures contemporary debates and research on judging. The dualism accepts that judges control legal thought. Brian Tamanaha, in *Beyond the Formalist-Realist Divide: The Role of Politics in Judging*, concludes that it leads to an inevitable dominance of politics in adjudication. Richard Posner recently redefined the dualism in *Reflections on Judging*, emphasizing the importance of experience over legal axioms.

2. The judge must "develop a theory of the constitution, in the shape of a complex set of principles and policies that justify that scheme of government, just as the chess referee is driven to develop a theory about the character of his game. He must develop that theory by

Hart's sense of oscillation derives from imposing a *static* conception of law upon shifting foundations. It results from the notion that there must be *one true theory* of uncertainty. When uncertain cases arise between the logical space of settled legal knowledge, according to the static perspective these cases expose "gaps" left open by the network of legal doctrine. They have to be filled in by judicial "legislation," unless an account can be given whereby they are deducible within a background system of "principles." This attitude assumes that the law has a conceptual boundary and consists of a set of propositional entities. The static perspective carries with it a commitment to the stable and *comprehensive* existence of an immediately apprehendable body of conceptual material, the "body of legal doctrine."[3]

Hart concludes in his essay that "these two are, in my view, illusions, though they have much of value to teach the jurist in his waking hours. The truth, perhaps unexciting, is that sometimes judges do one and sometimes the other. It is not of course a matter of indifference but of very great importance which they do and when and how they do it. That is a topic for another occasion." Although Hart never elaborated on this prescient comment, to the effect that judges "sometimes do one and sometimes the other," it seems clear that Holmes would have agreed with him.

Holmes's diachronic view has an explanatory account of Hart's oscillation. It sees the new case as often arising from conflicts between forms or patterns of prior knowledge and practice. Sometimes resolution might be easy, at other times difficult, depending on the clarity, breadth, and degree of active social commitment to competing schemes or patterns. If a broader conflict awaits legal resolution, that conflict may not necessarily be

---

referring alternately to political philosophy and institutional detail. He must generate possible theories against justifying different aspects of the scheme and test the theories against the broader institution." Dworkin, *Taking Rights Seriously*, 107.

3. The phenomenon of oscillation between opposing theories of uncertainty has been noted in epistemology by Hilary Putnam and John McDowell, in contexts that bear comparison to law. Putnam, in *Reason, Truth and History*, decries the "gestalt switch" between objective and subjective, or internalist and externalist, theories, where (you might say the "nightmare" of) relativism haunts (the "dream" of) objective access to reality; ix–x, 49–54. McDowell, in *Mind and World*, writes: "I have claimed that we are prone to fall into an intolerable oscillation: in one phase we are drawn to an objective reality, and in the other phase we recoil into an appeal to the Given, which turns out to be useless." Ibid., 23. Putnam's and McDowell's coping strategies, like those of analytical legal theorists, fail to consider the influence on the appearance of uncertainty from actual "phases" in the social continuum of inductive inquiry.

summed up within the terms and conditions of one case. Alexander Bickel's troublesome "first case" may be but a limited exemplar, only hinting at the full scope of an emergent problem. Edward Levi demonstrated that it could take a century or more before some troublesome classifications are resolved, if indeed they ever completely are.

The diachronic view advances a different approach to epistemic justification from either formalism or realism. Formalism seeks validation by deduction from accepted principles, while realism often reduces to a subjective behavioral account. The latter is the epistemic nightmare, the former the unrealistic dream. Drawing on analytical foundations, both attribute legal certainty and validation to "common origin or common recognition."[4] Social inductivism seeks validation in the contingent process I have called convergence. This is justification viewed not through a single lens or mind, but through the eventual consensus and active commitment of "many minds," and it relies upon the success of legal inquiry to address the often intricate social interactions that Lon Fuller emphasized.

A caveat is in order. Anyone who has practiced law, and especially trial law, knows that the continuum model cannot account for every kind of legal difficulty and complexity, given the American lawyer's resourcefulness in utilizing any procedural and substantive objection that might either prevail or at least obstruct or delay the day of reckoning for a client. Some cases are more deductive than others; many tax cases arrive as logical puzzles. Administrative law may raise a one-time question of efficiency or uniformity. Statutory cases may implicate questions of legislative purpose. But any case may include an emerging social dispute, one that a legal text, agency, or regulation fails or refuses to resolve.[5]

Meanwhile, jurisdiction has greatly increased under the constitutional "due process" clause, extending to abortion, gender rights, medically assisted death, free expression, religion, private property, even family law and eventually into bioethics. Formalism and realism, the dream and the nightmare, will continue to plague resolution of these issues when presented or left entirely to the judiciary—which they are, by contemporary analytical legal theory. The voluminous literature on legal realism and formalism suggests that, within that paradigm, there is no alternative to

4. Postema, "Law's System," 85; see chap. 8, n. 3.

5. For an analysis of other sources of legal uncertainty, see Brian Bix, *Law, Language, and Legal Determinacy*, and "Indeterminacy and Good Faith: Politics and Legitimacy."

accepting the political dimension of judging.[6] Holmes, Hand, Bickel, and Levi were able to see the flaw of a fixation on judges having ultimate discretion. The assumption that unaided judges must make final decisions, whether as matter of judicial fiat or armchair balancing of competing principles, commits American law to a definitive struggle over the nomination and confirmation of qualified judges.

In his diachronic inductive turn, Holmes does not deny the importance of political choice, but seeks rather to contextualize it in a process of inquiry that can be left either more, or less, open to extralegal feedback, depending upon the nature of the problem and the scope of judicial rationalization. It is a process driven by conflicts, encountered in a succession of stages of understanding (in the emergent "situation sense") and resolution (in the convergence of opposing poles toward a formula). In this view, the relation of case to law (call it the C/L relation, where C is the case and L represents the propositional content of law) is not constant with regard to any given uncertain case. The C/L relation may look more like Hart's nightmare in an early stage, and more like the noble dream in a later one, where judgments of similarity and difference converge. In the process of negotiated convergence, the law pursues the functions of coordination so obviously critical to Lon Fuller.

How did Holmes arrive at this insight, and what is involved in the idea of convergence, a term he did not use? A continuum was already implicit in Mill's thinking, reflected in his *Autobiography*. His liberal and meliorist faith was well known to Holmes and his peers in New England, a confidence that better ideas gain traction from experience and education, and meliorist practice will replace axiomatic creed. In his early reflections on law and philosophy, Holmes may have wondered how to reconcile Mill's account with his own experience. He had joined the Union Army as an abolitionist. Before resigning in 1864 he had become convinced (as he had written to his sister) that the Union cause was hopeless, and that his country would be permanently divided.[7] The contingency of history was on his mind even as he immersed himself in the study of philosophy and law. Mill's meliorist faith itself had to be reconceived.

6. Hart assumed that politics was removed from adjudication by the positivist separation, while realists have accepted that adjudication, especially at the highest level, is ultimately political. Brian Tamanaha writes, "A balanced realism accepts (indeed embraces) that social factors and considerations play into judicial decision making in various ways." *Beyond the Formalist-Realist Divide*, 193.

7. Howe, *The Shaping Years*, 138.

Regarding the meaning of "philosophy" in his 1876 letter to Emerson, consider Mill's own use of the term in his *Autobiography*: "whatever may be the practical value of a true philosophy of these matters," wrote Mill, "it is hardly possible to exaggerate the mischiefs of a false one"—and he commented that as "prejudice can only be successfully combated by philosophy, no way can really be made against it permanently until it has been shown not to have philosophy on its side."[8] Mill's use of the term "philosophy" was the same as Holmes's reference in the letter to Emerson, referring primarily to the empirical tradition.

Mill also records in the *Autobiography* that his reason for writing *A System of Logic* was to refute the "a priori view of human knowledge," and his work was written as a "text-book of the opposite doctrine—that which derives all knowledge from experience."[9] For Bacon and Mill, axioms were a reactionary force. For Holmes after the Civil War, they came from both sides of the national conflict, radical as well as reactionary; the greater danger lay in ideology and polarization. Hence Holmes challenged jurisprudence (1) to remove the definition of legal uncertainty from the uncertain case to the uncertain problem, (2) to transfer dependency on the logic of legal argument to that of underlying conflicts, and (3) to abandon an individualist, judge-centric posture in recognition of the social dimensions of public inquiry. These are the core insights of his theory, and (among all legal theorists) he is almost alone.

His historical explanation in *The Common Law*, of a change from moral to external standards, has widely escaped recognition as holding that particular experience establishes the general rule by specification, and of the social dimension of comparing competing patterns of belief and practice. I have long emphasized that the path of the early essays is essential evidence for his developed philosophy. As Holmes wrote to his friend and former coeditor Arthur Sedgwick in 1879, "My object in writing these articles is

8. Mill, *Autobiography*, 133–34:

> The notion that truths external to the mind may be known by intuition or consciousness, independently of observation and experience, is, I am persuaded, in these times, the great intellectual support of false doctrines and bad institutions. By the aid of this theory, every inveterate belief and every intense feeling, of which the origin is not remembered, is enabled to dispense with the obligation of justifying itself by reason, and is erected into its own self-sufficient voucher and justification. There never was such an instrument devised for consecrating all deep-seated prejudices.

9. Ibid., 133.

to take up from time to time the cardinal principles and conceptions of the law and make a new and more fundamental analysis of them—For the purpose of constructing a new Jurisprudence or New First Book of the law." This is an astonishingly ambitious claim. Perhaps the full significance of what Holmes did in the 1870s has been inaccessible, until other alternatives to jurisprudence have been so exhaustively explored that they can only be characterized as leading either to an impossible "dream," or to a "nightmare."

Let's retrace his sources, starting with the passage heading this chapter where Mill, writing six years after Holmes visited him in London, comments on the climate of changing beliefs and opinions. Mill viewed his era as a "period of transition," and observed that "some particular body of doctrine in time rallies the majority round it, organizes social institutions and modes of action conformably to itself, education impresses this new creed upon the new generations without the mental processes that have led to it, and by degrees it acquires the very same power of compression, so long exercised by the creeds of which it had taken the place." But Mill expressed this with an optimism of relatively peaceful times.

Holmes met Mill in mid-1866 while still engaged with philosophy and science. His father had gained renown in a scientific paper grounded in inductive method. Well before he attended Harvard, logical method was recognized in New England as a critical issue for philosophy; induction had long roots at the college, not limited to science.[10] When Holmes used the word "logic" in *The Common Law* (the life of the law is not logic but experience), he was not so much *rejecting* logic as agreeing with Mill's rejection of Richard Whately's *version* of logic; and he was reinventing it in the process. Professor Bowen had published his treatise on logic in 1864, highlighting the opposing views of Mill and Whewell. Peirce in late 1866 was analyzing the syllogism, induction, and the problem of similarity, and challenging Mill's dependence, for inductive method, on inherent similarities in nature.

Mill was keenly aware of a role for contention in the growth of knowledge. After his death in 1873, Chauncey Wright summed up his influence:

> [Mill] sincerely welcomed intelligent and earnest opposition with a deference due to truth itself, and to a just regard to the diversities in men's minds from differences of education and natural dispositions. These diversities even appeared

10. Flower and Murphey, *A History of Philosophy in America*, 1:365–87.

> to him essential to the completeness of the examination which the evidences of truth demand. Opinions positively erroneous, if intelligent and honest, are not without their value, since the progress of truth is a succession of mistakes and corrections. Truth itself, unassailed by erroneous opinion, would soon degenerate into narrowness and error.[11]

Clearly, then, *revision* was crucial to Mill's account of progress; revision of *ideas* was the central goal of free expression in his *On Liberty*. Holmes would reconsider the nature of revision, and its relation to conduct, in the resolution of contesting situations. Revision, in the cumulative understanding of a contested "situation," would gain increasing attention from Llewellyn, Levi, Dewey, and Bickel.

Wright, in his comment on Mill, addresses the role of error in finding truth, which resonates with Holmes's observation of the survival of vengeance in the forms of legal liability:

> The human mind cannot afford to forget its past aberrations. These, as well as its true discoveries, are indispensable guides; nor can it ever afford to begin from the *starting point* [my italics] in its search for truth, in accordance with the too confident method of more ambitious philosophers.[12]

When Wright refers to "ambitious philosophers" who confidently assume a "starting point" of inquiry, he means the hypothetical starting point embedded in the classical empirical model of the relation of observer to object, reinforced by the Cartesian separation of mind and world, that underlay the problematic of early modern philosophy.

Mill's *Logic* was a major effort toward allaying this concern; he sought a more "realistic" view of empiricism than the universal doubt from which Descartes began, leading Descartes to privilege (in the sense of *starting* with) "clear and distinct ideas," as in the latter's *cogito ergo sum*. Mill's response to Descartes is summarized in a passage from the *Logic*:

> When mankind first formed the idea of studying phenomena according to a stricter and surer method than that which they had in the first instance spontaneously adopted, they did not, conformably to the well-meant but impracticable precept of Descartes, set out from the supposition that nothing had been

11. Wright, *Philosophical Writings*, 122.
12. Ibid.

> already ascertained. Many of the uniformities existing among phenomena are so constant, and so open to observation, as to force themselves upon involuntary recognition.[13]

Mill here dismisses "set[ting] out from" universal doubt as an "impractical" starting point; explanation for human knowledge is instead to be found in "constant uniformities open to observation."

In showing instead "what really takes place," Mill was seeking (in contemporary philosophical jargon) to "naturalize" the Cartesian dualism, to bring it close to the actual nature of perception. As noted above in chapter 6, Mill's more "realistic" account of conceiving these uniformities is the act of sheer "comparison." But Mill's naturalization did not go far enough for Holmes. Even after disagreeing with Descartes over the hypothetical universal doubt, Mill's "we" retained a modified ideal-observer perspective (let's call it an "armchair" as opposed to a "main street" view), an implied detachment putatively able to make essential comparisons at once, and commit them to language.[14] Unlike Holmes, he sought to explain understanding through a process dependent on a unitary and somehow omniscient mind. Consider his definition of induction (watching carefully for the operation of a universally representative mind):

> For the present inquiry, Induction may be defined, the operation of discovering and proving general propositions. . . . [G]enerals are but collections of particulars, definite in kind but indefinite in number; and on the other hand, whenever the evidence which we derive from observation of known cases justifies us in drawing an inference respecting even one unknown case, we should on the same evidence be justified in drawing a similar inference with respect to a whole class of cases. The inference either does not hold, or it holds in all cases of a certain description; in all cases which, in *certain definable respects* [my italics], resemble those we have observed.[15]

13. Mill, *Logic*, 1:368, bk. 3, chap. 4, "Of Laws of Nature."

14. Mill's naturalization fell short also for Dewey, for comparable reasons: "Those who, like John Stuart Mill, have systematically criticized the traditional theory and who have attempted to build a logic in accord with modern scientific practices, have disastrously compromised their case by basing their logical constructions ultimately upon psychological theories that reduced 'experience' to mental states and external associations among them, instead of upon the actual conduct of scientific inquiry." Dewey, *Logic*, 81.

15. Mill, *Logic*, 1:328.

Here Mill's "collections of particulars" offers what I have called a "container" theory of perceived similarity, somehow unquestioningly gathering particular experience into "respects" both "certain" and "definable." Conceptions, he says, "do not develop themselves from within, but are impressed upon *the mind* [my italics] from without," and "every conception which can be made the instrument for connecting a set of facts, might have been originally evolved from those very facts."

In case the universal mind is not yet obvious, ask yourself how Mill can conclude that the process of comparison can find, in every case of inductive inquiry, a plain and obvious resemblance in "certain definable respects," a resemblance that all inquirers would immediately agree upon. A realistic account of *revision* is absent from this process of sheer comparison. What, after all, might prompt the universal mind, operating alone and without external criticism, to *revise* the comparison, and how might that take place?[16]

When Holmes came to consider Mill's *Logic* in November of 1866, Peirce had just questioned Mill's account of resemblance with objections that were presumably fresh in his mind. Meetings with Wright had encouraged him to read both sides of Mill's debate with Whewell; John Herschel had highlighted the problem as one of "constructing" general propositions. In coming upon Mill's use of the Mansfield story as a criticism of the syllogism, which Mill there described as an aspect of judicial decisions, Holmes must have wondered whether Mill had adequately addressed Herschel's question: "What is the act or series of acts of the mind in constructing general propositions, and when constructed, in what manner do we rest in them as expressive of truth?"

Holmes's 1870 essay can be viewed as proposing an alternative (although still hypothetical) "starting point" of inquiry; he revised the Mansfield story to introduce retrospective and participatory generalization. I see this as replacing Mill's radical empiricism and bald comparison, retaining the former but amending the latter: the general is still akin to a con-

16. Ibid., 2:193, 195, in chap. 2, "On Abstraction, or the Formation of Conceptions": This is part of Mill's argument against Whewell's version of Kepler's attribution of an ellipse to the path of the planet Mars. If you answer my question by saying the universal mind can revise *itself* from new experience, that just changes my question to "Whose experience?" If the reference to *education* is Mill's answer ("education impresses this new creed upon the new generations without the mental processes that have led to it"), there must be something else at work other than those "mental processes" of concept formation, something closer to the working of *multiple* minds, in a continuum of inquiry.

tainer (or, as Holmes says, a cluster) of particulars, but it is an eventual and consensual product of "many minds." While it debuts in 1870 as a putative *starting* point, it is soon revised as a *mid*-point, in the 1873 line-drawing essay, placing conceptual development within the (already heavily conceptualized) flow of experience.[17] Recall Wright's comment above, that the human mind cannot "afford to begin from the starting point," suggesting that the idea of a *real* starting point of inquiry will always be misleading. The idea has been endemic in logical theory, as a model for conceiving the relation of observation, experience, and conceptual content.

The diachronic model of social induction revises the classical observer model of empiricism. The classical model assumes three separate elements, (1) an observing mind (the expository "we"), (2) raw unconceptualized experience, and (3) the introduction of "conceptual relations" based upon similarities and differences that make understanding raw experience possible. The difficulty is that, from day one, there has been no single separate observing mind. Raw experience has been consistently encountered afresh by communities of often fractious individuals. Each individual and community has had its own purposes and intentions, although many of these have presumably been shared. Language is their medium of communication and belief, developing, representing, and displaying the recognition of similarity and difference, as well as (most of the time) the necessary convergence of intentions. Language has solidified that recognition into belief, even in the very notion of "observer" and "object"; the universal observing mind is itself a construct of language and discourse.[18]

To put this in contemporary philosophical jargon, I might suggest that Holmes was not only "naturalizing the Cartesian dualism," he was

17. This bears comparison with Wilfrid Sellars's and John McDowell's analytical account of "the space of reasons." McDowell, *Mind and World*, 5–13, 14–18, 42–43. "The dualism of conceptual scheme and 'empirical content,' of scheme and Given, is a response to [the worry about grounding conceptual freedom in experience]. The point of the dualism is that it allows us to acknowledge an external constraint on our freedom to deploy our empirical concepts. Empirical justifications depend on rational relations, relations within the space of reasons." Ibid., 5–6. For Holmes, the space of reasons is encountered through the practical need to find similarity in the resolution of actual conflicts, and is a progression through, rather than a dualism of, scheme and content. Compare McDowell's analytical "Given" to Holmes's "In our less theological and more scientific day, we explain an object by tracing the order and process of its growth and development from a starting point assumed as given." "Law in Science," *CW*, 3:406.

18. On the pragmatist reaction against an "Overmind" or "intelligibilizing Mind in nature," see Joseph Margolis, *The Unraveling of Scientism*, 14.

naturalizing the *dialectic*, the process of contested inquiry. Influenced by Wright, he was abandoning the attribution of certainty or validation to any starting point, common origin, or Cartesian process of recognition.

For Holmes's 1870 model of inquiry, the impingement of experience on knowledge begins with the necessity of a common need: resolution of particular disputes that advance cognition as well as (when unresolved) threaten the social order. The new dispute is at first conceived as entirely novel or original (like injury from a new practice or innovation). Over time, further experience establishes both similarities and differences in relation to the emerging sense of a core problem. While the original injury may *suggest* a general problem, it must be more precisely determined, or "specified," before a general rule can be adopted through practice.

In the process of comparison, consideration is naturally given to the nature and requirements of competing purposive activities, to what Lon Fuller called the "intermeshing anticipations" (or expectations) of those involved in the affected activities. Holmes's emphasis on "foreseeability" encompasses the multiplicity of factors involved in these early determinations; as he wrote in 1873, "A more modern example [Holmes had been discussing changes in the liability of innkeepers] is to be found in the rule of the road. After a sufficient amount of *fighting*, a practice is worked out, and a corresponding *expectation* generated. Then this is judicially noticed by the courts, and it is laid down as a rule of law that men are bound to in this instance what by general consent they are *expected* to do" (my italics).[19]

The "starting point" that he intimated in 1870 was amended by the 1873 account of the "growth" of legal knowledge, first written in a footnote to Kent's *Commentaries*.[20] Holmes now outlines a model in which the conceptual matter of law, if I may again cautiously use that phrase, is a retrospective evaluation of opposing precedents viewed as clusters. The image of clusters suggests a spare and radical empiricism; if indeed the facts of prior cases in the clusters are subject to constant reargument and reemphasis, the presumption of a fixed "body of doctrine" is necessarily deflated. Holmes's first example was the boundary dispute in *Beadel v.*

19. Holmes, "The Theory of Torts," 657; Kellogg, *Formative Essays*, 122; *CW*, 1:329. Both Lon Fuller and Holmes noted the obvious fact that the law has recognized contrasting customs or principles in different jurisdictions, Fuller with regard to jaywalking in New York versus San Francisco, Holmes on different standards of fencing cattle in Western states. Holmes, *The Common Law*, 124; *CW*, 3:194.

20. *CW*, 2:198.

Perry. There, you recall, a succession of disputes over the right to build a structure near a boundary led eventually to a "mathematical" formula for structural height and distance from the boundary, thereby reconciling the general property rights of landowners, both to build and to have access to "light and air."

I take it from Holmes's use of these examples that he finds from the record of prior cases that disputes in the earlier cases provide piecemeal information to be abstracted into what ultimately is concluded to be the core problem. The same may be said of the process described by Edward Levi, the problems recounted by Alexander Bickel, or Cass Sunstein's example of prosecutions of doctors for assisting patient suicide. In early instances, the actions and interests of opposing litigants are diverse. In such cases, trial lawyers may (and do) commonly offer anything favorable to a client, perhaps ranging (in the boundary case) from the use and aesthetics of the structure to the purposes and conduct of the litigants.[21] I'll try to flesh this out.

Take the example that Holmes mentions in his 1873 paper quoted above, the emergence of English "rule[s] of the road." In America we drive on the right; in Britain they drive on the left. Even so, I am reasonably familiar with the rules that relate to driving a rental car on English streets and highways, for example, in those confusing clockwise "roundabouts." When Holmes talks about a practice being worked out through a "sufficient amount of fighting," Holmes would have us imagine disputes over vehicular collisions, for which there is yet no settled rule—for example, when and how drivers first entered what might have been an *early* English roundabout.

Going back to that hypothetical time, I can imagine myself as the trial counsel representing Ms. Quickly, who was struck by a truck when she blithely dashed into that early roundabout (assuming, if you will, that there was a complete absence of accepted driver conduct). I will naturally engage in exhaustive discovery to bring up everything favorable to her case, including her being late to church, and her unimpeachable character (and the fact that the truck was carrying a cargo of scandalous literature),

21. This is typical of what takes place before the "mathematical formula" renders other considerations irrelevant. Trial lawyers who stray too far from what seems to be the core issue are used to being reined in by the trial judge on grounds of relevance; Holmes noted in the 1873 essay that modifications in the law are first recognized in the rules of evidence, n. 26 below. This process of finding relevance can be described as the "retirement of reasons" in normative induction. See my "The Snake and the Roundabout: Ethical Particularism and the Patterns of Normative Induction."

anything to sway the judge or jury. Counsel for the truck driver will raise countervailing arguments such as his need for income and duty to advance the interests of commerce. Holmes's point is that, once the rule establishing a presumptive right of way has taken hold for any vehicle *already* in the roundabout, none of this is relevant.[22]

I mentioned near the end of the last chapter that ethical generalism has come under attack in moral philosophy. It might be useful here to consider the contemporary debate between moral particularism and generalism. The newly invigorated particularism emphasizes the multiplicity and variety of reasons for any particular ethical decision, reasons that can shift polarity from case to case, whereas generalism focuses upon situations in which a limited set of reasons can dictate the same result.[23] As a generalist position, R. M. Hare's doctrine of universalizability claims that when a particular action is judged morally wrong, this is so on account of a discrete set of nonmoral (factual) properties. Consistency demands that any action that shares these properties is also wrong:

> Universalizability can be explained in various equivalent ways; it comes to this, that if we make different moral judgments about situations which we admit to be identical in their universal descriptive properties, we contradict ourselves.[24]

Ethical particularism has consistently contended on numerous grounds (not material for my purposes) that the generalist's "list of relevant properties," required to support universalization, cannot coherently be limited.[25] It has challenged the very notion of identicality in normative life.

Without engaging this debate in depth, I simply note its relevance for the specification and convergence that Holmes identifies in *legal* adjudi-

22. Readers familiar with Holmes will recall that Holmes used the figure of "Mrs. Quickly" to illustrate the same point in "The Path of the Law": "The reason why a lawyer does not mention that his client wore a white hat when he made a contract, while Mrs. Quickly would be sure to dwell upon it along with the parcel gilt goblet and the sea-coal fire, is that he foresees that the public force will act in the same way whatever his client had upon his head." Holmes, *CW*, 3:391.

23. Jonathan Dancy, "The Particularist's Progress," in Brad Hooker and Margaret Little, eds., *Moral Particularism*, 131: "For the main aim of my particularist position is to break the stranglehold of a certain conception of how moral reasons function—the generalist conception under which what is a moral reason in one situation is necessarily the same reason whenever it occurs."

24. R. M. Hare, *Moral Thinking*, 21.

25. David Bakhurst, "Ethical Particularism in Context," in Hooker and Little, eds., *Moral Particularism*, 162–63; see Jonathan Dancy on "mere comparison," in ibid., 149.

cation. In the early or novel case, the list of relevant properties is long. There are aggravating and mitigating factors everywhere you look, on both sides, and moral particularism does not contemplate restrictive rules of relevant evidence.[26] Generalism *in law* is a product of establishing a commitment to finite expectations in a given problematic situation. It often occurs, *ceteris paribus*, at a later stage of inquiry, if relevant properties can be winnowed down to a formula.[27] But Hare insists, nevertheless, regarding moral generalism:

> The thesis of universalizability, which is one of the main elements in a true account of the structure of moral thinking, has the consequence that it is a misuse of the word "ought" to say "You ought, but I can conceive of another situation, identical in all its properties to this one, except that the corresponding person ought not."[28]

This assumes that the initial or early decision, that I may have won by aggressive advocacy for Ms. Quickly (on a determination based on all the factors that I presented, although the judge ruled as irrelevant her grades in elementary school), is universalizable (even if wrong in retrospect) in some meaningful way. The notion of abstract universalizability in any particular normative context may be a product of classical logic, but not of real life. The classical debate over moral generalism and particularism has been in large part an abstract one, divorced from the legal concern with actual disputes.

This highlights a practical difference between law and morals, or at least moral *theorizing*: the motivation toward legal specification comes from the need to resolve urgent social conflicts.[29] Physical or economic harm or loss

26. Mrs. Quickly is arguably blameworthy only in law, not (perhaps according to Dancy) in morals. Holmes notes that "[m]odifications in the law are recognized much sooner in the rules of evidence than in pleading, where precedents remain of record." Holmes, "The Theory of Torts"; Kellogg, *Formative Essays*, 121; *CW*, 329. See Dancy, *Moral Reasons*, x: "[I]t is common to hear that moral rules, or moral theory, cannot cope with the rich multiplicity of lived situations."

27. As, e.g., in Edward Levi's demise of the concept of dangerous instrumentality. *Introduction to Legal Reasoning*, 24. For the pertinence of social inductivism to the debate over ethical particularism, see my "The Snake and the Roundabout."

28. Hare, *Moral Thinking*, 10.

29. But I note that Holmes's 1899 speech to the New York Bar Association, where he viewed the law as an anthropological document of the prevalent ideas and ideals in society, applied the notion of entrenchment in the continuum of inquiry (which he described there

has occurred, and one party or the other must bear the cost. And the problem of *one* hard case may become a *continuing* problem, which requires more than a one-time settlement on particular grounds—as with Cass Sunstein's "incompletely theorized agreements." For resolution to succeed, relevance and admissibility of evidence must be gradually refined, as practices are evaluated and adjusted to meet Lon Fuller's requirements for the operation of a system of law, conceived as a *successful* system. As Fuller consistently wrote, "Law is not a datum, but an achievement that needs ever to be renewed."[30]

The reader may be thinking that the judicial feedback loop resembles incremental legislation. Indeed, it is similar; legislation too is directed toward urgent problems, and *ideally* takes place only after extensive (and inclusive) committee hearings on the kinds of matters that Fuller considered critical. Such was putatively the case regarding labor organization and picketing at the workplace, eventually regulated by the National Labor Relations Act in 1934. The feedback loop may also seem a grossly inefficient way to achieve solutions to intractable problems, but if a problem is deeply ingrained in conflicting patterns of conduct, there may be some advantage to incremental exploration through litigation. Legislative solutions are only lately removing the issues of medically assisted death from the courts. They are having less success with other controversies. Holmes's process of convergence implies more than a cognitive dimension to the analyzing and reconciling process. There must also be a convergence of communal practice and *action*. Resolution of the uncertain case requires revising an *actual* context, not just a conceptual *sense* of context, because a larger problem may be implicated in the specific dispute.

Whether legal change comes through legislation or litigation, the process I have outlined is obviously open to abuse. That might be a relevant

as "the change of emphasis which I have called the law of fashion") to nonlegal forms of human inquiry, including morals; "the law of fashion has prevailed even in the realm of morals." Holmes, *CW*, 3:407.

30. Fuller's "eunomics" was "the study of good order and workable social arrangements." On the difference between a law and a good law he wrote, "In the field of purposive human activity, which includes both steam engines and the law, value and being are not two different things, but two aspects of an integral reality." Lon Fuller, *The Law in Quest of Itself*, 11. Fuller asked how the law really works to maintain order: people "need the support of intermeshing anticipations that will let them know what their opposite numbers will do, or that will at least enable them to gauge the general scope of the repertory from which responses to their actions will be drawn." Ibid. See generally, Kenneth Winston, ed., *Selected Essays of Lon L. Fuller*.

observation for social critics of the analytical scheme, where the social context of law is largely irrelevant. The diachronic model opens inquiry into *how* social factors influence the law. They do not do so through a purely doctrinal judicial pipeline, but are introduced in the more protracted and interactive process recounted by Edward Levi.

An example of blindness to this fact is the focus of analytical jurisprudence on semantic vagueness as a primary source of legal indeterminacy. Timothy Endicott opens *Vagueness in Law* with the following comment:

> I argue that vagueness, and resultant indeterminacies, are essential features of law. Although not all laws are vague, legal systems necessarily include vague laws. When the law is vague, the result is that people's legal rights and duties and powers are indeterminate in some (not in all) cases.
>
> The indeterminacy claim seems to make the ideal of the rule of law unattainable: to the extent that legal rights and duties are indeterminate, we cannot be ruled by law. The indeterminacy claim is a threat to what I will call "the standard view of adjudication," the view that the judge's task is just to give effect to the legal rights and duties of the parties.[31]

This will appear unrealistic to a trial lawyer. Vagueness is certainly endemic in legal as well as common *language*, but where a practical problem surrounding a vague term is critical, the law engages in specification. It is in that process that abuse (in the sense of capture of the process by special interests) is most likely to take place. The analytical model of indeterminacy attributes all such mischief (and its cure) to the judiciary, whereas the social model sees it as largely rooted outside the legal system.

The classic case of analytical vagueness is the "Sorites" or "heap" paradox, attributed to Eubulides of Miletus, a contemporary of Aristotle. As Timothy Williamson describes it in *Vagueness*,

> Does one grain of wheat make a heap? Do two grains of wheat make a heap? . . . Do ten grains of wheat make a heap? It is to be understood that the grains are properly piled up, and that a heap must contain reasonably many grains. If you admit that one grain does not make a heap, and are unwilling to make a fuss about the addition of any single grain, you are eventually forced to admit that ten thousand grains do not make a heap.[32]

31. Timothy A. O. Endicott, *Vagueness in Law*, 1.
32. Timothy Williamson, *Vagueness*, 8.

This ignores that specification may occur regarding the meaning of "heap" in a contested situation where practical outcomes are at stake.

Imagine an English-speaking country that has adopted a proviso that the price of a day's labor is a "heap" of grains of wheat. Disputes are adjudicable in an English-style common law system. Problems arise among the affected communities due to the patently vague term. Cases of alleged underpayment are brought into court. It should not be surprising eventually to find a settled precedent specifying fairly precise dimensions of this use of "heap." (If instead the rule said "heap of olives," or indeed "apples," the precedent could become numerically precise.)

In the first "heap" case, someone sued for insufficient payment, arguing to a jury that a spoon-sized heap was too little—and won. Then another worker sued with the claim that a keg-sized heap was too little—and lost. More cases brought to light various considerations, such as the hours and effort required, working conditions, and so on. Eventually a precedent emerged, but only after findings on all manner of testimony, most of which would later be ruled irrelevant.[33] Opposing interests, of workers, managers, or others with a practical stake, had brought particular considerations to bear on the decisions, finally resulting in a rule. The term "heap" will now have acquired a contextual standard of similarity, whose fairness will depend far less on judicial fiat than upon the balance of evidence presented.[34]

This reveals another important implication of the famous remark in the opening paragraph of Holmes's *The Common Law*, "the life of the law has not been logic." I have said that he was following Mill's critique of classical logic. But if Mill sensed that there was a problem with vagueness, he failed to address it, noting (after the passages cited above),

> This want of clearness, or, as it may be otherwise called,
> this vagueness in the general conception, may be owing either to

33. For those conversant with ethical particularism, this represents the *retirement* of reasons through development of a *practice*; see my "The Snake and the Roundabout."

34. Endicott mentions the "standard model" of adjudication, and says that the law provides for its own determinacy (or "regulates its own creation"), citing Aristotle. That only leaves the entire matter in the hands of judges. "The conclusion is that judges have a duty to give (in fact *impose*) resolution. Resolution is a basic requirement of the rule of law." *Vagueness in Law*, 197–98. For Timothy Williamson, vagueness is "epistemic." *Vagueness*, xi. See also "Vagueness and Political Choice in Law," in Geert Keil and Ralf Poscher, eds., *Vagueness and the Law: Philosophical and Legal Perspectives*; Luke William Hunt, "What the Epistemic Account of Vagueness Means for Legal Interpretation," 29–54.

> our having no accurate knowledge of the objects themselves, or merely to our not having carefully compared them.

Holmes, in bringing a detailed knowledge of common law from Kent's *Commentaries* to his reading of Mill, addressed the complexity of vagueness in his move toward a social inductivism. He completed Mill's criticism of formal and classical logic, from which vagueness is viewed as an epistemic dilemma. Hilary Putnam put this dilemma as follows in 1983:

> Modern logic teachers would probably tell their students: "in Logic we assume—or pretend—that all terms have somehow been made precise." According to [G. E. L.] Owen, Aristotle—and even Plato—worried about this pretense. Is it a pretense that we have done something that we—or some conceivable cognitive extension of ourselves—could in principle do? Or a pretense that we have done a "we know not what it would be like"? And who is truly more sophisticated: the modern logic teacher, for whom this is no problem, or the founders of the subject?

It seems that part of the motivation for moving logic into formal symbols had, as one of its driving reasons, escaping the vagueness of language.[35]

Holmes's social conception of logical inquiry addresses the manner in which specification emerges from borderline cases. It also accounts for the emergence of normativity from experience, since (like Fuller) Holmes did not draw a firm conceptual line between fact and value. If, as Fuller maintained, social facts have both normative and empirical dimension, Holmes demonstrated how they *acquire* precise normativity through socially informed judgments of prudence. Patterns of activity in a given area are not at first encountered because they have already been validated as morally correct. It is when a disturbance occurs that they are evaluated in context, from the standpoint of prudence and foreseeability. The law is always opening new inquiries *in medias res*, and revising prior stable concepts to keep them stable and relevant.

This might suggest that a primary interest in the continuum model is one of order and stability. Holmes was less interested than Peirce in the

35. Hilary Putnam, *Realism and Reason: Philosophical Papers, Volume 3*, 271. Putnam suggests here that classical logic doesn't apply unless similarity is not at issue. See also his *The Collapse of the Fact/Value Distinction*, 12, and "Rethinking Mathematical Necessity," 245. See also G. E. L. Owen, *Logic, Science and Dialectic*, 153–60, 164, 213–15, 221ff.

vexing problem of precisely defining "truth." Peirce's conclusion was that truth is an end point of inquiry, the attainment of a settled and stable belief after the process of inquiry, stimulated by doubt, had reached its final expression. James would deploy the much criticized expression "cash-value." John Dewey would drop use of the word "truth" in favor of "warranted assertibility."

Holmes did not articulate an end point to inquiry, but I have suggested that "entrenchment" would be a useful way to understand his overall view. His occasional reference to "my Can't Helps" reflected a recognition that individuals have different and often opposing views; but, of course, his imagery did not stop there, suggesting a skeptical relativism of pluralist "can't helps," in a static global incommensurable multiverse. The multiple individual "can't helps" simply must be commensurated, wherever and whenever that may be necessary for civilization to continue.

The notion of our personal "can't helps" suggests that knowledge is not accessible through a universal mind. Nor can anyone presently know the future; it is radically open, but it is also radically precarious. This view does not necessarily close off *any* answer to the question of validity. If there is an end point of inquiry, it has to do with more than just language, and propositional "conceptual matter"; it must also include the element of human conduct, and it must be radically normative. Order and stability are more than cooperationless predication or predicationless cooperation.

Any successful conclusions of social inquiry must, in an important respect, conform with the world at large. Social inductivism does not imply that the procedures and ends of justification are relativist products of differing conventions, and that their authority is purely "contextual," confined to a purely practical element, its "cash value." Induction is not (as John McDowell puts it) a "frictionless spinning in the void."[36] As with Holmes's remark about law, social induction must always seek, even if never reaching, "consistency."[37] Taken in its full context, consistency implicates more than

36. John McDowell, *Mind and World*, 66; moral reality is disclosed to us in its full objectivity only in connection with rule-governed behavior, *Mind, Value and Reality*, 58–65, 203–12, 221–62.

37. "What has been said will explain the failure of all theories which consider the law only from its formal side, whether they attempt to deduce the *corpus* from *a priori* postulates, or fall into the humbler error of supposing the science of the law to reside in the *elegantia juris*, or logical cohesion of part with part. The truth is, that the law is always approaching, and never reaching, consistency. It is forever adopting new principles from life at one end, and it always retains old ones from history at the other, which have not yet been absorbed or

a deductive, propositional, purely conceptual quality of existence. It implicates a full accounting of human conduct toward coordinate purposes, nothing less than the survival and flourishing of the human race, and its entire account (filled as it is with religious tradition) of knowledge, accomplishment, and values.

Does Holmes's theory close off any ascent through legal inquiry to larger questions, and does his conception contemplate room for moral progress and justification? Holmes didn't avoid the word "truth," but he used it shockingly, as in "the majority vote of the nation that can lick all the others."[38] This is clearly hyperbole, but exactly how it fits in needs to be addressed. If there is a starting point in social induction, it consists of human *action*, and it is always purposive, whether for sheer observation, communication, flourishing, or survival. Entrenchment then reaches the embodiment of the broadest possible sharing of human purposes.

Mark Howe's defense of Holmes took the position that he did not have *any* foundational view, that he was basically agnostic, but that this was nevertheless harmless, considering that "human values" can be "constructive" when not conceived as "absolutes." I have argued that his perspective must be reconceived as a view that foundations are themselves contingent upon constant human striving; they are not limited to mere "assertion." Foundations are vital, and must be found amidst contested situations. If serious conflicts do not reach resolution, they can lead to violent destruction.

This is an aspect of the question raised in chapter 6, how to understand the theory of validation implicit in the social process of legal inquiry. Social inductivism hardly denies, but rather advances, the idea of an ascent from local uncertainty to global improvement, in the very *idea* of the moral absolute; it advances understanding of "what really takes place" when humans *seek* it. Holmes's position should not be conceived as a negative skepticism

---

sloughed off. It will become entirely consistent only when it ceases to grow." Holmes, *Common Law*, 32; *CW*, 3:133.

38. "When I say a thing is true I mean that I can't help believing it and nothing more. But as I observe that the cosmos is not always limited by my Can't Helps I don't bother about absolute truth or even inquire whether there is such a thing, but define the Truth as the system of my limitations. I may add that as other men are subject to a certain number, not all, of my Can't Helps, intercourse is possible. When I was young I used to define the truth as the majority vote of that nation that can lick all the others. So we may define the present war as an inquiry concerning truth." Letter to Learned Hand, June 22, 1918.

of Mill's meliorism, but as an improvement, as a fully realistic voluntarist meliorism, giving due attention to how knowledge is rooted in conflict, how conflict itself is malleable, and how it can be further understood and improved, as it already has been, through both empirical science and the common law tradition.

This brings me to the problem of validation of legal knowledge.

CHAPTER TEN

Validation

This chapter explores Holmes's approach to inductive validation, through a disagreement with Judge Learned Hand over the law of free expression in time of war.

* * *

You say that I strike at the sacred right to kill the other fellow when he disagrees. The horrible possibility silenced me when you said it. Now, I say, "Not at all, kill him for the love of Christ and in the name of God, but always realize that he may be the saint and you the devil. Go your way with a strong arm and a swift shining sword, in full consciousness that what you kill for, and what you may die for, some smart chap like Laski may write a book and prove is all nonsense."—U.S. District Judge Learned Hand to Justice Holmes, June 22, 1918

Judge Learned Hand wrote this passage in a letter to Holmes soon after the two had fortuitously met and talked on the train from New York to Boston—as it happens, during critical battles in Europe. In the news was Belleau Wood, near the Marne River, the apex of Germany's late push in France to win the great conflict before American troops had fully deployed. Captain Lloyd Williams had famously replied to a French soldier urging the arriving U.S. Marines to retreat: "Retreat? Hell, we just got here!" Williams did not survive the costly stand. Fifty-six years earlier, struck while leading a company of Union infantry, a recovering Holmes had expressed relief that his chest wound at Ball's Bluff had entered from the front, and he would later worry that the shot through his neck at Antietam came through the back.

Hand had been "silenced" by a remark, shocked as others have been by a brash Holmes comment. Discussing free expression in time of war, Holmes had said there is a natural right to resort to violence. He would respond to Hand's letter with the even more shocking comment that "the present war is an inquiry concerning truth." Rather than discovery of truth through the machine gun, Holmes's hyperbolic reply addresses the fundamental problem of validation, putting the matter of truth finding within the recurring philosophical framework of *dialectic*, the opposition of arguments. Dialectic is ubiquitous, and Holmes's comments apply John Stuart Mill's probing concern about *realism*: what, in the interaction of opposing arguments, is "really tak[ing] place?" How, in other words, might one *naturalize* the dialectical aspect of human understanding?

Hand was a forty-five-year-old federal district judge the year before when confronted with a trial under the newly enacted Espionage Act, which among other things prohibited the mailing of publications that "willfully obstruct the recruiting or enlistment service of the United States." Shortly after passage, the federal government sought to prohibit the mailing of the forthcoming issue of Max Eastman's monthly journal, *The Masses*, which had a circulation of roughly twenty thousand. Heavily laden with Eastman's general views on the need for social and economic reorganization in the United States, it opposed American involvement in World War I. The government argued that "to arouse discontent and disaffection among the people with the prosecution of the war and with the draft tends to promote a mutinous and insubordinate temper among the troops." Hand had enjoined the government's action.

It was on June 19, 1918, as the battle for Belleau Wood was raging and seven months before Holmes would be faced with the same issue in *Schenck v. United States*, that Hand was on his way by train to his summer home in Cornish, New Hampshire, when he chanced to share part of the long train ride in conversation with Holmes, thirty-one years his senior, northward bound for his summer house in Beverly Farms, Massachusetts, at the end of the Supreme Court term. Hand had recently had his decision overruled in favor of the government by the U.S. Court of Appeals for the Second Circuit. He had espoused a more "objective" test than Holmes would adopt in *Schenk*, and looked to the literal words of the alleged obstruction (as the *Schenck* defense later vainly urged the Supreme Court to do). Hand recognized that his position "seemed to meet with practically no professional approval whatever," and he found himself in a profound disagreement with Holmes.

Soon after the train ride, on June 22, Hand wrote to Holmes:

> Dear Mr. Justice–
>
> I gave up more easily than I now feel disposed about Tolerance on Wednesday. Here I take my stand. Opinions are at best provisional hypotheses, incom-

pletely tested. The more they are tested, after the tests are well scrutinized, the more assurance we may assume, but they are never absolutes. So we must be tolerant of opposite opinions or varying opinions by the very fact of our incredulity of our own. . . .

You say that I strike at the sacred right to kill the other fellow when he disagrees. The horrible possibility silenced me when you said it. Now, I say, "Not at all, kill him for the love of Christ and in the name of God, but always realize that he may be the saint and you the devil. Go your way with a strong arm and a swift shining sword, in full consciousness that what you kill for, and what you may die for, some smart chap like Laski may write a book and prove is all nonsense" [my italics] . . .

I sat under the Bo Tree and these truths were revealed to me. Tolerance is the twin of Incredulity, but there is no inconsistency in cutting off the heads of as many as you please; that is a natural right. Only, and here we may differ, I do say that you may not cut off heads, (except for limited periods and then only when you want to very much indeed), because the victims insist upon saying things which look against Provisional Hypothesis Number Twenty-Six, the verification of which to date may be found in its proper place in the card catalogue. Generally, I insist, you must allow the possibility that if our heads are spared, other cards may be added under that sub-title which will have, perhaps, an important modification. All this seems to me so perfectly self-evident, self-explanatory and rigidly applicable to the most complicated situations that I hesitate to linger upon it, lest I should seem tolerant of any different [*sic*] of opinion concerning it.

I greatly enjoyed my good fortune in meeting you on the train.

Faithfully yours,

Learned Hand

In a letter dated just two days later Holmes replied:

Dear Hand

Rarely does a letter hit me so exactly where I live as yours, and unless you are spoiling for a fight I agree with it throughout. My only qualification, if any, would be that free speech stands no differently than freedom from vaccination. The occasions would be rarer when you cared enough to stop it but if for any reason you did care enough you wouldn't care a damn for the suggestion that you were acting on a provisional hypothesis and might be wrong. That is the condition of every act. You tempt me to repeat an apologue that I got off to my wife in front of the statue of [radical abolitionist William Lloyd] Garrison on

Commonwealth Avenue, Boston, many years ago. I said—If I were an official person I should say nothing shall induce me to do honor to a man who broke the fundamental condition of social life by bidding the very structure of society perish rather than he not have his way—Expressed in terms of morals, to be sure, but still, his way. If I were a son of Garrison I should reply—Fool, not to see that every great reform has seemed to threaten the structure of society,—but that society has not perished, because man is a social animal, and with every turn falls into a new pattern like the Kaleidoscope. If I were a philosopher I should say—Fools both, not to see that you are the two blades (conservative and radical) of the shears that cut out the future. But if I were the ironical man in the back of the philosopher's head I should conclude—Greatest fool of all, Thou—not to see that man's destiny is to fight. Therefore take thy place on the one side or the other, if with the added grace of knowing that the Enemy is as good a man as thou, so much the better, but kill him if thou Canst. All of which seems in accord with you. If I may repeat another chestnut of ancient date and printed in later years—When I say a thing is true I mean that I can't help believing it and nothing more. But as I observe that the cosmos is not always limited by my Can't Helps I don't bother about absolute truth or even inquire whether there is such a thing, but define the Truth as the system of my limitations. I may add that as other men are subject to a certain number, not all, of my Can't Helps, intercourse is possible. When I was young I used to define the truth as the majority vote of that nation that can lick all the others. So we may define the present war as an inquiry concerning truth. Of course you won't suspect me of thinking with levity on that subject because of my levitical speech. I enjoyed our meeting as much as you possibly could have and should have tried to prolong it to Boston but I feared my wife would worry.

Sincerely yours
O. W. Holmes

The reply is a perfect summary of Holmes's lifelong theorizing, and of his distinctive brand of, if you will, philosophical pragmatism. The shocking comment on vaccination refers to his sense of the scope of uncertainty in the continuum of inquiry—a sense that Hand was seeking to disturb. Did Holmes really think that truth is discovered through the machine gun? Not quite that the world war would settle discovery of the real; rather, the remarks can be seen as suggesting a radical naturalizing of the underlying dialectical process and its relation to *validation*, the process of justifying the human perception of normative (and if I may follow other writers, natural) *reality*.

To guide us safely through this, I will survey the literature that differentiates social inductivism from other pragmatisms, in particular the new analytical pragmatism of contemporary scholars. Along the way, you have only to keep in mind that what Holmes's letter contains, and is missing from a vast literature in philosophy, is the continuum of inquiry, which is ultimately not a weakening but a strengthening force. The social continuum of inquiry is what the ironical man in the back of the philosopher's head has in mind, when he calls the philosopher the greatest fool of all, and says that humanity's destiny is to fight.

To fight in Holmes's full sense (borrowing a favorite word from Lon Fuller) is to *strive*, for meaning and principle. This final chapter, in closing out many themes of the book, brings the war metaphor to reach a wider audience, not just those who are invested in jurisprudence and philosophy, but also their children and grandchildren, the "millennials" captured by digital devices and clever reality games; now may be my chance to get their attention. Philosophy per se may never appeal to them, but what has been happening there is not so far removed from the computer war game, only the opposing strategists (in this text) are different: Descartes and Hume, Kant and Hegel, Whewell and Mill, then Wright, Peirce, James, Holmes and Dewey, and more recently, Hart and Dworkin, and now Rorty, Wittgenstein, Quine, and Robert Brandom.

If Holmes's metaphor must be reduced to Hand's card catalog, it may never interest the new generation. Better to see it as another transcendent and cosmic battle against dark forces, a war for the future of our existence itself.[1] For what Holmes apparently saw after the Civil War is that philosophy is engaged in a *real* battle for the future, over the patterns of global belief and conduct, the ultimate battle for the validation of human understanding.

As suggested at the end of chapter 9, the theory of validation implicit in the social process of legal inquiry is not banal "conventionalism." It hardly denies, but rather advances, understanding of the ascent from local uncertainty to global resolution, to understanding the very *enacted* idea of the moral absolute, in its *actual* garb. No one can deny the necessity of validation, indeed of ultimate and transcendent validation; it is felt as both existent and fundamental throughout science and morals. Validation

1. "The world is worth fighting for!" Phrase spoken by a "nerdy female scientist" protagonist named Mei in the computer war game *Overwatch*, as reported in article about video game addiction, *Washington Post*, December 6, 2016, p. C9.

arrives through contested inquiry, which provides its foundation. But few see it as instantiated in partial, precarious, and often divided form (even in the origins of philosophy[2]). Why should contemporary philosophy not recognize this, that above the card catalog there is a transcendent war, and not just a game?

Analytical theory follows a long tradition in philosophy that seeks a secure standing inferential "track" (Wittgenstein's image) for all validation, but social induction reveals an experiential one that actually obtains. In a word, humanity's destiny is either to fight for validation, preferably through the peaceful process of convergence, or lose it.[3]

It is evident from its origins that Holmes's social induction is genealogically related to pragmatism; but that label was inconveniently captured after Dewey's death by analytical writers and attitudes. There are now two warring narratives over pragmatism, which I will explore through a leading *analytical* strategist in this particular battle, Robert Brandom. His recent essay in *Pragmatism, Law and Language* addresses the very problem of legal indeterminacy that has concerned the preceding chapters, and it clarifies how these attitudes are opposed to Holmes. Titled "A Hegelian Model of Concept Determination," it begins by recognizing the connection of legal knowledge with the root philosophical problem of validation:

> The specter of indeterminacy haunts the philosophy of law. . . . The engagement of early modern philosophy with skepticism traced out an arc, from the epistemological skepticism from which Descartes recoiled to the more radical semantic skepticism that Kant was concerned to forestall.

Here Brandom connects legal "indeterminacy" (which Holmes of course saw as *uncertainty*) with the larger issue of philosophical realism and the "early modern" legacy from Descartes and Hume to Kant and Hegel. The

2. "In one sense philosophy is for Plato identical with dialectic; in another it achieves its culmination in dialectic." Friedrich Solmsen, "Dialectic without the Forms." "It was partly because Aristotle had to work out for himself the theory and methodology of dialectic that he made himself into the first logician philosopher." Gilbert Ryle, "Dialectic in the Academy." Can the global philosophical dialectic be associated with the local emergence of conceptualism through everyday disputes? I think Holmes implied as much in his 1899 address to the New York Bar Association.

3. Just like Thurgood Marshall litigating against segregated educational institutions through the NAACP Legal Defense Fund, or Richard Epstein advocating in *Supreme Neglect*. See chap. 6, n. 21, and accompanying text.

matter is thus connected with the foundations of knowledge, the fulcrum that also anchored Holmes's interest from 1865 on. Where then does Brandom look for an answer?

He goes on in this essay to find that G. W. F. Hegel's famous dialectical movement of the *geist*—roughly, the conscious spirit of the world, the movement from thesis to antithesis and ultimately to synthesis—provided an answer, indeed *the* answer. Brandom finds this in Hegel's shift to *vernunft* and away from Kant's *verstand*, to the historical rather than purely rationalist answer of Kant. Here is how he applies Hegel's famous "historical dialectic" to law:

> We might start with the observation that we want to say both that judges are responsible *for* the law, and that judges are responsible *to* the law. Hegel's account of the reciprocal recognitive structure of the process by which legal concepts and principles are determined provides a way of understanding these symmetric claims according to which we can be entitled to both. . . .
>
> In offering a rationale, a justification for a decision, the judge presents what is in effect a rational reconstruction of the tradition that makes it visible as authoritative insofar as, so presented, the tradition at once *determines* the conceptual content one is adjudicating the application of and *reveals* what the content is, and so how the current question of applicability ought to be decided.[4]

This account of legal validation, like Ronald Dworkin's appeal to principle, is immediate, inherent, and reassuringly automatic. Brandom's "reciprocal recognitive structure" descends from Hegelian philosophy like divine grace, as an unearned warrant for the resolution of any difficult case by individual judges. Although Brandom's deference to history may make him seem closer to Holmes than to Kant, Hegel's phantom dialectic does not go nearly as far as Holmes's fully naturalized and contingent historical perspective, grounding validation in hard-won resolution of concrete

4. The full title of Brandom's essay is "A Hegelian Model of Concept Determination: The Normative Fine Structure of the Judges' Chain Novel." Graham Hubbs in a useful introduction (to *Pragmatism, Law, and Language*, the volume in which Brandom's essay appears) makes a case for several distinct contemporary versions of pragmatism, which (to me) do not appear inconsistent with Ralph Sleeper's version of one basic distinction (see n. 12 below). Brandom has maintained that his reading of Hegel is associated with the influence of Wilfrid Sellars (see *From Empiricism to Expressivism: Brandom Reads Sellars*, 201–4), while Joseph Margolis, in *Pragmatism Ascendent*, argues that Brandom's adoption of Wilfrid Sellars as a Hegelian is "incoherent" (26).

disputes, and the continuing struggle for consensual convergence as an alternative to revenge and violence.

Holmes's own occasional comments on Hegel were mostly dismissive (there is an allusion in his letter to Hegel's dialectic in the philosopher's "conservative and radical shears that cut out the future"). The diaries and later letters show Holmes had read and continued to read Hegel, though he would call doing so a "bore" and a "blight."[5] All accounts suggest that Hegel had been brought into the many discussions among Holmes, Peirce, Wright, and James. One of these is James's 1912 "look back into the [eighteen] sixties," revealing how and why Holmes would not have viewed Hegel as a kindred spirit. The empiricism of Francis Bacon shines through James's account, describing a Hegel, unlike Brandom's, lumped with Kant as an "idealist," not fully engaged in factual historical inquiry but rather in "conceptualism." Opening with a Baconian tone, James urges a revival of empiricism, to which he (like Mill in the previous chapter) assigns the laudatory term "philosophical":

> Fortunately, our age seems to be growing philosophical again—still in the ashes live the wonted fires. Oxford, long the seed-bed, for the English world, of the idealism inspired by Kant and Hegel, has recently become the nursery of a very different way of thinking. . . . It looks a little as if the ancient english empiricism, so long put out of fashion here by nobler sounding germanic formulas, might be repluming itself and getting ready for a stronger flight than ever.[6]

James then recalls the earlier influence for him and his contemporaries of the empiricism of Mill, Bain, and Hamilton; "Reduced to their most pregnant difference, *empiricism means the habit of explaining wholes by parts, and rationalism means the habit of explaining parts by wholes*" (James's italics).[7] In the accompanying essay "Hegel and His Method," James launches a surprisingly harsh critique:

> The vision in [Hegel's] case was that of a world in which reason holds all things in solution and accounts for all the irrationality that superficially appears by taking it up as a moment into itself.

5. Howe, ed., *Holmes-Pollock Letters*, 2:75, 152; see also 1:44, 188; 2:71; Holmes, *Common Law*, *CW*, 3:136, 220ff.

6. William James, *A Pluralistic Universe*, 3.

7. Ibid., 7–8.

This "superficial" account of irrationality refers to Hegel's inhering, invisible dialectic of concepts, that Holmes would envision more concretely as "clusters" of actual case-specific disputes. James continues:

> Great injustice is done to Hegel by treating him as primarily a reasoner. He is in reality a naively observant man, only beset with a perverse preference for the use of technical and logical jargon. . . . His passion for the slipshod in the way of sentences, his unprincipled playing fast and loose with terms; his dreadful vocabulary, calling what completes a thing its "negation," for example; his systematic refusal to let you know whether he is talking logic or physics or psychology, his whole deliberately adopted policy of ambiguity and vagueness. . . .
>
> This dogging of everything by its negative, its fate, its undoing, this perpetual moving on to something future which shall supersede the present, this is the hegelian intuition of the essential provisionality, and consequent unreality, of everything empirical and finite.[8]

James pulls no punches in calling Hegel's idea of truth a "dogmatic ideal, the postulate, uncriticized, undoubted, and unchallenged," and (in a quote from Shakespeare that resonates with Holmes's letter to Hand) James observes that "death once dead for it, there's no more dying then."[9] For

8. Ibid., 85–89. Holmes writes in *The Common Law*: "Hegel . . . puts [punishment] in his quasi-mathematical form, that, wrong being the negation of right, punishment is the negation of that negation, or retribution." *CW*, 3:135.

9. James, *A Pluralistic Universe*, 102–3, quoting Shakespeare, Sonnet 168. James says that *ideas* alone don't fight: "Let the *mental idea* of the thing work in your thought all alone, [Hegel] fancied, and just the same consequences will follow. It will be negated by the opposite ideas that dog it, and can survive only by entering, along with them, into some kind of treaty. This treaty will be an instance of the so-called 'higher synthesis' of everything with its negative; and Hegel's originality lay in transporting the process from the sphere of percepts to that of concepts and treating it as the universal method by which every kind of life, logical, physical, or psychological, is mediated. Not to the sensible facts as such, then, did Hegel point for the secret of what keeps existence going, but rather to the conceptual way of treating them. Concepts were not in his eyes the static self-contained things that previous logicians had supposed, but were germinative, and passed beyond themselves into each other, by what he called their immanent dialectic." Ibid., 91–92.

James's view of Hegel was not always entirely negative; Perry observed that notwithstanding the harsh criticism "[h]e had always had a sneaking fondness for Hegel, but insisted on taking liberties with him. He liked him in undress, stripped of his logical regalia. There was, he thought, a homely Hegelian insight: the fact that things contaminate one another, thus becoming something other than themselves." Ralph Barton Perry, *The Thought and Character of William James*, 329.

Holmes, a life-or-death struggle for validation *is* the dialectic, and the dying will never cease, though it may be controlled through successful practices, like law's convergence.

Where does Brandom get his reformed Hegel? This can best be understood as part of the two warring narratives to which I alluded. Brandom has outlined a widely accepted account of pragmatism to which this book may contribute to a counternarrative. The crucial event was the posthumous capture of John Dewey into the analytical camp by Richard Rorty, under the banner of linguistic theory that Rorty deployed to bring all of pragmatism into the analytical tent in 1979.[10] Brandom assumes that the ground for this had been prepared by the insights of Bertrand Russell, Gottlob Frege, Ludwig Wittgenstein, Wilfrid Sellars, W. V. Quine, and other analytical philosophers.

According to this account, the early pragmatists like Dewey and James were mere anticipators of logical and linguistic positivism, just as Holmes has supposedly been of legal positivism and realism. They were "rejectionist" rather than properly "revisionist," meaning that their achievement was to reject the methods of early modern philosophy and pave the way for linguistic analysis, which would itself later become pragmatic (in a different sense) by focusing not on linguistic *meaning* but *use*, following Ludwig Wittgenstein. Even Hegel would be brought transformed into this new pragmatic revision, grounded in language as the essence of experience.[11]

10. Richard Rorty, *Philosophy and the Mirror of Nature*. For the resistant counternarrative I draw on Ralph Sleeper, *Necessity of Pragmatism*, and Joseph Margolis, *Pragmatism's Advantage*. See also my "Who Owns Pragmatism?"

11. "The new notion of determinateness Hegel proposes is an essentially *temporally perspectival* [Brandom's italics] one," "Hegelian Model of Concept Determination," 36. Brandom writes elsewhere that the two pillars of pragmatism are empiricism and naturalism. "[W. V.] Quine thought one could save at least the naturalist program by retreating semantically to the level of reference and truth-conditions. James and Dewey appeal to the same sort of methodological pragmatism in support of more sweeping sorts of semantic revisionism—pursuing programs that Rorty, for instance, argues should be understood as more rejectionist than properly revisionist. And under the banner 'Don't look to the meaning, look to the use,' Wittgenstein further radicalizes the pragmatist critique of semantics. Pointing out, to begin with, that one cannot assume that uses of singular terms have the job of picking out objects, nor that declarative sentences are in the business of stating facts, he goes on to deny, in effect, that such uses even form a privileged center on the basis of which one can understand more peripheral ones. ('Language,' he says, has no downtown.')" Robert Brandom, *Between Saying and Doing: Towards an Analytic Pragmatism*, 3–5; see also his *Perspectives on Pragmatism: Classical, Recent, and Contemporary* and *From Empiricism to Expressivism: Brandom Reads*

This story (the now-conventional narrative) was never accepted by a core group of Dewey scholars, who insisted that Dewey had already traveled further down a genuinely pragmatic road than Wittgenstein ever would.[12] So incensed were they by the dominance of analytical topics and papers among academic philosophers in the mid-twentieth century, and by the regular rejection of their own papers submitted to meetings of the American Philosophical Association, that they founded alternative organizations, published comprehensive original Dewey, Peirce, and other writings, and built an alternative literature of "classical" pragmatism (free of stringent analytical postulates) that has been mostly dismissed by the still-dominant analytical community.[13] Ralph Sleeper wearily explained this in 1986, from the standpoint of the neglected scholars:

> When A. J. Ayer published his *Language, Truth, and Logic* in 1936, thereby capturing a title that could well have served for the volume that Dewey was working on at the time, the philosophical tide was running in his favor. Mainstream logic was preeminently the mathematical and symbolic logic descended from Frege and Russell, but shorn of its earlier metaphysical pretensions, and mainstream epistemology and philosophy of science were already under the influence of the logical empiricism evolved by the Vienna Circle from the nineteenth century scientific positivism of Comte. Ayer's reformulation of Hume's famous division of all meaningful statements into the exclusive categories of the analytic and the synthetic, on the basis of his own principle of verification, had the effect of directing these two powerful mainstream currents into a mighty confluence that threatened to carry all philosophy with it.

Sleeper refers here to the book *Logic: The Theory of Inquiry* that Dewey published two years later, but was "virtually ignored":

Sellars. Huw Price advances this agenda in setting forth an analytical view of naturalism in *Expressivism, Pragmatism and Representationalism*, 3–5.

12. Ralph Sleeper, *The Necessity of Pragmatism: John Dewey's Conception of Philosophy*, 119, 148–49, 171, 212; the outstanding difference between Holmes and Wittgenstein lies in the former's activism and the latter's quietism, in Wittgenstein's deflation of philosophical problems as rooted in language and meaning, translatable into "games," rather than as battles for local and global belief.

13. The principal organizations are the Charles S. Peirce Society and the Society for the Advancement of American Philosophy, but there are also active societies for the study of Dewey, Josiah Royce, George Santayana, Jane Addams, W. E. B. DuBois, and other pragmatic philosophers.

> It was not just that Dewey's book was difficult to a degree verging on incomprehensibility, or that it appeared not to be about logic at all in the sense in which that term was currently used, or that hardly anyone noticed that it was a book about language and meaning, or even that Dewey insisted on using vaguely defined terms such as *warranted assertability* in place of the crisper, more definite *truth*. It was also that even Dewey's most sympathetic critics seemed unable to grasp its relevance to the mainstream currents of the day.[14] (Sleeper's italics)

I should add to this that Holmes was an indirect victim of Sleeper's "mighty confluence," and that the failure to recognize his keen insights into what Dewey later called the continuum of inquiry allowed the powerful analytical current to flood unobstructed throughout the theory of law.[15]

Sleeper's counternarrative is a penetrating assessment of Dewey's career. Dewey had begun as a Hegelian, and had lately added his own account of the continuum to naturalize Hegel's dialectic.[16] Sleeper argues,

14. Ibid., 134.

15. While this claim obviously warrants more support than an offhand comment, it is the drift of my chap. 8, noting the influence of Waismann and J. L. Austin on Hart; see Lacey, *The Nightmare and the Noble Dream*, 128–40. Through Hart, analytical *legal* philosophy in both England and America came through Waismann and Austin, while American analytical philosophy in general has been largely stimulated by Quine, as well as by Wilfrid Sellars's 1956 *Empiricism and the Philosophy of Mind* (published with an introduction by Richard Rorty and a study guide by Robert Brandom). Richard Rorty observes in his introduction that "Austin's criticism of Ayer in his posthumous *Sense and Sensibilia* played the role in Britain which Sellars's article played in America."

A notable exception to the analytical current in jurisprudence is the critical study of legal history, greatly stimulated in 1984 by Robert Gordon's critique of evolutionary functionalism (see chap. 3, n. 19). Gordon's argument is that by taking the world as we know it as largely determined by impersonal social forces, evolutionary functionalism obscures the ways in which these seemingly inevitable processes are actually manufactured by people who claim (and believe themselves) to be only passively adapting to such processes. The social nature of human beings reveals itself not through constant responses to their environments but through an astonishing diversity of cultural responses and, most remarkable of all, a repeatedly demonstrated capacity to reimagine their situations so as to generate novel responses. Robert Gordon, "Critical Legal Histories," 70–71.

16. Dewey "admired Hegel for having healed the breach between the analytical and the synthetic by grounding his logic in the historical process." Sleeper, *Necessity of Pragmatism*, 98; see also 3–4, 17–18, 23–25. "Dewey's Hegelianism was not based on the metaphysics of the absolute. . . . For Dewey the appeal of Hegelianism rested rather on the logic of synthesis, which 'supplied a demand for unification that was doubtless an intense emotional craving, and yet was a hunger that only an intellectualized subject-matter could satisfy. . . . Hegel's synthesis of subject and object, matter and spirit, the divine and human, was, however, no

and I think clearly shows, that Dewey drew on Hegel to pass through and beyond Quine's rejection of Hume's and Kant's division of propositions into analytic and synthetic, and reconfigured the role of formal logic as a stage in a socialized process of inquiry ("Logical forms accrue to subject matter when the latter is subjected to controlled inquiry.") Experience was as paramount for Dewey as it was for Francis Bacon, and existence was as problematic for him as it was for Holmes. But Dewey's explanations in his *Logic* failed to gain a wide audience, and he despaired until the end of effectively getting his point—which undermined the presumptive primacy and essentialism of formal logic—across.[17]

I can best illuminate this by showing where Dewey's insight is not just imprecise but incomplete, and how Holmes (whom Dewey praised effusively in his 1958 *Experience and Nature*[18]) contributes vital relevance and force to it. But (as Holmes and Hand would agree) the final proof in this debate lies not in the card catalog but in the real world of American experience, including legal and constitutional experience.

Where precisely does Dewey differ from Holmes? One place to look is his use of the phrase "controlled inquiry." He writes emphatically (the italics are his): "*Inquiry is the controlled or directed transformation of an indeterminate situation into one that is so determinate in its constituent distinctions and relations as to convert the elements of the original situation into a unified whole.*" Here he builds on Peirce's doubt-belief scheme, as well as Peirce's privileged role of the community in inquiry.[19] But if indeed inquiry is always being "controlled or directed," who or what is doing it? Mill's

---

intellectual formula; it operated as an immense release, a liberation. Hegel's treatment of human culture, of institutions and the arts, involved the same dissolution of hard-and-fast dividing walls, and had a special attraction for me." Ibid. 18.

17. Sleeper, *Necessity of Pragmatism*, 116, 135, 194–95, 205.

18. Discussing "the relationship between existence and value, or as the problem is often put, between the real and the ideal," Dewey observed of Holmes:

> I gladly borrow the words of one of our greatest American philosophers; with their poetry they may succeed in conveying where dry prose fails. Justice Holmes has written: "The mode in which the inevitable comes to pass is through effort. Consciously or unconsciously we all strive to make the kind of world that we like. And although with Spinoza we may regard criticism of the past as futile, there is every reason for doing all that we can to make a future such as we desire." He then goes on to say, "there is every reason also for trying to make our desires intelligent. The trouble is that our ideals for the most part are inarticulate, and that even if we have made them definite we have very little experimental knowledge of the way to bring them about." (Dewey, *Experience and Nature*, 417–18)

19. Dewey, *Logic*, 104–5; Sleeper, *Necessity of Pragmatism*, 140.

universal omniscient mind? A committee of inordinately agreeable philosophers? What is the nature of Dewey's resultant "unified wholes?" He says too little about the mess that can occur if and when things *don't* unify.

Hegel's phantom dialectic had worked autonomously and automatically within an imaginary conceptual ecosphere. Dewey's naturalization removed the mythical structure but failed to replace it with a convincing everyday account of what "really takes place." Here is a typical passage from his *Logic*, in which Dewey uses law as an example:

> All of these formal legal conceptions are operational in nature. They formulate and define ways of operation on the part of those engaged in the transactions into which a number of persons or groups enter as "parties," and the ways of operation followed by those who have jurisdiction in deciding whether established forms have been complied with, together with the existential consequences of failure of observation. The forms in question are not fixed and eternal. They change, though as a rule too slowly, with changes in the habitual transactions in which individuals and groups engage and the changes that occur in the consequences of these transactions. (102)

The reference here to parties as groups, choosing operational forms in a changing context, compares well with the insights of Edward Levi and Holmes; but Dewey gives only a vague sense of control over the inquiry, and how or why it succeeds or fails. What he misses is the often protracted struggle, which Holmes and Levi both saw in battles over similarity. The fact that Dewey mainly sees inquiry as leading toward "unified wholes" undermines his admitted sense of precariousness, the prospect of potential failure. Dewey may have (as Brandom claims) "naturalized" the subject-object dualism of Descartes and early modern philosophy, but he failed to fully and convincingly naturalize the *dialectic*.[20]

20. In Sleeper's account, Dewey "distanced himself from the prevailing rigorous formal techniques," but his target was the very dogma of empiricism descended from Hume that insisted on the categorical distinction between analytic and synthetic. The key is his view of logical forms, that they "accrue to subject-matter when the latter is subjected to controlled inquiry. . . . These formal conceptions arise out of the ordinary transactions; they are not imposed upon them from on high or from any external and *a priori* source. But when they are formed they are also *formative*; they regulate the proper conduct of the activities out of which they develop." Sleeper, *Necessity of Pragmatism*, 101–2. In defending his idea of objectivity Dewey relied on "progressive derivation, through differentiation under environing conditions, from a common ancestry." Dewey's model for inquiry drew on analogies to biological development. Sleeper

I should not discredit Dewey's notion of any kind of human control over the dialectic; otherwise, how has civilization (so far) survived? In Holmes's historical account, the mechanism has changed. Some degree of control over the blood feud in the vengeance era came from enforced surrender of the offending person or thing.[21] With the advent of the external standard, control was derived (ideally, with common law or analogous mechanisms) through case-specific comparison and adjustment, enforced often by the sheriff of course, but at its best when judicial input is restrained and appropriately retrospective. The common law process of dispute resolution is itself evolving, and becomes more precarious when Baconian discipline is lost, the worse when ideology is unleashed and runs rampant. That is when the conflict and the dying can get *out* of control. Hence Holmes warns lawyers and judges that their choice of method has profound implications, and no single judge in a critical matter can be sure of getting it right.

With these thoughts in mind, I return to free expression in time of war.[22]

Learned Hand had studied philosophy at Harvard under the giants of classical pragmatism, William James, George Santayana, and Josiah Royce, and seriously considered a career in philosophy.[23] His approach to uncertainty, and his form of judicial certainty, were models of Baconian empiricism.[24] He developed an intimate understanding of commercial and

---

comments that it is "tangled texts" like this that "deserve, but scarcely inspire, careful and contextual reading." Compare Waldron, *Law and Disagreement*, 162: "[E]ach conception of the good generates a direct competitor to the conception of justice which is putatively the recipient of allegiance in overlapping consensus." See also Stuart Hampshire, *Justice Is Conflict.*

21. Holmes, *The Common Law*, *CW*, 117–32.

22. Full credit and considerable thanks are due to the late Professor Gerald Gunther of Stanford Law School, whose *Learned Hand: The Man and the Judge* was the inspiration for the narrative of this chapter, originally published as my 1987 article in the *American Scholar*, "Learned Hand and the Great Train Ride." See also Thomas Healy, *The Great Dissent: How Oliver Wendell Holmes Changed His Mind—and Changed the History of Free Speech in America* (examining multiple influences that illuminate Holmes's conversion in *Abrams v. U.S.*).

In *Abrams* in 1919, Holmes would dissent when the Court sustained the convictions of five Russian-born men who were prosecuted under the Espionage Act of 1917, as it had been amended by the Sedition Act of 1918, for "provoking and encouraging" resistance to the government's war efforts (and its hostile maneuvers toward Russia) through a series of pamphlets.

23. Gunther, *Learned Hand*, xii, 33.

24. In 1924 Hand was elevated by President Warren Harding from the federal trial court, where he ruled in the *Masses* case, to the U.S. Court of Appeals for the Second Circuit, with jurisdiction over the world's leading financial center, where he dealt with the majority of important federal commercial litigation, much of it having national and international implications.

financial transactions. To assist him in admiralty cases and the movement of ships, Hand kept charts and dividers in his chambers and was known to correct counsel in open court on the intimate details of offshore geodetics from memory. In his familiarity with the precise conditions surrounding recurring detail lay the key to his expertise as a generalist. "It is the merit of the common law," as Holmes had said, "that it decides the case first and determines the principle afterwards."

Along with dealing in the main with relatively concrete matters, it was also Hand's task as a judge, particularly in resolving conflicts among discrete governmental bodies and their various branches, and determining the limits on their authority, to interpret the legal implications of sweeping constitutional phrases. Here the uncertainty factor reached its highest and, as Justice Frankfurter observed, Hand avoided axioms and sought to rule with factual precision, recognizing the preliminary and tentative place of the "early case," avoiding grand rationalization:

> When considerations of such magnitude influence if they do not underlie the accommodations that determine important adjudications, it is not surprising that on occasion we find in Learned Hand, as in Holmes, a certain vagueness of formulation and a penumbral scope to decisions. This is a manifestation of clarity of thought. It is the kind of clarity, which, in Professor Whitehead's phrase, "leaves the darkness unobscured."[25]

Less than two years after Hand had been overruled in the *Masses* case, Holmes would write the opinion of the Supreme Court in *Schenck v. United States*, upholding the criminal conviction of Charles T. Schenck, general secretary of the Socialist Party, for conspiracy to violate the Espionage Act by mailing fifteen thousand circulars to men who had been called and accepted for military service. The circular, drawing on socialist doctrine, inveighed against conscription, called it unconstitutional, and beseeched, "Do not submit to intimidation." But the entire discussion, as Holmes conceded, "in form at least confined itself to peaceful measures such as repeal of the Act."

The principal constitutional argument in defense of Schenck was that the explicit words used were protected: two of the strongest expressions in his circular were said to be quoted from "well known public men." To this Holmes memorably replied:

25. Kellogg, "Learned Hand and the Great Train Ride," 478.

> We admit that in many places and in ordinary times the defendants in saying all that was said in the circular would have been within their constitutional rights. But the character of every act depends upon the circumstances in which it is done. The most stringent protection of free speech would not protect a man in falsely shouting fire in a theater and causing a panic. The question in every case is whether the words used are used in such circumstances and are of such a nature to create a clear and present danger that they will bring about the substantive evils that Congress has a right to prevent.

Thus was born the "clear and present danger" test, in a case supporting, not overruling, punishment for speech.

In their correspondence after the train ride, Holmes's letter of June 24, with its statement that "free speech stands no differently than freedom from vaccination," was not answered by Hand. The two would correspond again in early 1919, around the time of *Schenck* and subsequent rulings by the Supreme Court in the *Frohwerk* (1919) and *Debs* (1919) cases, in which Holmes continued to acquiesce in convictions under the Espionage Act, as *satisfying* the "clear and present danger" test when "circumstances" provided a rationale. This correspondence culminated in Hand's relief and congratulations eight months later, when Holmes finally opposed a conviction in his famous dissent in *Abrams v. United States*.

In analyzing *Masses*, Hand had concluded at once that a clear, objective test applicable to the literal character of language was required to prevent juries from convicting in the heat of the moment. There would have to be a direct incitement, independent of "circumstances." Although Holmes never appreciated this, in *Abrams* he did at last appear to set free speech apart from other freedoms with the following language:

> [W]hen men have realized that time has upset many fighting faiths, they may come to believe even more than they believe the very foundations of their own conduct that the ultimate good desired is better reached by free trade in ideas—that the best test of truth is the power of the thought to get itself accepted in the competition of the market, and that truth is the only ground upon which their wishes safely can be carried out. That, at any rate, is the theory of our Constitution. It is an experiment, as all life is an experiment. Every year if not every day we have to wager our salvation upon some prophecy based upon imperfect knowledge. While that experiment is part of our system I think that we should be eternally vigilant against attempts to check the expression of opinions that we loathe and believe to be fraught with death, unless they

> so imminently threaten immediate interference with the lawful and pressing purposes of the law that an immediate check is required to save the country.

While the *Abrams* dissent resonates with the same philosophical point that Hand made to Holmes in his letter of June 22, 1918, all Holmes did in reaching an opposite conclusion was to infuse a stronger emphasis into the element of "present" in "clear and present danger." As Hand's private correspondence reveals, he believed that this alone would not prevent juries from convicting for something short of the imminent threat to lawful and pressing purposes; only a standard prohibiting outright incitement to violence would serve.

The pertinent history following the train ride is filled with ironies. Such was the acclamation of his *Abrams* dissent among informed circles of opinion—touched with a sense of relief over the mere suggestion of *some* limit—that Holmes's "clear and present danger" test would be enshrined by Harvard law professor Zechariah Chafee Jr., and would (for a while) occupy a dominant place in First Amendment doctrine. Yet, in the wake of World War II, the continuum resumed.

When the courts turned to the prosecution of suspected Communist Party members under the Smith Act, the limit that Holmes had roughly sketched in his *Abrams* dissent turned out to provide more confusion than protection. Hand, now chief judge of the respected but subordinate U.S. Court of Appeals for the Second Circuit, having had his *Masses* doctrine rejected as a trial judge, dutifully followed Supreme Court precedent, doing his best to refine and clarify the "clear and present danger" test in *Dennis v. United States* ("whether the gravity of the evil, discounted by its improbability, justifies such invasion of free speech as is necessary to avoid the danger"). For his pains he was roundly criticized for promoting a "balancing" test, as opposed to one drawn from "principle." The debate was joined by Justices Hugo Black, who saw the First Amendment as an absolute, and Frankfurter, who gave extreme deference to legislative purposes. The growing debate over judicial power would extend to other areas of constitutional doctrine long after Hand's death.

Later, history vindicated Hand's original position.[26] As is sometimes the case when a controversy refuses to rest, a discrete point of greatest friction

26. There is a divergence of opinion regarding Hand's continued commitment to his *Masses* test, and even to free expression itself, in his interpretation of the clear and present danger test in affirming the convictions in *U.S. v. Dennis*. Thomas Healy, whose valuable

is exposed by persistent and skillful advocacy. That point was the same on which Learned Hand's mind had quickly pounced in 1917, and it was put before the Court forty years later in arguments honed and sharpened by continued resistance to prosecutions under the Smith Act. The defendants in *Yates v. United States* (1957) had challenged the trial court's instructions to the jury—perhaps the only procedure through which to raise it—for failure to provide adequate guidance on the distinction between expounding abstractions and advocating action. The government replied that "the true constitutional dividing line is not between inciting and abstract advocacy of forcible overthrow [of government], but rather between advocacy as such, irrespective of its inciting qualities, and the mere discussion or exposition of violent overthrow as an abstract theory." The issue was finally joined.

Justice John Marshall Harlan, writing for a near unanimous court (only Justice Thomas C. Clark dissented), rejected the government's position, finding that the jury instructions had ignored "any issue as to the character of the advocacy in terms of its capacity to stir listeners to forcible action." Intent alone was not enough, and to be unlawful the speech must have urged illegal conduct: "Vague references to 'revolutionary' or 'militant' action of an unspecified character, which are found in the evidence, might in addition be given too great weight by the jury in the absence of more precise instructions."

This opinion, with those such as *Brandenburg v. Ohio* (1969) that built upon it, demonstrates that Hand's *Masses* doctrine has substantially prevailed. It has prevailed, I should add, in this country, for now. Over much of the world it would hardly be given any serious thought, even by a formal, public forum of review sufficiently endowed like our Supreme Court to elucidate the advocacy/incitement distinction and implement it. But Judge Hand would be the first to deny that there is any inherent textual content necessitating such a distinction, to be drawn from the language of the First Amendment. He was instead drawn to it from a trained sense of the imperfections of the jury trial—the zeal and resources of the prosecutor considered against the impressionable reactions of a jury—and the likely effect on political discourse from convictions based in part on anomalous "circumstances."

---

study details other influences on Holmes, takes the position that the clear and present danger test provides all that is needed to protect free expression, and downplays the importance of the *Yates* Court's adoption of Hand's emphasis on incitement. See Gunther, *Learned Hand*, 603–4, and Healy, *The Great Dissent*, 246.

As philosophers, Hand and Holmes were remarkably close; both shared the view that no model of reality will or can be finally enshrined for all time. Their approach to pragmatism opposed illusions of certainty in life, including those of analytical linguistic "pragmatism." As James had observed of "conceptualism," "death once dead for it, there's no more dying then." Fractiousness and conflict were accepted by Hand and Holmes, even while ignored to this day by the static vision of analytical philosophy.

Hand's exposition of the value of free expression, set forth in his first letter to Holmes, is admirably restated in Holmes's *Abrams* dissent. Perhaps Holmes could have been moved toward an objective *Masses*-type formula, had he lived another generation. But he was born into an era of armed conflict of a scale greater than anything Americans have recently known. Yet he was open-minded in the face of Hand's outcry, and always recognized the need for creative thought, for Peirce's "abduction," for such principled anticipation of experience as Hand exemplified. Free expression, for both men, was and remains a supreme product of American creative thought. It has become entrenched and stabilized through experience, inside and outside the courtroom.

It might be said that Holmes and Hand, rather than being innocent of importing their own worldviews, simply adopted a modified social Darwinism, in which the struggle to survive provided the dominant context for their legal thinking. But this is grossly simplistic and ignores the profound achievement of protected free expression. It also ignores the fact that Holmes himself cut short any form of reading evolutionary theory into law, with his famous dissent in *Lochner v. New York* (1905), where the Court struck down state regulation of working hours as violating a laissez-faire view of contract, with his comment, "The Fourteenth Amendment does not enact Mr. Herbert Spencer's *Social Statics*."

For those who believe that all thinking is paradigmatic, the most that can be alleged of a Hand/Holmes paradigm is that it was a paradigm against paradigms, an antiparadigm. Such was the respect for uncertainty of their shared vision of reality that it carried within it the prospect of its own error, failure, even demise. It was not a vision of utopia upon which their republic had been founded, but one of experiment, with a sense that nothing profoundly important could be absolutely fixed and certain, unavailing constant human striving.

So what, then, was the use of the Constitution, and how does it protect something so fundamental as free expression? What it did was not altogether different from what the common law has come to do in numerous experiments with free and private institutions in England: it focused the inquiry, it forced the question, repeatedly. This is what is meant by First Amendment jurisdiction: it asks whether the public purpose is consistent with free expression in a continuing succession of urgent but particular controversies, in which the stakes are high and all are held to account; and it has asked it relentlessly.

This is the foundation for freedom, more secure than analytical theory or the principle-as-generalization, the un-Baconian axiom, that Holmes in 1894 called "the empty general proposition which teaches nothing but a benevolent yearning." It is secured by a wall of factual inquiry that cannot be torn down unless every constructing brick is clearly seen to be removed with it. In this process particular answers are more formidable than any axiom. If they are to be reconsidered and the wall dismantled, it will have to be done under full public scrutiny, providing ample opportunity, for those on the other side, if they are willing, to join the fight.

"Clear and present danger" now plays a subordinate role in First Amendment decision making; the objective test does not address every situation. The answers have not come from any inherent content in the document, from patent logical inconsistencies between congressional and constitutional language, or from bland and empty axioms; they have arisen from a so far sensible, but dogged and principled, response to the specific exigencies of maintaining a democracy through world war, and on into a risky and uncertain future.

In the largest sense, the objective test for First Amendment cases in national security is itself an experiment, which is to say a choice. We have taken it, and it is not perfect, as many will claim throughout the twenty-first century. Perhaps it's wrong—in the sense that only a nation willing to ignore the distinction between advocacy and direct incitement can survive another century as reckless and cruel as the last one. Holmes seems at first to have thought so, and to this sentiment we hear the echo of Hand's response: "The horrible possibility silenced me when you said it. Now, I say, 'Not at all, kill him for the love of Christ and in the name of God, but always realize that he may be the saint and you the devil.'"

Looking back, who is to say that the real tragedy of the twentieth century—the killing of tens of millions of innocent men, women, and children—cannot be traced to the very engine Judge Hand had in mind when he responded to Holmes about the certainty of devils who thought they were saints. It was this form of righteousness that Hand sought to undermine when he drew the line in *United States v. Masses*. If Hand was right about this, it follows that such killing should not have taken place, and cannot recommence, without the illusion of certainty. It is a kind of certainty that *we*, in the United States, having had the question placed upon us by common law and our Constitution, and the choice proposed by Holmes and Hand, have chosen to unmask, so leaving the darkness unobscured.

Bibliography

Alexander, Larry, and Kenneth Kress. "Against Legal Principles." In *Law and Interpretation*, edited by Andrei Marmor, 279–327. Oxford: Clarendon Press, 1995.

Alexy, Robert. *The Argument from Injustice*. Translated by Bonnie L. and Stanley L. Paulson. Oxford: Clarendon Press, 2002.

Allen, C. K. *Law in the Making*. Oxford: Clarendon Press, 1930.

Altman, Andrew. *Critical Legal Studies: A Liberal Critique*. Princeton, NJ: Princeton University Press, 1990.

———. "Legal Realism, Critical Legal Studies, and Dworkin." *Philosophy & Public Affairs* 15 (Summer 1986): 205–35.

Altshuler, Albert W. *Law without Values: The Life, Work and Legacy of Justice Holmes*. Chicago: University of Chicago Press, 1999.

Apel, Karl-Otto, and Charles S. Peirce. *From Pragmatism to Pragmaticism*. Translated by John Michael Krois. Amherst: University of Massachusetts Press, 1981.

Austin, John. *Lectures on Jurisprudence; or, The Philosophy of Positive Law*. London: John Murray, 1869.

Austin, J. L. *Philosophical Papers*. 3rd ed. Edited by J. O. Urmson and G. J. Warnock. Oxford: Oxford University Press, 1979.

Bacon, Francis. *Novum Organum*. Translated and edited by Peter Urbach and John Gibson. Chicago and La Salle, IL: Open Court, 1994.

Baker, Liva. *The Justice from Beacon Hill: The Life and Times of Oliver Wendell Holmes*. New York: HarperCollins, 1991.

Barnes, Barry, David Bloor, and John Hanson. *Scientific Knowledge: A Sociological Analysis*. Chicago: University of Chicago Press, 1996.

Bickel, Alexander. *The Least Dangerous Branch*. Indianapolis and New York: Bobbs-Merrill Co., 1962.

Bix, Brian. "Indeterminacy and Good Faith: Politics and Legitimacy." Minnesota Legal Studies Research Paper No. 16–29 (2016). https://papers.ssrn.com/sol3/papers.cfm?abstract_id=2842602##.

———. *Law, Language, and Legal Determinacy*. Oxford: Clarendon Press, 1993.

Bloom, Alan. *The Closing of the American Mind: How Higher Education Has Failed Democracy and Impoverished the Souls of Today's Students*. New York: Simon & Schuster, 1987.

Bobbitt, Philip Chase. "The Age of Consent." *Yale Law Journal* 123 (May 2014): 2334, 2336.

———. *Constitutional Fate: Theory of the Constitution*. Oxford and New York: Oxford University Press, 1982.

———. *Constitutional Interpretation*. Oxford and Cambridge, MA: Blackwell, 1991.

———. *The Shield of Achilles: War, Peace and the Course of History*. New York: Alfred Knopf, 2002.

———. *Terror and Consent: The Wars for the Twenty-First Century*. New York: Alfred Knopf, 2008.

Bowen, Francis. *A Treatise on Logic: Or the Laws of Pure Thought; Comprising Both the Aristotelic and Hamiltonian Analyses of Logical Forms and Some Chapters of Applied Logic*. Cambridge, MA: Sever and Francis, 1864.

Brandom, Robert. *Between Saying and Doing: Towards an Analytic Pragmatism*. Oxford: Oxford University Press, 2008.

———. *From Empiricism to Expressivism: Brandom Reads Sellars*. Cambridge, MA, and London: Harvard University Press, 2015.

———. "A Hegelian Model of Concept Determination: The Normative Fine Structure of the Judges' Chain Novel." In *Pragmatism, Law, and Language*, edited by Graham Hubbs and Douglas Lind. New York and London: Routledge, 2014.

———. *Perspectives on Pragmatism: Classical, Recent, and Contemporary*. Cambridge, MA, and London: Harvard University Press, 2011.

Brent, Joseph. *Charles S. Peirce: A Life*. Bloomington and Indianapolis: Indiana University Press, 1998.

Brint, Michael, and William Weaver, ed. *Pragmatism in Law and Society*. Boulder, CO: Westview Press, 1991.

Burton, Steven J. *The Path of the Law and Its Influence: The Legacy of Oliver Wendell Holmes, Jr.* Cambridge: Cambridge University Press, 2000.

Butler, Brian. *Law as a Democratic Means: Democratic Experimentalism and Constitutional Law*. Chicago: University of Chicago Press, 2016.

Calabresi, Guido. *A Common Law for the Age of Statutes*. Cambridge, MA: Harvard University Press, 1982.

———. "An Introduction to Legal Thought: Four Approaches to Law and to the Allocation of Body Parts." *Stanford Law Review* 55 (2003): 2113.

Cane, Peter. *The Hart-Fuller Debate in the Twenty-First Century*. Oxford and Portland, OR: Hart Publishing, 2010.

Cardozo, Benjamin N. *The Nature of the Judicial Process*. New Haven, CT, and London: Yale University Press, 1921.

Cartwright, Nancy. *The Dappled World: A Study of the Boundaries of Science*. Cambridge: Cambridge University Press, 1999.

Clouser, K. Danner, and Bernard Gert. "A Critique of Principlism." *Journal of Medicine and Philosophy* 15 (1990): 219–23.

Cohen, Adam. *Imbeciles: The Supreme Court, American Eugenics, and the Sterilization of Carrie Buck*. New York: Penguin Press, 2016.

Cross, Rupert. *Precedent in English Law*. Oxford: Clarendon Press, 1977.

d'Amato, Anthony. "A New (and Better) Interpretation of Holmes's Prediction Theory of Law." Faculty Working Papers, Paper No. 163 (2008). http://scholarlycommons.law.northwestern.edu/facultyworkingpapers/163.

Dancy, Jonathan. *Ethics without Principles*. Oxford: Clarendon Press, 2004.

———. *Moral Reasons*. Oxford and Cambridge, MA: Blackwell 1993.

Dewey, John. *Experience and Nature*. New York: Dover Publications, 1958.

———. "Logical Method and Law." *Cornell Law Review* 10 (1924): 17.

———. *Logic: The Theory of Inquiry*. New York: Henry Holt and Co., 1938.

Dreier, James, ed. *Contemporary Debates in Moral Theory*. Oxford and Cambridge, MA: Blackwell, 2006.

Duxbury, Neil. *Patterns of American Jurisprudence*. Oxford: Clarendon Press, 1995.

Dworkin, Ronald. *Justice in Robes*. Cambridge, MA, and London: Belknap Press, 2006.

———. *Law's Empire*. Cambridge, MA, and London: Belknap Press, 1986.

———. *Taking Rights Seriously*. Cambridge, MA: Harvard University Press, 1977.

Eisenberg, Melvin A. *The Nature of the Common Law*. Cambridge, MA: Harvard University Press, 1988.

Endicott, Timothy. *Vagueness in Law*. Oxford and New York: Oxford University Press, 2000.

Epstein, Richard. *Supreme Neglect*. Oxford and New York: Oxford University Press, 2008.

Finnis, John. *Natural Law and Natural Rights*. Oxford: Oxford University Press, 1979.

Fisch, Max H. "Was There a Metaphysical Club in Cambridge?" In *Studies in the Philosophy of Charles Sanders Peirce*, edited by Edward Moore and Richard S. Robin. Amherst: University of Massachusetts Press, 1964.

Fisch, Max H., Christian J. W. Kloesel, Edward C. Moore, Don D. Roberts, Lynn A. Ziegler, Nathan Houser, Marc Simon, Ursula Niklas, Andre' De Tienne, Cornelis de Waal, Jonathan K. Eller, and Albert Lewis, eds. *Writings of Charles S. Peirce: A Chronological Edition*. 6 vols. Bloomington: Indiana University Press, 1982–2000.

Flower, Elizabeth, and Murray G. Murphey. *A History of Philosophy in America*. 2 vols. New York: Capricorn Books, 1977.

Foot, Philippa. *Theories of Ethics*. Oxford: Oxford University Press, 1967.

———. *Virtues and Vices*. Berkeley and Los Angeles: University of California Press, 1978.

Francis, Leslie. "Applied Ethics: Misnomer for a Field?" Presidential address delivered at the ninetieth Pacific Division meeting of the American Philosophical Association in San Francisco, April 1, 2016.

Frank, Jerome. *Law and the Modern Mind*. New York: Doubleday and Co., 1963.

Friedmann, Wolfgang. *Legal Theory*. New York: Columbia University Press, 1967.

Friedrich, Carl Joachim. *The Philosophy of Law in Historical Perspective*. 2nd ed. Chicago: University of Chicago Press, 1963.

Fuller, Lon L. "American Legal Philosophy at Mid-Century." *Journal of Legal Education* 6 (1954): 457–85.

———. *The Law in Quest of Itself*. Boston: Beacon Press, 1940.

———. *The Morality of Law*. New Haven, CT, and London: Yale University Press, 1964.

———. *The Principles of Social Order: Selected Essays of Lon L. Fuller*. Edited by Kenneth Winston. Oxford and Portland, OR: Hart Publishing, 2001.

———. "Reason and Fiat in Case Law." *Harvard Law Review* 59 (1946).

Fuller, Steve. *Social Epistemology*. Bloomington and Indianapolis: Indiana University Press, 1988.

———. *Thomas Kuhn: A Philosophical History for Our Times*. Chicago and London: University of Chicago Press, 2000.

George, Robert P., ed. *Natural Law Theory*. Oxford: Oxford University Press, 1992.

Gilmore, Grant. *Ages of American Law*. New Haven, CT, and London: Yale University Press, 1977.

———. *Death of Contract*. Columbus: Ohio State University Press, 1974.

Glock, Hans-Johann. "The Influence of Wittgenstein on American Philosophy." In *Oxford Handbook of American Philosophy*, ed. Cheryl Misak. Oxford: Oxford University Press, 2008.

———. *What Is Analytical Philosophy?* Cambridge: Cambridge University Press, 2008.

Goldman, Alvin I. *Knowledge in a Social World*. Oxford: Clarendon Press, 1999.

———. *Reliabilism and Contemporary Epistemology: Essays*. Oxford and New York: Oxford University Press. 2012.

Goldstein, Laurence, ed. *Precedent in Law*. New York and Oxford: Clarendon Press, 1987.

Goodman, Nelson. *Fact, Fiction, and Forecast*. New York and Indianapolis: Bobbs-Merrill Co., 1955.

———. *Problems and Prospects*. New York and Indianapolis: Bobbs-Merrill Co., 1972.

———. "Seven Strictures on Similarity." In his *Problems and Prospects*, 437. Indianapolis and New York: Bobbs-Merrill Co., 1972.

Gordon, Robert W. "The Arrival of Critical Historicism." *Stanford Law Review* 49 (1997): 1023.

———. "Critical Legal Histories." *Stanford Law Review* 36 (1984): 57.

———. "Critical Legal Histories Revisited: A Response." *Law & Social Inquiry* 37 (2012): 202.

———. *The Legacy of Oliver Wendell Holmes Jr.* Edinburgh: Edinburgh University Press, 1992.

———. "The Past as Authority and as Social Critic." In *The Historic Turn in the Human Sciences*, ed. Terence McDonald. Ann Arbor: University of Michigan Press, 1996.

Gottlieb, Stephen E. "The Paradox of Balancing Significant Interests." *Hastings Law Journal* 45 (1994): 825.

———, ed. *Public Values in Constitutional Law*. Ann Arbor: University of Michigan Press, 1993.

Gray, John Chipman. *The Nature and Sources of the Law*. Gloucester, MA: Peter Smith, 1972.

Gunther, Gerald. "Learned Hand and the Origins of Modern First Amendment Doctrine: Some Fragments of History." *Stanford Law Review* 27 (1975): 719.

———. *Learned Hand: The Man and the Judge*. New York: Alfred Knopf, 1994.

Haack, Susan. 1978. *Philosophies of Logic*. Cambridge: Cambridge University Press.

Habermas, Jürgen. *Between Facts and Norms*. Cambridge, MA: MIT Press, 1996.

Hacking, Ian. *The Social Construction of What?* Cambridge, MA: Harvard University Press, 1999.

Hale, Matthew. *The History of the Common Law of England* (1713). Chicago and London: University of Chicago Press, 1971.

Hamilton, William. *Lectures on Metaphysics and Logic*. 4 vols. Edited by Henry L. Mansel and John Veitch. Edinburgh: Blackwell, 1859–60.

Hampshire, Stuart. *Justice Is Conflict*. Princeton, NJ: Princeton University Press, 2000.

Hand, Learned. *The Bill of Rights*. Cambridge, MA: Harvard University Press, 1958.

Hanson, N. R. *Patterns of Discovery: An Inquiry into the Conceptual Foundations of Science*. Cambridge: Cambridge University Press, 1958.

Hare, R. M. *The Language of Morals*. Oxford: Oxford University Press, 1952.

———. *Moral Thinking*. Oxford: Clarendon Press, 1981.

Hart, H. L. A. *The Concept of Law*. Oxford: Clarendon Press, 1961.

———. "Discretion." *Harvard Law Review* 127 (December 2013): 636, 665.

———. *Essays in Jurisprudence and Philosophy*. Oxford: Clarendon Press, 1983.

Hartshorne, Charles, and Paul Weiss, eds. *Collected Papers of Charles Sanders Peirce*. Cambridge, MA: Belknap Press, 1978.

Hayek, Friedrich. *The Constitution of Liberty*. Chicago: University of Chicago Press, 1960.

Healy, Thomas. 2013. *The Great Dissent: How Oliver Wendell Holmes Changed His Mind—and Changed the History of Free Speech in America*. New York: Metropolitan Books, Henry Holt and Co., 2013.

Hegel, G. W. F. *Elements of the Philosophy of Right*. Translated by T. M. Knox. Oxford: Oxford University Press, 1978.

———. *Science of Logic*. Translated by A. V. Miller. Atlantic Highlands, NJ: Humanities Press International, 1989.

Herget, James E. *American Jurisprudence, 1870–1970: A History*. Houston: Rice University Press, 1990.

Herschel, John. "Whewell on Inductive Sciences." Review of the *History* and the *Philosophy*. *Quarterly Review* 68 (1841): 177–238.

Hesse, Mary. *The Structure of Scientific Inference*. London and Basingstoke: MacMillan Press, 1974.

Hobbes, Thomas. *Leviathan; or, The Matter, Forme, and Power of a Commonwealth Ecclesiasticall and Civil*. New York: Collier Books, 1962.

Holmes, Oliver Wendell, Jr. *The Collected Works of Justice Holmes: Complete Public Writings and Selected Opinions of Oliver Wendell Holmes*. Edited by Sheldon M. Novick. Chicago and London: University of Chicago Press, 1995.

———. *The Common Law*. Boston: Little Brown and Co., 1881.

Honneth, Axel. *Freedom's Right*. New York: Columbia University Press, 2014.

Hooker, Brad, and Margaret Little, ed. *Moral Particularism*. Oxford and New York: Oxford University Press, 2000.

Horwitz, Morton. *The Transformation of American Law, 1870–1960: The Crisis of Legal Orthodoxy*. New York and Oxford: Oxford University Press, 1992.

Howe, Mark De Wolfe, ed. *Holmes-Pollock Letters*. Cambridge, MA: Harvard University Press, 1946.

———. *Justice Oliver Wendell Holmes: The Proving Years, 1871–1882*. Cambridge, MA: Belknap Press, 1963.

———. *Justice Oliver Wendell Holmes: The Shaping Years, 1841–1870*. Cambridge, MA: Belknap Press, 1957.

———. "The Positivism of Mr. Justice Holmes." *Harvard Law Review* 64 (February 1951): 529, 537–38.

Hubbs, Graham, and Douglas Lind, eds. *Pragmatism, Law, and Language*. New York and London: Routledge, 2014.

Hume, David. *An Enquiry concerning the Principles of Morals*. London: A. Miller, 1751.

———. *A Treatise of Human Nature*. New York: E. P. Dutton, 1949.

Hunt, Luke William. "What the Epistemic Account of Vagueness Means for Legal Interpretation." *Law and Philosophy* 35, no. 1 (February 2016).

Hurst, James Willard. *Justice Holmes on Legal History*. New York: Macmillan Co., 1964.

Iltis, Carolyn. "D'Alembert and the Vis Viva Controversy." *Studies in History and Philosophy of Science* 1, no. 2 (1970): 135.

James, William. 1995. *Correspondence of William James*. 4 vols. Edited by Ignas K. Skrupskelis and Elizabeth M. Berkeley. Charlottesville: University Press of Virginia, 1992–2004.

———. *A Pluralistic Universe*. London: Longmans, Green and Co., 1912.

Keil, G., and R. Poscher, eds. *Vagueness in Law: Philosophical and Legal Approaches*. Oxford: Oxford University Press, 2016.

Kellogg, Frederic R. "The Abuse of Principle: Analytical Philosophy and the Doubtful Case." *Archiv fur Rechts-und Sozialphilosophie* 97 (2011): 218.

———. *The Formative Essays of Justice Holmes: The Making of an American Legal Philosophy*. Westport, CT, and London: Greenwood Press, 1984.

———. "Hobbes, Holmes, and Dewey: Pragmatism and the Problem of Order." *Social Science Research Network* (2010). https://ssrn.com/abstract=1655307.

———. "Holistic Pragmatism and Law: Morton White on Justice Oliver Wendell Holmes," with reply by White, "Holmes and Hart on Prediction and Legal Obligation," *Transactions of the Charles S. Peirce Society* 60 (Fall 2004): 559, 569.

———. "Learned Hand and the Great Train Ride." *American Scholar* 56 (Autumn 1987): 471.

———. *Oliver Wendell Holmes Jr., Legal Theory, and Judicial Restraint*. Cambridge: Cambridge University Press, 2007.

———. "The Snake and the Roundabout: Ethical Particularism and the Patterns of Normative Induction." *Duc in Altum Cadernos de Direito* 8, no. 16 (December 2016). https://papers.ssrn.com/sol3/papers.cfm?abstract_id=2888196.

———. "What Precisely Is a 'Hard' Case? Waldron, Dworkin and Judicial Recourse to Principle." *Social Science Research Network* (2013). https://papers.ssrn.com/sol3/papers.cfm?abstract_id=2220839.

———. "Who Owns Pragmatism?" *Journal of Speculative Philosophy*, n.s., 6 (1992): 67–80.

Kelsen, Hans. *General Theory of Law and State*. New York: Russell and Russell, 1961.

Kornblith, Hilary. *Inductive Inference and Its Natural Ground: An Essay in Naturalistic Epistemology*. Cambridge, MA: MIT Press, 1995.

Kuklick, Bruce. *The Rise of American Philosophy, Cambridge, Massachusetts, 1860–1930*. New Haven, CT, and London: Yale University Press, 1977.

Lacey, Nicola. *A Life of H. L. A. Hart: The Nightmare and the Noble Dream*. Oxford: Oxford University Press, 2004.

———. "The Path Not Taken: H. L. A. Hart's Harvard Essay on Discretion." *Harvard Law Review* 127 (2014): 636.

Lacey, Nicola, and Hanna Pickard. "From the Consulting Room to the Court Room? Taking the Clinical Model of Responsibility without Blame into the Legal Realm." *Oxford Journal of Legal Studies* 33 (2013): 1–29.

Laudan, Larry. *Progress and Its Problems*. Berkeley, Los Angeles, and London: University of California Press, 1977.

Leiter, Brian. *The Future for Philosophy*. Oxford: Clarendon Press, 2004.

———. *Naturalizing Jurisprudence: Essays on American Legal Realism and Naturalism in Legal Philosophy*. Oxford: Oxford University Press, 2007.

———, ed. *Objectivity in Law and Morals*. Cambridge: Cambridge University Press, 2001.

———. "Rethinking Legal Realism: Toward a Naturalized Jurisprudence." *Texas Law Review* 76 (1997): 267.

Levi, Edward. *An Introduction to Legal Reasoning*. Chicago and London: University of Chicago Press, 1949.

Little, Eleanor. "The Early Reading of Justice Oliver Wendell Holmes." *Harvard Library Bulletin* 8 (1954): 163.

Llewellyn, Karl N. *The Bramble Bush: Our Law and Its Study*. New York: Oceana, 1960.

———. *The Common Law Tradition: Deciding Appeals*. Boston: Little Brown and Co., 1960.

———. *Jurisprudence: Realism in Theory and Practice*. Chicago: University of Chicago Press, 1962.

———. "The Status of the Rule of Judicial Precedent." *University of Cincinnati Law Review* 14 (1940): 208.

———. *The Theory of Rules*. Edited by Frederick Schauer. Chicago: University of Chicago Press, 2011.

Lyotard, Jean-Francois. *The Postmodern Condition*. Minneapolis: University of Minnesota Press, 1988.

Madden, Edward H. *Chauncey Wright and the Foundations of Pragmatism*. Seattle: University of Washington Press, 1963.

Maher, Chauncey. *The Pittsburgh School of Philosophy: Sellars, McDowell, Brandom*. New York and London: Routledge, 2012.

Manicas, Peter. *Logic as Philosophy*. New York: Van Norstrand Rheinhold Co., 1971.

Mansel, Henry. *Prolegomena Logica: An Inquiry into the Psychological Character of Logical Processes*. London, 1851; 2nd ed. enlarged, 1860.

Margolis, Joseph. *Pragmatism Ascendent*. Stanford, CA: Stanford University Press, 2012.

———. *Pragmatism's Advantage*. Stanford, CA: Stanford University Press, 2010.

———. *The Unraveling of Scientism*. Ithaca, NY, and London: Cornell University Press, 2003.

Marmor, Andrei. *Interpretation and Legal Theory*. Oxford: Clarendon Press, 1992.

McDowell, John. *Mind, Value and Reality*. Cambridge, MA, and London: Harvard University Press, 1998.

———. *Mind and World*. Cambridge, MA, and London: Harvard University Press, 1994.

McIntyre, Alisdair. *Whose Justice? Which Rationality?* Notre Dame, IN: University of Notre Dame Press, 1988.

Menand, Louis. *The Metaphysical Club*. New York: Farrar, Straus and Giroux, 2001.

Mendenhall, Allen. *Oliver Wendell Holmes Jr., Pragmatism, and the Jurisprudence of Agon: Aesthetic Dissent and the Common Law*. Lewisburg, PA: Bucknell University Press, 2017.

Mill, John Stuart. *The Collected Works of John Stuart Mill*. John Robson, general editor. 33 vols. Toronto: University of Toronto Press; London: Routledge and Kegan Paul, 1963–91.

———. *A System of Logic Ratiocinative and Inductive*. 2 vols. London: Longmans, Green, Reader and Dyer, 1872.

Milsom, S. F. C. *Historical Foundations of the Common Law*. London: Butterworths, 1969.

———. *A Natural History of the Common Law*. New York: Columbia University Press, 2003.

Misak, Cheryl. *The American Pragmatists*. Oxford and New York: Oxford University Press, 2013.

———, ed. *The Cambridge Companion to Peirce*. Cambridge: Cambridge University Press, 2004.

———. *Truth and the End of Inquiry*. Oxford and New York: Oxford University Press, 1991.

Murphey, Murray G. *C. I. Lewis: The Last Great Pragmatist*. Albany: State University of New York Press, 2005.

Novick, Sheldon M., ed. *The Collected Works of Justice Holmes: Complete Public Writings and Selected Opinions of Oliver Wendell Holmes*. Chicago and London: University of Chicago Press, 1995.

———. *Honorable Justice*. Boston and London: Little Brown and Co., 1989.

Oliphant, Herman. "A Return to Stare Decisis." *American Bar Association Journal* 14 (1928).

Owen, G. E. L., ed. *Aristotle on Dialectic, The Topics: Proceedings of the Third Symposium Aristotelicum*. Oxford: Clarendon Press, 1968.

———. *Logic, Science and Dialectic*. Edited by Martha Nussbaum. Ithaca, NY: Cornell University Press, 1986.

Patterson, Dennis. "Can We Please Stop Doing This? By the Way, Postema Was Right." In *Metaphilosophy of Law*, edited by Pawel Banas, Adam Dyrda, and Tomasz Gizbert-Studnicki. London, New York, New Delhi, and Sydney: Bloomsbury Publishing, 2016.

Peirce, Charles S. *Collected Papers of Charles Sanders Peirce*. Edited by Charles Hartshorne and Paul Weiss. Cambridge, MA: Belknap Press, 1978.

Perry, Ralph Barton. *The Thought and Character of William James*. Cambridge, MA: Harvard University Press, 1948.

Posner, Richard. *Law, Pragmatism, and Democracy*. Cambridge, MA, and London: Harvard University Press, 2003.

———. *The Problems of Jurisprudence*. Cambridge, MA, and London: Harvard University Press, 1990.

———. *Reflections on Judging*. Cambridge, MA, and London: Harvard University Press, 2013.

Postema, Gerald. "Law's System: The Necessity of System in Common Law." *New Zealand Law Review* 69 (2014): 12.

———. "Legal Positivism: Early Foundations." SSRN, 2015. https://www.researchgate.net/publication/228278311.

———. *A Treatise of Legal Philosophy and General Jurisprudence*. Volume 11, *Legal Philosophy in the Twentieth Century: The Common Law World*. Dordrecht: Springer Netherlands, 2011.

Pound, Roscoe. *The Spirit of the Common Law*. Boston: Beacon Press, 1921.

Price, Huw. *Expressivism, Pragmatism and Representationalism*. Cambridge: Cambridge University Press, 2013.

Putnam, Hilary. *The Collapse of the Fact/Value Dichotomy*. Cambridge, MA, and London: Harvard University Press, 2002.

———. *Meaning and the Moral Sciences*. Boston and London: Routledge and Kegan Paul, 1978.

———. *Mind, Language and Reality*. Cambridge, MA, and London: Harvard University Press, 1975.

———. *Philosophy of Logic*. New York and London: Harper & Row, 1971.

———. *Realism and Reason: Philosophical Papers, Volume 3*. Cambridge and London: Cambridge University Press, 1983.

———. *Reason Truth and History*. Cambridge, MA, and London: Harvard University Press, 1981.

———. "Rethinking Mathematical Necessity." In *Words and Life*. Cambridge, MA, and London: Harvard University Press, 1994.

Quine, W. V. *Elements of Logic*. Cambridge, MA, and London: Harvard University Press, 1966.

———. *Philosophy of Logic*. Cambridge, MA, and London: Harvard University Press, 1970.

———. "Two Dogmas of Empiricism." In *From a Logical Point of View*. Cambridge, MA, and London: Harvard University Press, 1953.

———. *Word and Object*. Cambridge, MA: MIT Press, 1960.

Quine, W. V., and J. S. Ullian, *The Web of Belief*. New York: Random House, 1978.

Rabban, David M. "From Maine to Maitland via America." *Cambridge Law Journal* 68 (2009): 410.

———. *Law's History: American Legal Thought and the Transatlantic Turn to History*. Cambridge and New York: Cambridge University Press, 2013.

Rawls, John. *A Theory of Justice*. Cambridge, MA, and London: Harvard University Press, 1971.

———. "Two Concepts of Rules" (1955). Reprinted in *Theories of Ethics*, by Philippa Foot. Oxford: Oxford University Press, 1967.

Raz, Joseph. *The Concept of a Legal System*. Oxford: Clarendon Press, 1970.

Rogers, Melvin L. *The Undiscovered Dewey*. New York: Columbia University Press, 2009.

Rorty, Richard. *Philosophy and the Mirror of Nature*. Princeton, NJ: Princeton University Press, 1979.

Rosenberg, David. 1995. *The Hidden Holmes: His Theory of Torts in History*. Cambridge, MA, and London: Cambridge University Press, 1995.

Russell, Bertrand. "Logic as the Essence of Philosophy." In *Our Knowledge of the External World*. London: Allen and Unwin, 1914.

———. *The Problems of Philosophy*. New York: Henry Holt and Co., 1912.

Ryle, Gilbert. "Dialectic in the Academy." In *Aristotle on Dialectic, The Topics: Proceedings of the Third Symposium Aristotelicum*, edited by G. E. L. Owen, 73. Oxford: Clarendon Press, 1968.

Schauer, Frederick. "A Critical Guide to Vehicles in the Park." *New York University Law Review* 83, no. 4 (October 2008).

———. "Do Cases Make Bad Law?" *University of Chicago Law Review* 73 (Summer 2006): 883.

———. "Legal Realism Untamed." *Texas Law Review* 91 (2013): 749.

———. *Playing by the Rules: A Philosophical Examination of Rule-Based Decision-Making in Law and Life*. Oxford: Clarendon Press, 1991.

Schlegel, John Henry. *American Legal Realism and Empirical Social Science*. Chapel Hill and London: University of North Carolina Press, 1995.

Schneider, Herbert, *A History of American Philosophy*. New York: Liberal Arts Press, 1946.

Sellars, Wilfrid. *Empiricism and the Philosophy of Mind: With an Introduction by Richard Rorty and a Study Guide by Robert Brandom*. Cambridge, MA: Harvard University Press, 1997.

———. "Language, Rules and Behavior." In *John Dewey: Philosopher of Science and Freedom; A Symposium*, ed. Sidney Hook, 289–315. New York: Barnes and Noble, 1949.

Sen, Amartya. *The Idea of Justice*. London and New York: Allen Lane, 2009.

Shapin, Steven, and Simon Shaffer. 1985. *Leviathan and the Air-Pump: Hobbes, Boyle, and the Experimental Life*. Princeton, NJ: Princeton University Press.

Shaw, Geoffrey. "H. L. A. Hart's Lost Essay." *Harvard Law Review* 127 (2014): 674.

Sherry, Suzanna. "Property Is the New Privacy: The Coming Constitutional Revolution." *Harvard Law Review* 128 (2015): 1452.

Sleeper, Ralph W. *The Necessity of Pragmatism*. New Haven, CT: Yale University Press, 1986.

Snyder, Laura J. *The Philosophical Breakfast Club*. New York: Broadway Books, 2011

———. *Reforming Philosophy: A Victorian Debate on Science and Society*. Chicago and London: University of Chicago Press, 2006.

Solmsen, Friedrich. "Dialectic without the Forms." In *Aristotle on Dialectic, The Topics: Proceedings of the Third Symposium Aristotelicum*, ed. G. E. L. Owen, 49. Oxford: Clarendon Press, 1968.

Spann, Girardeau A. "Simple Justice." *Georgetown Law Journal* 73 (1985): 1041, 1060.

Stone, Julius. *The Province and Function of Law: Law as Logic, Justice and Social Control, a Study in Jurisprudence*. Cambridge, MA: Harvard University Press, 1950.

———. *Social Dimensions of Law and Justice*. Stanford, CA: Stanford University Press, 1966.

Sullivan, Kathleen M. "Categorization, Balancing, and Government Interests." In *Public Values in Constitutional Law*, ed. Stephen E. Gottlieb. Ann Arbor: University of Michigan Press, 1993.

Summers, Robert S. 1984. *Lon L. Fuller*. Stanford, CA: Stanford University Press.

Sunstein, Cass. *One Case at a Time: Judicial Minimalism on the Supreme Court*. Cambridge, MA: Harvard University Press, 1999.

Tamanaha, Brian. *Beyond the Formalist-Realist Divide: The Role of Politics in Judging*. Princeton, NJ, and Oxford: Princeton University Press, 2010.

Thayer, James B., ed. *Letters of Chauncey Wright, with Some Account of His Life*. Cambridge, MA: John Wilson and Son, 1878.

Thomson, William. *An Outline of the Necessary Laws of Thought*. London, 1849.

Tushnet, Mark V. "Anti-Formalism in Recent Constitutional Theory." *Michigan Law Review* 83 (1984): 1502.

———. "Defending the Indeterminacy Thesis." In *Analyzing Law*, edited by Brian Bix. Oxford: Clarendon Press, 1998.

———. *Making Civil Rights Law: Thurgood Marshall and the Supreme Court, 1936–1961*. London: Oxford University Press, 1994.

———. *Making Constitutional Law: Thurgood Marshall and the Supreme Court, 1961–1991*. New York: Oxford University Press, 1997.

Twining, William. *Karl Llewellyn and the Realist Movement*. Norman: University of Oklahoma Press, 1973.

Unger, Roberto. *The Critical Legal Studies Movement*. Cambridge, MA: Harvard University Press, 1983.

Utz, Stephen, "Maine's Ancient Law and Legal Theory." *Connecticut Law Review* 16 (1984): 821.

Viets, Henry R., MD. "A Mind Prepared: O. W. Holmes and 'The Contagiousness of Puerperal Fever,' 1843." *Bulletin of the Medical Library Association* 31 (October 1943): 319–25.

Waismann, Friedrich. *The Principles of Linguistic Philosophy*. New York: St. Martin's Press, 1965.

———. "Verifiability." In *Logic and Language, the First Series*, ed. Antony Flew. Oxford: Blackwell, 1960.

Waldron, Jeremy. "Did Dworkin Ever Answer the Crits?" In *Exploring Law's Empire: The Jurisprudence of Ronald Dworkin*, ed. Scott Hershovitz. Oxford: Oxford Scholarship Online, 2009.

———. "The Irrelevance of Moral Objectivity." In *Natural Law Theory*, ed. Robert P. George. Oxford: Oxford University Press, 1992.

———. *Law and Disagreement*. Oxford: Oxford University Press, 1999.

Waluchow, W. J. *Inclusive Legal Positivism*. Oxford: Clarendon Press, 1994.

Weir, Robert F., ed. *Physician Assisted Suicide*. Bloomington and Indianapolis: Indiana University Press, 1997.

Whewell, William. *History of the Inductive Sciences, from the Earliest to the Present Time*. 3rd ed. 3 vols. London: John W. Parker, 1857.

———. "Modern Science—Inductive Philosophy." Review of John Herschel, *Preliminary Discourse on the Study of Natural Philosophy* (1830). *Quarterly Review* 45 (1831): 374, 379.

———. *The Philosophy of the Inductive Sciences, Founded upon Their History*. 2nd ed. 2 vols. London: John W. Parker, 1847.

———. "Remarks on the Review of the Philosophy of the Inductive Sciences." Reply to DeMorgan. *Athenaeum*, no. 672 (1840): 3–8.

White, G. Edward. *Justice Oliver Wendell Holmes: Law and the Inner Self*. New York and Oxford: Oxford University Press, 1993.

Williams, Bernard. *Ethics and the Limits of Philosophy*. Cambridge, MA: Harvard University Press, 1985.

———. *In the Beginning Was the Deed*. Princeton, NJ, and Oxford: Princeton University Press, 2005.

Williamson, Timothy. *Vagueness*. London and New York: Routledge, 1994.

Winston, Kenneth, ed. *The Principles of Social Order: Selected Essays of Lon L. Fuller*. Oxford and Portland, OR: Hart Publishing, 2001.

Woodiwiss, Anthony. *Rights v. Conspiracy: A Sociological Essay on the History of Labour Law in the United States*. New York and Oxford: Berg, 1990.

Wright, Chauncey. *The Philosophical Writings of Chauncey Wright: Representative Selections*. New York: Liberal Arts Press, 1958.

———. "The Philosophy of Herbert Spencer." In *Philosophical Discussions*, ed. Charles Eliot Norton. New York: Burt Franklin, 1977.

Young, Robert. *Medically Assisted Death*. Cambridge: Cambridge University Press, 2007.

Index